TALKING ABOUT SINGLE PAYER

Health Care Equality for America

James F. Burdick, MD

Near Horizons Publishing

For information about permission to reproduce selections from this book, write to
Near Horizons Publishing LLC
PO Box 1283, St. Michaels, MD 21663

Book and cover design by Ruwa Studio, ruwastudio.com.
Set in Adobe Caslon Pro and Novecento Wide.

Figures 2 and 4 and OpEds in the Appendix used by permission.

Library of Congress Cataloging-in-Publication Data
Burdick, James F., 1941- author.
        Talking about single payer : health care equality for
America / James F. Burdick.
        pages cm
        Includes bibliographical references and index.
        ISBN 978-0-9970545-0-7 paperback
        ISBN 978-0-9970545-1-4 Kindle
        ISBN 978-0-9970545-2-1 ePub
        ISBN 978-0-9970545-3-8 hardcover

        1. Health care reform--United States.
    2. Single-payer health care--United States.   I. Title.

RA445.B867 2016   362.10973
                       QBI16-600034

Printed in the United States of America on acid-free paper.

CONTENTS

APPRECIATION

I owe a singular debt of gratitude to Alan Adelson for the existence of this book. His contribution of powerfully incisive editing of the details and substance was incalculably valuable. And he cared about it. Thanks, Al.

In addition, thanks to several stalwarts who read a previous version and gave me plenty of positive and negative feedback that contributed to this final book. They were: Mike Abecassis, Mary Burdick, John Cameron, Michael Kandel, Jeff Kaplan, John and Fredelle Robinson, Paul Scheel and Audra Wolfe.

Special thanks to those who took time from their busy lives to be interviewed (more details elsewhere in the book): Gerry Anderson, Phil Boling, Charles Bond, Jo Ivey Boufford, Joshua Cohen, "Buz" Cooper, Tom Daschle, Ray Drasga, Jim Duderstadt, Jon Fielding, Nortin Hadler, Ida Hellander, Matthew Katz, Andreas Lapaucis, Jack Lewin, Frank Opelka, Liana Orsolini, Jack Ostrich, Adam Owens, Peter Pronovost, Gene Ransom, Jack Rowe, Bernie Sanders, Steve Schroeder, Arloc Sherman, Tommy Thompson, Andy Warshaw, Sam Wells, Quentin Young and Richard Zorza.

Finally, blessed with many wonderful friends, I have had extraordinary support over the 15 years I spent getting this together. You kept me going, sometimes with insightful scoffing, more commonly a warm encouraging "How's your book coming along?" Thanks to all. Here are everyone I can remember, in hopes that I have left no one out: Judy Adelson, Peter Agre, David and Betsy Allison, Ken Andreoni, Chris and Dave Batten, Dan and Lorna Berman, Jessica Berry, Mary Bowers, Robert Brook, Doug and Mary Brown, Bob Brugger, John and Nikki Burdick, Joshua Burdick, Tom and Lucy Burge, Marion and Arthur Bushel, Anne Canfield, Carolyn Clancy, Mandy Cohen,

Paul and Linda Colombani, Peter and Susan Cookson, Jocelyn Cowern, Betty Crandall, Joe Craver, Mike Cross-Barnett, David Custy, John and Judy Dean, Meghana DeSale, Brock and Laurel Dew, Paul Eggers, Shan Ferguson, Alan and Faith Friedman, Rachel and Bill Fissell, Pierre-Gerlier Forest, Richard Frank, Julie Freischlag, Naomi Freundlich, Gloria Galloway, John and Joy Garrett, John Goodell, Tim Goodell, Sue Greene, Andrew Greene, Doc and Evie Hersperger, Robert Higgins, Sam Hopkins, Barbara Jablin, Jack Jones, Lauren and Seth Karp, Dale Kaufman, Mike Klag, Doug Krug, Ken and Nancy LaCombe, Barbro and Ernst Larsson, Lois Levin, Charles Locke, Susie Lorand, Warren and Meighan Maley, Adrian Martin, John and Anne Martin, Ron and Eileen Martin, Don McCanne, Stan and Babs Minken, Eric Naumberg, Vincente Navarro, Richard Peck, Tom Peters, Joan Petty, Mike Posner and Carol Owen, Peter J. Prescott, Adi Ratner, Lloyd Ratner, Norm and Joan Rattray, Evelyn Rattray, Gene Rich, Betty Robinson, Walter and Jane Rolland, Max Romano, Shirley Sallet, David Sklar, Michelle Snyder, Dave and Sandy Spector, Gigi Spicer, Bill and Marie Stacy, Anne Stey, Anne Stiller, Barry Straube, Brigitte Sullivan, Breck and Michele Taylor, Jw Thurber, Heli and Bill Tomford, Sean Tunis, Jim Warren, John and Mary Lou Welch, Helaine White, Budd Whitebook, Ladd Wiley, Modena Wilson, M.K. Woolfrey, Linda Ziff, Gazi Zibari and Joan Zorza.

INTRODUCTION

For over a quarter of a century I worked in blood vessel surgery and organ transplantation to make patients better through disconnecting and reconnecting arteries and veins in various types of operations. Sometimes this was to improve flow to an existing part of a patient and sometimes it was to provide blood flow to a new part: a transplanted organ such as a kidney, liver or pancreas. It is a huge satisfaction to arrive on the morning after an operation to restore flow in a leg blood vessel and find the patient happily wiggling her toes and exclaiming that her foot feels warm again, or to share a recent kidney transplant recipient's delight in an outpouring of urine after years of no urination on dialysis, or to see a patient with a liver I transplanted recovering quickly from the stupor of liver failure. As a busy doctor, I had little time to think about the big picture. For many people who had health care coverage and were referred for treatment, it was my good fortune to have been able to fix things in this way. But over the years, thoughts came increasingly to weigh on me of those without insurance who were shut out of care.

Fifteen years ago, when the Clinton health reform plan failed, I began to feel that something was missing, something so fundamental that it seemed hard to understand why almost no one mentioned it: The doctors were missing from the design.

This book corrects that error. It describes a powerful role for doctors in the novel national stucture that I propose to allow us to move beyond the incomplete successes of the Patient Protection and Affordable Care Act (ACA). Opinions from a variety of authorities are quoted to provide rich independent sources of understanding about the complex realities and difficult choices we face. Much of this is relevant to any systematic improvement in the U.S.

health care system, but out of it emerges in particular a compelling argument in favor of a national single payer system giving access to care for everyone.

These convictions issue in part from my career as an active clinician and health care administrator. I have seen problems from the inside which has given me a clear vision of the power that only doctors can bring to saving our health care system.

Organ transplantation is organized nationally in the U.S. to provide best use of the special gift of life that a donated organ represents. It is overseen by a public-private organization with a board of practicing doctors and others who make clinical rules and follow up on results. I was fortunate to participate as President of this organization, UNOS, and later to work in the federal government as Director of the Division of Transplantation, Health Resources Services Administration/Dept. of Health and Human Services overseeing the federal Organ Procurement Transplant Network. Through seeing the professional input and federal involvement in organ transplantation from both sides, I understand and appreciate the effectiveness of this administrative approach. I am confident that national professional responsibility for clinical care can be applied to the national system for American health care.

One of the most important reasons that single-payer health plans have failed to take hold in American politics is the fear that government-sponsored health care will put health decisions in the hands of government bureaucrats, leading to rationing, red-tape, and cost overruns. My plan removes those obstacles by putting decision-making powers in the hands of trusted medical professionals, backed by empirical research and a robust electronic medical records system. Doctors can unite behind my plan to help ensure passage of a single-payer plan that will provide quality, affordable health care to all Americans. Most single payer health plan proposals include some sort of decision-making board. The difference, in the case of the Health Security Board in my proposal, is its private character.

Health care and its delivery involve a complex of issues and all must be considered for such a major restructuring. Costs, issues regarding doctors and hospitals, drugs, devices, diagnostic tests, electronic medical records, professional involvement and the general social challenges in our country are all part of the single payer system talked about in this book.. The final structure proposed in the last chapter is my vision for how best to serve patients through a synthesis of all of these topics.

Among the elements in that final structure proposed are some significant and novel approaches. The Doctors' Board concept appears occasionally in the shadows of other writing but never before as fundamental to a whole system.

The necessity for states to play a large role has often been passed over or made redundant with federal processes in depictions of national systems. The novel definitions of what doctors do and how to measure quality are new. Also new is the concept that we can liberate doctors by ensuring they are trained well then letting them practice unhindered, with retrospective electronic medical record follow up by the Doctors' Board for oversight of quality. And the reality that we can best succeed only with a total approach that recognizes the other problems in our society, as emphasized in this book, is absent or given little significance in most other works about health care reform.

The ideas here are not just my opinions—far from it. I have gathered disparate views from knowledgeable individuals through a series of interviews and researched the literature extensively to underscore a variety of important perspectives.

Somewhat by chance, this book was born as the U.S. presidential campaign was gearing up at the beginning of 2016. It is dedicated to answers for present and future health care system questions. These novel insights will help any candidate to do better by American health care, now and for years to come. But since it is impossible to overlook topical connections to the election year, I give my personal endorsement at the end of the book.

CHAPTER ONE
SINGLE PAYER

The United States, with its prominent private health care industry, has failed to deliver a program that ensures health care coverage for its citizens. Funding health care with a single payer system is the best way to satisfy this need for our country.[1] Convinced of the fundamental common sense of some variety of single payer program but concerned about possible problems, years ago I evolved the proposal for how to make it work. I describe it in this first chapter. With its novel major role for doctors, the system I describe begins to answer questions raised in public and academic discourse of recent decades. Figure 1 shows this simple, basic plan.

Since there is no existing national program there is no actual single payer system for academic study. Moreover, there is not much general discussion about single payer among either politicians or in the public. For this reason I decided to obtain the series of interviews previewed at the end of this chapter to find out what people would say about single payer. I am grateful to the many who were ready and willing to talk about single payer. Their thoughts are presented as part of the discussions on the topics dealt with in this book.

From the varied observations and consideration of recent political and technical developments, I will show that single payer is the clear theoretical favorite, but with important practical enhancements to consider that I incorporate in the updated concept later.

To establish the basic idea, I interviewed an early advocate, Dr. Quentin Young. He has been part of the Physicians for a National Health Program, a strong single payer advocacy organization, since it was started in 1987 by Drs.

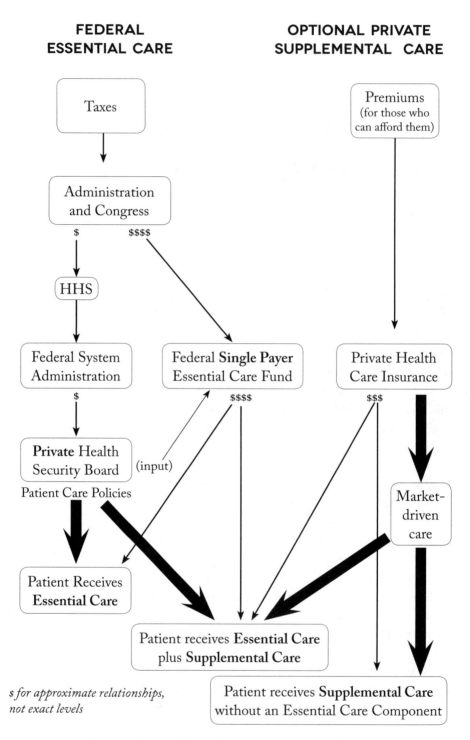

FEDERAL ESSENTIAL CARE

OPTIONAL PRIVATE SUPPLEMENTAL CARE

Taxes

Premiums
(for those who
can afford them)

Administration
and Congress

$ $$$$

HHS

Federal System
Administration

$

Private Health
Security Board

Patient Care Policies

Federal **Single Payer**
Essential Care Fund

$$$$

(input)

Private Health
Care Insurance

$$$

Market-
driven
care

Patient Receives
Essential Care

Patient receives **Essential Care**
plus **Supplemental Care**

Patient receives **Supplemental Care**
without an Essential Care Component

*$ for approximate relationships,
not exact levels*

Figure 1. General Single Payer Essential Care System

David Himmelstein and Steffie Woolhandler and Dr. Young served a term as PNHP President in the early years. Although universal health care coverage based on a national government program was well underway in other countries by then, the persistent, dedicated advocacy of this social modernization for the U.S. started with the PNHP through these early proponents, with increasing support as it has grown to its current 19,000 members.

During his 61 years practicing as an internist in Chicago, Dr. Young had a singular history—at least equal to any other American physician—of prominent, widely based liberal activism for social change in civil rights and public health. Our conversation was inspiring. Now over 90, the vision of reform to which he has devoted so much over the years shone through: "The public wants the coverage—if you don't have coverage and you have a major illness, you die. . . . I'll make this generalization. Health care is a necessity—not something you can take like candy. We're not doing well in covering the whole population and people know that. So I hope we can develop a national health program." He had advice about other practical considerations that will be found later in the book but it is worth keeping his enduring fundamental social precept in mind as we consider health care reform.

Quality in any health care system would benefit from improved involvement of medical professionals. From thinking about the need for doctors to have a fundamental role, it was an easy step to understand that the simplicity of a single payer system would maximize the effectiveness of doctors' input.

In this chapter we start with a look at our country's health care needs now, examine the basics of how we can structure a national health program, then consider how that mechanism can be made to work. In later chapters we will consider the many other challenging issues facing American health care, and the detailed decisions necessary to establish a fair, effective, workable single payer system.

THE PROBLEM

The need for more substantial reform is acute. Although individual Americans generally receive excellent care from their doctors, there are many large problems left over beyond that. Overall, about 15% of Americans were without health care coverage in 2014 after a major impact of the Affordable Care Act.[2] But the problem goes far beyond the uninsured. Typical testimonials from those who can afford to be covered include: "Don't take away my Medicare," and, "I want to be able to continue to see the same doctor." Even people with insurance now feel threatened. Recent polling indicates that the public wants universal coverage. As Nobel prize-winning economist Dr. Paul Krugman has written, the public is more supportive of this social welfare than the centrist Democratic members of Congress. For our government, health care coverage is a veiled public health issue. If the 45,000 people who die each year due to the lack of health coverage[3] were to be dying instead from some bizarre new infectious disease, it would matter.

Too often a sick patient in America may be threatened not only by the illness but by the worry of how much the treatment will cost, unlike in other countries. Of course this is particularly true for the uninsured but also pertains to those who have insurance but are not well-to-do. For them, the questions of whether the care is covered and what the copayment will cost loom large. There was considerable public interest in the run-up to the passage of Obamacare. A Harris Interactive–Health Day poll found that 84% of people 45–64 years old with insurance still were worried about being able to pay for health care in 2009.[4] Other polls underscore this: over 80% said that changing health care to make it more affordable is very important.[5] When compared to other issues, 30 to 50% said improved affordability is more important than anything else.[6,7] In the NYTimes/CBS News poll of June 2009 cited by Paul Krugman, 72% supported a government-sponsored health plan that would compete with private plans. Even with Republicans it is a toss-up with 50% support. Fifty percent overall thought the government would be better at providing health care and 59% said that the government would be better at containing costs. The percent in agreement with each of these increased quite a bit over the 2007 responses. These concerns of those with insurance have not changed since the ACA.

Listen to Jonni in Anchorage, KY (before 2010, in Obama's Health Care Stories for America): He had survived cancer the year before and was in remission. He was laid off for a year and survived on his 401k and credit cards "while I fought for my life." His hopes for financial recovery included refinancing his house but were not realized because there were too many expenses not reimbursed through the insurance company. In addition to the resulting debt, his ongoing medical expenses including premium, copayments, and coinsurance will be 40% of his net pay for the next five years. "Add the bills the insurance rejects and makes excuses for and I'm bankrupt many times over. I've worked for the last 25 years and always had health insurance. Little did I know that when I needed it, I would be abandoned by the system. I am effectively bankrupt but alive." Talk about a fighting spirit ! But however praiseworthy his resolve is, Americans must do better than that for its citizens.

There are many examples of responsible, working citizens who are being dragged down by the traps in U.S. health care coverage. Incredibly, in Kaiser Family Foundation data, of the 22% who had trouble paying their medical bills in 2008, 4% had declared bankruptcy due to medical expenses.[8] A recent study by Dr. David Himmelstein and other members of the Physicians for a National Health Program (PNHP) predicted over 800,000 bankruptcies due to illness in 2009.[9] Very commonly this happens in spite of the bankrupted person having had health insurance.[10] True, it seems likely that other factors are important in at least a reasonable fraction of these cases. But it is hard to avoid the conclusion that large numbers of bankruptcies would not have occurred had it not been for medical costs. Moreover, about 20% of people put off medical care or prescription medicine purchases because of cost[11] (this has been found repeatedly). So medical costs because we lack a national system are hurting the health of those who are still solvent.

Now that President Obama has signed the Patient Protection and Affordability Act of 2010 (ACA) into law, did Americans really get what they wanted? No. Americans want security, cost control and a fair shake in their health care. The Congress, influenced by the health insurance industry, threw out cost savings that would have been possible with single-payer and the public option. Then Congress turned around and opposed reform by citing the very costs they themselves had perpetuated. And insurance company excesses were not curbed effectively. Recently U.S. health insurance companies announced plans to raise premiums between 20 to 40% for 2016.[12] The recently proposed legislation to fend off the adverse tiering by which health insurers escape covering expensive patients is imperfect. The ACA gave us only partial reform—it still costs too much, leaves too many out, and is too dangerous to those who are in. The people wanted the direction the ACA took. They did not want the obstructionism and nay-saying that prevented it from going far enough.

Even so, a marvelous result of the tumult over health care was that Americans can now finally dream of the day when we will have a doctor for every family. The government does care. In spite of obstructionist states unwilling to take up the Medicaid Expansion and multiple legislative and judicial attacks, the ACA survives. Young adults can stay longer on their parents' insurance plan, coverage cannot be refused due to pre-existing conditions and some other industry abuses are curtailed. The law has provided for more quality driven health care decisions and has begun to slow the growth of our massive national health care budget. The Urban Institute documents that over 16 million more adults have insurance.[13] As the 2016 election buzz increases, it seems that the Republicans are winding down their attempts to repeal Obamacare.

Fortunately for Jonni in the example above, Kentucky was one of the states that endorsed the ACA, with "Kynect," a state program with a health insurance exchange and Medicaid expansion. So Jonni may find new help for health care coverage. But we have quite a long way to go. Recently, columnist Thomas Edsall reviewed reports that the public has been so unsettled by the battles and difficulties with the ACA that there is a reaction against any further reform.[14] Time will tell whether the public is that fickle. There are still at least 25 million Americans without health care coverage. Moreover many millions more have low value insurance that will leave them stranded if they become seriously ill. This endangerment will become increasingly real as illness strikes more and more people with inadequate insurance who are healthy today.

A BASIC SINGLE PAYER SYSTEM

An optimal health care system (Figure 1) must serve the following principles:

1. Patient care as the dominant consideration for essential care;
2. Incentives for best essential care and removal of market-based disincentives;
3. Essential care for everyone to be covered, decided by a national plan for quality;
4. Cost savings from the benefits of best care rather than by budget restrictions on care;
5. Electronic medical records to provide complete, seamless, national data for the system;
6. Supplemental care to be with no impact on essential care or the national budget.

Universal coverage specifics will be determined by professional oversight. We will explore how advancing technology will provide for this in Chapter 5. Care is funded by progressive taxation and there is no copayment or other charge at the time of treatment. Provision is made for those wishing and able to pay for additional supplemental care, although it would have no tax benefits. The government pays for all essential care plus a small amount for administration of the system. Supplemental care might include fancier surroundings for essential care and for other non-essential items, with protections against supplemental care causing any negative impact on essential care or cost to the taxpayer. As shown by Gerard Anderson and Bianca Frogner[15] in Figure 2, compared with the U.S., all other countries studied have a smaller but measurable amount of their health care budget from private means. To avoid the privileged impinging on everyone else's care and increasing our taxes, it will be necessary to plan for controlling supplemental care from the start.

There are many precedents for "Quasi-governmental" entities. These include Amtrak, the origin of the Rand Corporation and the Tennesee Valley Authority. Each of these serves a more limited segment of the population. The universal impact of health care access may magnify the visibility of the Health Security Board and thus promote transparency. Although most federal health care programs are completely run by the government, there is one medical "Quasi-governmental" exception: organ transplantation.

To provide for the evolution of organ allocation rules, a national transplant system was established in the U.S. by the National Organ Transplant Act in 1984. The national system called the Organ Procurement and Transplantation Network (OPTN) is a public-private partnership run by a nonprofit private corporation named UNOS (the United Network for Organ Sharing). This law was passed because of the special nature of organ transplantation, which is expensive, publicly visible, and requires oversight to keep it fair. Priority for allocation of organs from deceased donors (from someone who just died and there was consent for donation) is done by rules that include how urgently a recipient needs the transplant. Making transplantation policy requires experienced technical clinical understanding. The rules are generated by a private expert OPTN board composed of practicing transplant professionals and the public. The Board work is transparent, it operates through open meetings, and is guided by highly accurate data as provided for in the law. During my career as a transplant surgeon I was involved in this, including as UNOS President for a year and for a stint as the Director of the Division of Transplantation in the Health Resources Services Administration (HRSA) of The Department of Health and Human Services. This Division oversees the national program for the federal government. From my experience in how this works regarding technical clinical issues, fairness, ability to incorporate patient needs and professional/institutional considerations in the rules and its ability to serve government oversight in the citizens' interests, I believe that the OPTN/UNOS serves as a model for how a national system could work for medicine in general. Working in this national transplant system, supported by the staff at UNOS, I and my colleagues helped to arrange solutions for contentious organ allocation problems, correct patient safety issues with optimal policies, support institutions for improvement where needed—and, rarely, participated in penalizing institutions for misbehavior, all done by independent effort from the medical field with effective federal oversight in the background. Its

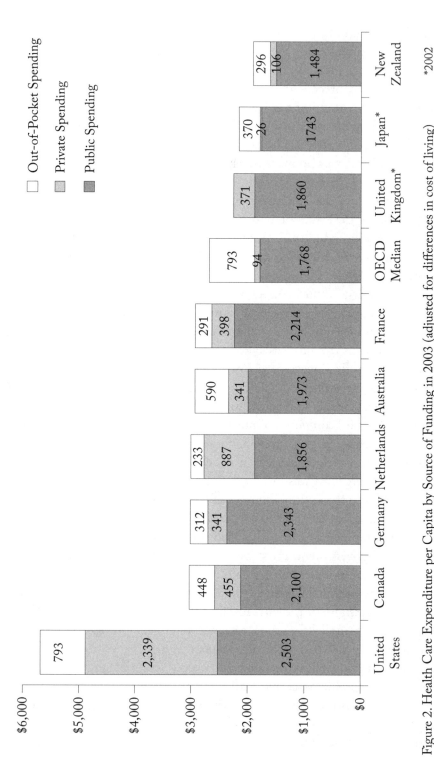

Figure 2. Health Care Expenditure per Capita by Source of Funding in 2003 (adjusted for differences in cost of living)
Source: OECD Health Data 2005; AIHW Health Expenditure Australia 2003–4

success proves that the concepts could be used to develop a general national system for overseeing essential care.

Although decisions by the OPTN are not directly about reimbursement or medical coverage, in practice they control patient care issues and the option of doing transplants at each institution. Decisions that affect the bottom lines of transplant programs are made regularly by the OPTN after these authoritative data-driven deliberations by the committees and the OPTN Board. This represents an effective way for professionals and other knowledgeable stakeholders to deal with a highly technical and evolving field, supporting innovation and patient equity. Cooperation is very good. The rules are generally followed without dispute. Troublesome non-compliance has been uncommon although occasionally programs are resistant to coming into line. Ultimately compliance has always been achieved and only rarely has misbehavior required a severe penalty. Granted, transplantation is a small field and its clinical programs are tied together by the need for donated organs. Nevertheless, the process works in this setting, controlling clinical decisions that have a financial impact for physicians and transplant institutions.

You may suspect me of bias, coming from my background in transplantation. But you can find the same view from a sociologist who studied the OPTN as an alternative to a pure federal process. In his book, "Medical Governance," David Weimer writes that the timeliness and authority with which the medical field can deal with clinical issues through the OPTN are advantages over a federal process.[16] This is a valuable academic confirmation of the practical potential for the role of the proposed Health Security Board.

This success in transplantation has confirmed my conviction that when given the authority, the medical profession can provide singular cost-effective oversight of clinical processes. Lessons learned from the history of other such public-private organizations mentioned above could help the Board of Health Security function.

PROS AND CONS OF SINGLE PAYER

There may be skepticism on the grounds that it is impossible to get doctors to agree about anything, or to govern themselves. But these are not laws of nature. Doctors can agree when the data are clear, and the facts will be clear for most guidelines. Care choices that are more uncertain will require a more tentative approach to guidelines, with the Board using clinical judgment and often determining an acceptable range of options, subject to refinement as the facts emerge over time. Patients must be helped by the medical team to have a clear understanding and make an informed decision when there are options. Acceptable deviations from the recommendations may occur, but in other cases the Board may find that failure to follow the rules requires redress. It is the doctors who can do that oversight authoritatively. We will see that purely administrative processes such as exist now, whether public or private, are a failure regarding clinical quality oversight. As electronic medical records mature after a misguided start, this capacity will facilitate data driven rules and monitoring. EMR will soon be a powerful force supporting doctors in health care reform. Many descriptions of the problems in U.S. health care delivery and the benefit of moving to a single payer system have represented position papers from PNHP members and other experts.[17] A large treatise supporting single payer was reported from the Institute of Medicine Committee on the Consequences of Being Uninsured with papers emerging from 2001–2004 and many other reports since have confirmed support for this reform.[18]

This version of single payer in Figure 1 has details that are in dispute. The PNHP feels that no supplemental care is permissible[19] but there are good arguments in favor of including supplemental care as we will see when we address this controversy in more detail in later chapters. The goal for Figure 1 is simply to be clear on the proposed mechanism: every citizen taxpayer pays for essential care through their taxes. They have an option to obtain additional, supplemental care, through insurance or out of pocket, just as they might decide to buy a car and obtain automobile insurance. Other variations that might apply to this concept have been suggested.[20] The practical argument in favor of planning for a fraction of the nation's health care provided through private means, such as from insurance or out of pocket, is that this exists in all other countries. Poorer access relative to private care has become an issue for people treated in the public system in most countries,[21] so access to care for people covered through essential care must be protected.

It will be particularly important to ensure that essential care patients have access that is equitable, because in the U.S. it is likely that many will choose to buy private insurance for supplemental care. There might be an incentive to give precedence to supplemental care patients when their care has a component of essential care if the payment is larger for supplemental care. A counter incentive to avoid this downward spiral is needed. For this it is important that all essential care be reimbursed by the single payer system. The extra reimbursement for supplemental care plus essential care would be only the difference between the amount paid for as essential care and the extra supplemental cost that is not covered under essential. An example of how this might be structured for a given episode of care is given in Figure 3. In this case, the essential care reimbursement is $100. At baseline, presuming access for essential care patients in the region is good, if a patient has supplemental coverage, the total reimbursement including the supplemental care reimbursement in this case might be $150. On the other hand, if access for essential care is poor because of the incentive to put supplemental care first, the essential care portion of the reimbursement for joint essential/supplemental care patients would be lowered, decreasing the total amount from supplemental plus essential coverage paid to the doctor or hospital and thus decreasing the incentive that favored supplemental patients. When access for patients with only essential care coverage improves, the essential care payments for the jointly reimbursed care will be restored back to the baseline essential amount plus the supplemental payment, totaling $150. Occasionally very rich patients might offer considerably more for the supplemental component. This might require employing more severe disincentives if it were common enough to seriously impact access to essential care.

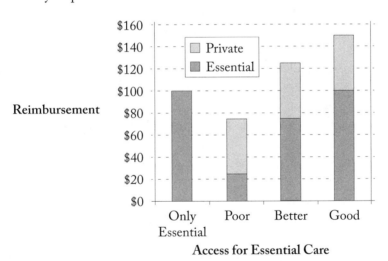

Figure 3. Incentive to maintain fair access by
adjustment of federal portion of fees paid.

It would not be necessary to make the measure, such as waiting times, mathematically equal for essential and supplemental care. It should be sufficient if the incentive keeps the difference within whatever reasonable range is chosen. Differences in the waiting times for treatment for cancer and urgent heart disease, for instance, will need to be kept short. Waiting times for more elective things can be somewhat longer, but also must be kept reasonably fair.

In creating our national health plan we have a great advantage compared with other countries: we can decide at the outset on the details of the mechanism in the U.S. to maintain equal access for everyone based on recent medical advances, unlike the older systems on other countries. Moreover, the Board will be able to adjust or change the specifics of the mechanism as necessary, based on first principles and data, not political posturing. Quality care for each patient remains the guiding principle.

Single payer has been sharply criticized from many directions. Hillary Clinton has said that she favors the Affordable Care Act but not single payer,[22] a damning proclamation, given her prominence. In a segment of a Hastings Center Report Dr. Ezekiel Emanuel, an oncologist and ethicist who was part of the Obamacare legislative team in the White House, strongly criticizes single payer as un-American.[23] The alternative to single payer is the proposal championed most learnedly by Harvard Business School's Michael Porter, PhD, who is a standard bearer for those challenging a national government payment program. He believes in "a value based market" for national health care insurance on the basis of market economics, unregulated by interference with free enterprise.[24] On the other hand, it is widely recognized that the conservative Republican establishment has no coherent proposal to compete with Obamacare, let alone to stand against a single national government payer system.

One argument by those who resist changing to a system that covers everyone such as single payer is the contention that things are not so bad with our health care here in the U.S. now. They deny or excuse our lower average survival compared with other countries; the illnesses that needlessly threaten those without insurance that make any care they do eventually get more expensive; and the impairment of our freedoms due to the tyranny of private health insurance rules. This denial of reality is partly due to intentional, malignant disinformation.

Other objections, although easily answerable, have substance that bears discussion. These will be addressed in more detail in later chapters. They include concerns about loss of patient or physician autonomy, loss of choice of doctor, poorer or less individualized quality, increased cost, long waiting times, squelched innovation and in general a loss of free market choice. But in the U.S. waiting times now are immeasurably long for the millions without insurance.[25] With a national system we can implement far better quality measures at considerably lower costs than we have today. There is free choice of care and caregiver in the system proposed in Figure 1. Much of the innovation we rely on for our medical advances comes from our strong government support of research in the U.S. and from drugs and devices developed in the nationalized health care systems of other developed countries. And a national program that provides necessary health care for all would address the critical fact that there cannot be a satisfactory functioning market for the actual process of deciding the clinical details about health care because good health cannot be balanced against money. Good health is priceless.

The objection to single payer based on claims that a government run program is un-American, that it will deny individual freedoms and that everyone should just take the responsibility to help themselves, is not really even about medical care. It is a misplaced longing for a simpler world, cynically nurtured by conservatives for their own ends—if not outright bigotry, and at any rate these dreams are not, in fact, provided for by American health care at present. The present dismal situation for so many of our citizens without a national health care coverage program can be considered far more "un-American." Moreover, given the VA, Medicare, and other federal medical programs, slightly over half of health care in the U.S is already government run—and there is no enthusiasm for giving these programs up.

No convincing arguments against reform by citing international experience are given by the conservative establishment, such as the Heritage Foundation, except that patients and doctors won't like national federal coverage for all Americans. Claims that single payer is not in the mainstream, is a disaster in all other developed countries, and, based on international comparisons, will not improve simplicity and quality and provide savings, all fail to reckon with the massive problems we have in the U.S. at present. We will review the arguments about social preferences and markets more as we discuss various aspects of reform, but it is worth just stating here that we have the most commoditized market-based health care system in the world and we have very serious fundamental problems with our national health care compared to other countries.

SINGLE PAYER CONVERSATIONS

In fact, there is considerable general support emerging for the single payer solution.[26] From all of this, frustrating questions emerge. Given the arguments for the advantages of universal national coverage for health care, why has the United States held out against it? Why is single payer so generally considered "off the table."? So often, single payer seems to be an unacceptable topic for discussion. Is it just the obvious political and corporate resistance? Can that be responsible for such an obstructive corrosion of common sense?

Or are there other things that need to be understood that create our national exception to the rule among developed countries? Academic observations relevant to single payer have been analyzed and published with various conclusions but, to be fair, since we do not have an actual U.S. single payer system to study scientifically (as one might isolate a molecule and prove that its mutation causes a disease) and since the systems in other countries are at best only arguably applicable to our possibilities, academic studies must remain inferential. Medical economics can provide a framework and analytic tools but are not a mechanism for solving human problems.[27] And there is the possibility of bias because of the very personal character of health care: (Dr. Uwe Reinhardt quoted by Frank Diamond[28] on vertical and horizontal health economists): "When we are vertical, we talk a tough game. 'Don't do marginally beneficial things.' When you are horizontal, even when you are an economist, on an operating table. . . ."

Similarly, news articles span the possibilities but without establishing a consensus that deems single payer a realistic consideration. The questions are unlikely to be answered by citing more and more articles—there is no indication that some undiscovered additional basic insight lurks in what has been written either in the popular or academic press. True, public discussion may be increasing somewhat, but it still seems that many academics as well as politicians feel justified in a condescending conservatism that precludes thoughtful scrutiny of this critical issue.

I decided that the way to get at these questions about single payer was to talk with some people who were likely to have thought out something to say about it. I initiated a series of interviews of knowledgeable people with backgrounds that would have led them naturally to think about a national health program and single payer, at least in passing. The process and a list of the interviewees are documented in the last section of the book. Interviewees were people that I knew or who were recommended to me, and who were willing to talk with me from various viewpoints about a single payer solution and health care reform in general. This certainly does not represent a scientifically valid poll. It is quite the opposite: The choice of participants was arbitrary and nonrandom, the questions were not uniform, the settings varied. No statistical analysis would be valid. Instead, perhaps it can be called a field trip, strolling through the human geography of thoughts about health care reform. Among the many insights that I will describe, two particular points emerged: it certainly is generally possible to discuss single payer in spite of the paucity of that conversation at present and, although single payer ranks high as a likely best option, there is plenty of room for deliberation about the details as we make further improvements in health care for America.

CHAPTER TWO
COSTS

Health care reform is up against a powerful pervasive conviction that it will cost too much. In this chapter we review the overall U.S. budget for health care now, with specifics about costs of private insurance and public government coverage, address administration and advertising which are two largely nonessential costs, and summarize the implications of these topics for possible cost control in single payer health care reform. Later chapters will relate the single payer concept to a variety of additional medical areas where savings could be found. The general economic advantage for the country with a single payer system will become evident.

Regardless of what they wanted to say about single payer, every one of the people I interviewed included costs in their comments. In view of the public concern in recent years about the huge amount that the United States spends on health care, perhaps I should not have been surprised about the range of opinions related to costs that I encountered. The discussion of the country's health care budget must at the least include federal programs, insurance and other private programs, public policy, clinical care and social change. I consulted with Dr. Stephen Schroeder, who has the remarkable distinction of expertise in all of these areas. During his career in the practice of Internal Medicine, he spent time in the Centers for Disease Control and Prevention, started a Health Maintenance Organization at George Washington University, was Chairman and CEO of the Robert Wood Johnson Foundation where he was instrumental in the remarkable success we have had in the U.S. with smoking cessation, and became a member of the Institute of Medicine. Presently he is Professor of Health and Health Care at U.C. San Francisco.

During our interview, Dr. Schroeder weighed in on several aspects, but overall expressed a somber pessimism that anything will be done soon about the relatively large U.S. health care budget: "You've got an industry that is almost ⅕ of the GDP with various components—the docs, the hospitals, the teaching hospitals, the device makers, big pharma, health insurance—companies that are very, very powerful—so I think the cost problem is going to stay with us." He doesn't see the political will to change.

Some expressed a more serious urgency to fix the problem. I invited former Sen. Alan Simpson to be interviewed and his office referred me to Charles Bond in Berkley, CA, a lawyer who, among other things, has done many presentations to medical and other groups on the status of health care. In Bond's view, "Health care is the world's largest bubble. It dwarfs any and all other bubbles . . . until the rational pricing of health care is addressed . . . you will have a bubble that is bursting and is going to become a serious problem." Others with that view whom we will see more of in later chapters included engineer and former college president James Duderstadt, PhD, and Drs. Jon Fielding, Jack Lewin, Frank Opelka and Sam Wells. Dr. Lewin: "We can't afford our health care system—it's unsustainable"

On the other hand, Dr. Schroeder's view that high health care costs are not at the point where they are likely to be addressed politically was shared by health policy professor Dr. Gerry Anderson ("There is no constituency for cost containment."), although tempered somewhat by surgeon Dr. Andy Warshaw: "The government is going to try through some of the provisions in the Medicare Access and CHIP Reauthorization Act but the final results of this are not established." Most unexpected was the relatively bland view of two people that I interviewed whose political sentiments I would have thought would be more in line politically with that of lawyer Bond (to whom I had been referred from "Deficit Scold"[1] Alan Simpson's office). One bland view was from former HHS Secretary Tommy Thompson who invoked recent encouraging news: "In different years I have different opinions on that, Jim. Right now I don't see us crashing. I think 5 years ago when it looked like we were going to break through 20% or 25% or 30% that—ah—it was going to be a runaway train that we could not control and therefore the potentiality of crashing was there. Now I don't see the crisis facing us as much." Similarly, from Dr. Jack Rowe, former head of Aetna, on whether health insurance costs are too high: "I see it differently. What I would say is that for the first time in over 40 years, the year over year increase in the unit price and the volume of health care services in the United States is less than the growth in GDP. It was 2 and a half points higher than GDP for 40 years and the proportion of GDP spent on health care rose inexorably. It is now flat or falling." (They were referring to the data showing total health expenditure as a % GDP 2010 to 2012 at 17.7–17.9%, cf, a 12% increase over years 2005–2009).[2]

This all is in the context of years of public alarm about rising health care costs. See *Money Driven Medicine* by Maggie Mahar,[3] the recent series of investigative articles in the New York Times by Elizabeth Rosenthal, *Paying until it Hurts*[4] and the Time Magazine article *Bitter Pill*[5] plus the subsequent book[6] by Steven Brill, among many other reports.

It seems that future health care reform, whether it involves single- or whatever- payer, will not succeed without a more general consensus on how serious the present cost burden is and what the prospective impact will be of reform on costs to the country and to each citizen. The present cost burden is the topic in this chapter. In later chapters on the system of health care and its reform, we will complete the cost discussion with consideration of what we are getting for our money and the how a national system will improve quality and lower the budget. Addressing the high cost and the value received for this spending by the country involves much of what health care reform is all about.

TRENDS IN HEALTH CARE COSTS

Overall, in 2013 the U.S. spent about $2.9 trillion on health care. The Centers for Medicare and Medicaid (CMS) broke this down as follows:[7]

Hospital care	$937
Physicians and clinical services	$587
Prescription drugs	$271
Dental services	$111
Other residential, health and personal care	$148
Nursing care and retirement facilities	$156
Other categories each < $100 bill.	$259

Until late in the 20th century, the national health care budget remained small and was not a prominent concern but, as Dr. Schroeder notes,[8] by 1971 the cost "had risen to 7.5% of the gross domestic product and was headed for an 'unsustainable' 10%". Of course, in defiance of unsustainability, the rise continued to just over 17% before leveling off since 2010. Note that the recent reprieve represents only a diminished rate of annual rise in health care spending, but not a retreat below 17% of GDP.

Both anticipation of the Affordable Care Act and its actual provisions may have contributed to the decreased growth in health care expenses,[9,10] but decreased spending may have also been due to the recession that persisted after the ACA took effect.[11] As the economy strengthens, this spending may return. At any rate, the decrease in growth of spending was tolerated and provides hope that there is potential to accommodate a downturn in spending with fiscal restraint in health care.

A dissenting thought about the fraction of GDP spent on health care, a view which I present as his vision of the future, not yet achievable, was from an insurance salesman I interviewed, Phil Boling: "It depends on how you look at it. If you are having your life improved or your life saved by medical care, that sounds like an investment in people's health. I mean, do we complain that too much of a percentage of GDP is spent on SUVs and pick up trucks and automobiles? No, they're products and services and people want to be able to buy them and use them and they should be able to do that, so health care is important and if we're getting a good return on that in terms of increased health, increased life span, the easing of pain, increased mobility, functionality and the ability to work when otherwise we might not be able to, that sounds like a pretty good investment to me. So if it's a certain percent of the GDP, I don't know if that's relevant."

Of course one problem with the high cost now is that there is too much else for which we need the money. Looking ahead hundreds of years, all the claptrap of our daily lives will become easier and less expensive—probably true whatever the SUV or iPhone equivalents are 500 years from now—but the one thing that will increasingly dominate our needs will be the too frail physical presence of our bodies within which we try to survive. So Phil Boling might be right in some future world. Perhaps health care will grow to 80% of GDP and consist of very fair, necessary patient care costs someday.

But for now, spending around $3 trillion annually for health care is a cause for concern for the country because it impacts the federal tax revenue available for other programs ranging from military defense to fragile social programs such as food stamps and unemployment benefits as well as effective, appropriate federal health care spending. Except for defense, these all suffer from the threat of funding cuts by those who decry big government. Spending to help the poorest Americans produces critical political disagreement in the U.S. On the one hand, those decrying economic harm from the increasing national debt condemn spending to help the poor as unjustifiable. But economist and New York Times columnist Paul Krugman castigates these complainers[12] noting that they really only advocate poorly disguised resistance to using some of our national wealth to help the less fortunate. Ironically, given our present economic situation, increasing government spending could actually help, not hurt, the economy in general. We seem to be managing, in the short run at least, with health care spending at 17% of GDP and an economy that is slowly but convincingly recovering from the frightful recession in the first decade of the 21st century. Nevertheless, a thrifty approach to health care spending without rationing or compromising quality is an important goal. There are other ways to increase government spending that would help Americans more. As we review various aspects of health care in this book, strategies for savings through health care reform will become apparent. We will also review realities about the relationship of health care costs to other social issues.

From the individual perspective, the cost of our health care is a personal financial issue for each of us. Together, Americans bear the burden of paying for it all since the national budget represents the total of taxes, premiums, copayments and other charges to those who can pay. And for the poorest among us, the high cost has been an impenetrable barrier to receiving timely, effective care.

For those who do get care, a few diseases dominate the reimbursement landscape. George Halverson, CEO of Kaiser Permanente, documents the five serious chronic diseases that are responsible for 70% of the nation's health care expenditure:[13] diabetes, congestive heart failure, coronary artery disease, asthma and depression. From his practical point of view on coverage, costs due to treatment of these illnesses are a principle challenge. From another perspective, chronic illness is a large part of the country's health care bill. Care for the ten percent of patients with chronic illness represents about 64% of the U.S. health care budget.[14] These are areas for attention in all of the aspects of health care that we will explore in the chapters to come.

Most important in thinking about health care expenses in general is the split between private (mostly insurance) funding and public funding, including Medicare, Medicaid, Children's Health Insurance Program and the Veterans Administration.

PRIVATE HEALTH INSURANCE

A bit less than one half of the health care budget in the U.S. is provided through private payments, mostly as health insurance. To receive care through private insurance you must disclose any health problems that you have. Under the Patient Protection and Affordable Care Act, your health problems cannot directly threaten your eligibility, but insurance companies may charge more to insure people who have pre-existing conditions and they can structure copayment levels and caregiver networks to discourage high risk populations.

You are fortunate if you are able to get sufficient coverage for a premium+deductible package that you can afford.

It turns out that these costs for the premiums and other aspects of insurance add up, even for healthy people. The Affordable Care Act introduced complexities such as mandates and rebates that helped many more get insurance, as well and imposed controls on some harmful insurance company practices, but the established picture from before that law is illustrative and unchanged in principle. In Maryland, an average family of four could get coverage for $876 a month.[15] This was neat: it had no deductible and no coinsurance. Of course that premium of over $10,000 a year might be a little over-the-top. Well, there was a plan for $345 a month. True, it had a $5,000 per person per year deductible and an annual out-of-pocket limit of $20,000—after the deductible—and 30% coinsurance (after copayment). Copayments are, for instance, $35 per person for a primary care visit. So you elect this insurance package and later the wife gets the flu, then becomes sicker and has a two-day stay in the hospital, needing a bronchoscopy for pneumonia. She fully recovers. The hospital bill? Let's guess it is $35,000, probably a low-ball estimate. You pay the first $5,000 on the deductible. You pay the 30% coinsurance: $9,000. Of course there was an office visit before and three in follow up: $140 for copayments. The antibiotics and decongestants for 10 more days cost $500, of which you pay the first $200 (pharmaceutical deductible) and a $65 copayment for "Tier 3" medicine. That comes to $14,405 out-of-pocket. After all, insurance did pick up the tab for over half of it. But that is just for this illness, not for any other care for your family this year, and in the meantime you paid $4,140 this year in premiums. Well, you could hope that no one would get sick next year. That's health care in America.

Before the ACA, most private insurance was supported by contributions from employers. Even though reliance on employer-based insurance is a feature of the ACA, employers have been changing from premium reimbursement to "account based" or "defined benefit" plans which shift the risk to the workers by providing them with a fixed amount, and expecting them to decide on the benefits they wish to elect. But for those still receiving the standard employment benefit, employers contribute to their employees' premiums for coverage. This is through plans established by each individual business. This is attractive because the employer contribution amount is not taxed as income. Typically the plan by which the employer makes these payments involves negotiations by the employer with a health insurance carrier. Horse trading occurs regarding how low the cost will be (to the employee but also to the employer) and how much the plan's features vary for executives compared with workers at low salary levels. Some items of care may also be negotiated away by the employer in order to get a financially acceptable package. A union representing employees may have some input during these negotiations, and then employees may have choices when they sign up. Nevertheless, the choices from this list of options will be negotiated with the insurance company mainly by the employer. For these reasons, before the insured patient gets to see the doctor, important decisions about their care—many outside the patient's control—have often been made. These conditions will partly dictate the care that the patient will (or will not) get.

Employer contributions can be a major advantage of a job because they do lessen the amount the employee must pay to get health insurance. But in addition to potentially restricting their health care options, there are hidden expenses. When employers pay part of their employees' health insurance premiums, the deal they make for their employees is likely to involve higher copayments and deductibles. This is in order to lower the shared amount of the premium paid by the employer.[16,17] And salaries for their employees are lower: the money the employer contributes to employee premiums is not likely to come out of the company's profits.[18] Finally, large businesses can unfairly restrict the better value "Cadillac" plans to top management.

These employer health premium contributions seem like nice tax breaks for those receiving them. But in the big picture this tax-free benefit for millions of workers raises taxes for everyone. At over $100 billion, it was our largest single federal tax subsidy.[19] For these reasons, tax breaks for higher-income employees are decreased in the ACA of 2010. That was controversial. Although cutting those tax breaks increases taxes for those with employer coverage, it is not quite as great a loss to these employees as would appear since it decreases the tax burden a little for everyone. And the freedom provided by the ACA to change jobs without worrying about health care is a boon to all.

When a person shows up for care (often to a care giver specified by his or her insurance), clerks will first check to be sure that appropriate insurance coverage is in place. If there is a copayment or deductible involved, it is secured either up front or arranged for at the time that the care needed by the patient is decided. Then the doctor provides, or arranges for, the needed care.

When the doctor enters the scene, most health care discussions presume that the actual care provided is settled according to what the doctor thinks, with nothing more to discuss. But considerable further time and expense by the doctor's staff, and often by the doctor, may be necessary in order to get the insurance company to agree to pay for the proposed care.[20] There is little in the ACA to protect doctors and patients from all of this.

Of course, this is the U.S. story. In most developed countries, the patient merely shows up and is cared for by the doctor, who is then reimbursed with no questions asked (and very little paperwork). We shall consider Sen. Sanders' views in greater detail later, but one of the delightful stories he told me illustrates this: He was curious, thinking of U.S. Social Security cards and the advanced "Carte Vitale," that citizens carry for health care in France. "We had young kids from the UK right in this room a couple of years ago and I said, "Show me your health care card, I'm interested in your health insurance card." And they looked at each other: "We have no card." They don't need a card or forms filled out to get health care at home.

Insurance is supposed to assure that people can share the risk to be able to afford health care. But in order to control costs, the insurance company functions by inserting market-based options for the potential patient—and their employer—that can cause choices that would decrease or prevent care. The possible options for coverage are pre-selected by the employer. A plan may require that the patient go to certain doctors or places for care. Alternatively, other choices may be discouraged by increased costs to the patient. In choosing care, patients need to decide whether they are willing and able to provide the copayments. Of course premiums are lower and more appealing if you select a plan that requires you to pay more for care if you get sick. And in the past, if you had a policy that you preferred instead, it would inhibit your changing jobs, although this problem is partially corrected now with the ACA.

Insurance companies are moving to policies with more individual payments at the time of service. The private insurance burden on employers and patients is increasing as insurance companies in general start to share more of the risk than previously. This trend is described by Dr. Jack Rowe. When I first met Dr. Rowe, he struck me as an energetic, irrepressible Fellow in Nephrology while I was a Surgical Fellow learning kidney transplantation. He was great to work with and I am not surprised to have learned of his later career. He says that because he felt that hemodialysis, a major part of nephrology, was too tame intellectually, he switched to gerontology. Part way through his academic career, he became the President of the Aetna Insurance Company. They needed help. The company was losing a million dollars a day. Relating the story, he says he tightened up the company's finances with thousands of layoffs, cancelled several money-losing contracts, settled a class-action law suit, and worked with doctors to institute programs on obesity and palliative care. In six years, Aetna became one of the most admired health care companies in the business, he claims. He is presently a Professor at the Columbia

University Millman School of Public Health where he teaches a graduate course called "Transforming Health Care."

Dr. Rowe on risk: "The way I look at it is the percent profit vs. the risk There's a general tendency towards self-insurance in the market with the employers being at risk—you're at Johns Hopkins Medicine. They're self-insured you know? They may have a stop loss policy. The insurance company that covers them has an administrative services-only contract. And that's growing so there's an increased share towards self insurance. Then you have all these government-sponsored programs where the government is at risk and what you see is that the insurance companies are generally taking less risk. They are making much less profit, but . . . any investor will tell you that your return should be risk adjusted. If you're taking a big risk you should receive a high return. If you're taking no risk, like treasury bills, you're going to get a low return. So . . . if you have a very big insurance company that is now basically running a very low risk business which provides administrative services, they'll make 5% on that maybe, at no risk: a risk free 5%."

Of course even a state government or a large employer may be able to self-insure because they have thousands of lives among which to spread the risk. Unfortunately risk-shifting is also being touted increasingly for individuals.[21] In the family with the spouse who required hospitalization as we described above, the risk to the individual when illness strikes is not shared. it is sheerly the beneficiary's problem.

The physician must often take the patient's financial status into consideration. Even then, time and money may be spent by the doctor making sure the insurance will indeed cover the care that is proposed. If you and the doctor manage to clear all these hurdles, then you can proceed to getting treated. Of course, the expense for all of this insurance business includes more than the costs of the actual care. You are also paying for the profits and additional administrative expenses for insurance payers, as well as the paperwork by doctors and hospitals, that results from all of this kerfuffle.[22] That is where much of the money you pay for health insurance coverage goes.

An illustration of just how tragically ridiculous all this can be was provided by Dr. Ben Carson, the well-known pediatric neurosurgeon at Johns Hopkins Hospital[23] who became a candidate in 2015 for the U.S. Presidency. Among his remarkable achievements is curing massive seizure disorders in young children by removing the affected half of the child's brain with an operation called a "hemispherectomy." The other half of the young brain is able to adapt and return the patient to a normal life. Although it was radical and new, Dr. Carson had done this successfully several times and then he was confronted with an insurance denial for another young patient. The company declared this to be "experimental" and so refused payment. After considerable back and forth by his staff and then Dr. Carson himself, dealing over and over with insurance officials who had no medical understanding, the company finally relented. The grudging letter from the company finally stipulated that "If the patient requires another hemispherectomy we will not pay for it." Dr. Carson and his staff ". . . laughed a long time."

INSURANCE ENDANGERMENT

The potential plight of people buying health care insurance as individuals rather than in a group plan reveals the bizarre unreality of health care coverage in the U.S. The fantastic bills cited by Elizabeth Rosenthal for doctors and hospitals and by Steven Brill for drug costs are largely examples of patients in the individual insurance markets. These represented the upper boundary of individual costs before the Affordable Care Act, and are diminished now where the state or federal exchanges are running well. Two issues remain. In the first place, although insurance companies are prohibited from refusing to cover patients with preexisting conditions, they can charge higher premiums for those people, at least until this is corrected.[24] Moreover, they can pick and choose geographically, deciding not to do business in areas where they may not make as much money. The areas skipped are unlikely to be a nest of well-to-do potential subscribers. Secondly, although the average premiums for insurance are not rising a lot with the ACA[25] as had been feared, this is partly because insurance companies can offer policies that cost less but are more restricted in coverage and require more copayments. Increasingly comprehensive plans start from a low amount of coverage, rated bronze, through silver then gold to the highest value, platinum, for the most extensive coverage provided. Leaving the misconstrued market justifications for all of this to the next chapter, it is important here to note that in disguise this is just like the example of the family in Maryland, when a plan with lower premiums was selected and then family expenses one year were unexpectedly high. After signing up for a silver plan, what is one to do when you contract a platinum illness? How that threat plays out will only be evident a few years into the ACA when the numbers of initially healthy people in these categories become sick and the damages from severe uncovered costs begin to accumulate. Although some of the regulations in the ACA will help, the uncertainty and churn of decisions by people trying to make the right guess does not make the system work beneficially.

    Dr. Don McCanne, health reform guru and blogger ("Quote-of-the-Day") for the Physicians for a National Health Program: "Thus the ACA Marketplace perpetuates instability of premiums, instability of plans selected, instability of provider networks, instability of out-of-pocket cost sharing, and instability of the innumerable devious insurer practices such as outrageous coinsurance for expensive drugs—a practice designed to chase chronically ill individuals away, dumping them on the insurer's competitors."[26]

This has all been about the people who are able to have private insurance.

U.S. PUBLIC COVERAGE

The intent of the ACA was to expand Medicaid eligibility around the country. But the Supreme Court ruled that the states are not required to accept the expanded criteria with its accompanying additional federal Medicaid payments. So out of political perversity, about half of the states have not improved their Medicaid eligibility. For those states that have taken up the ACA Medicaid expansion, poor people qualify for Medicaid if their income is up to about 133% of the Federal Poverty Level, given certain citizenship and residency requirements.

This improved coverage for the very poor was emphasized with characteristic optimism by Dr. Rowe: "The people who really got squeezed up until the Affordable Care Act, which I strongly support, by the way, are the single guys with limited incomes who didn't have families and didn't have access to Medicaid. They were the ones who were uninsured. There are also people who are retired and whose companies were not paying health insurance for them. There are 11 million of those, and there are the uninsured aliens, but I think they were getting squeezed. I think that people at the very low end at least have Medicaid now with the Affordable Care Act, those people are eligible for subsidy. So I think we've done a pretty good job of trying to cover the poorest of the country. I think the pressure was really at the next level where people were making decisions about insurance versus educating their kids and that's obviously ridiculous. It can't happen—I think everybody should be insured. I do think the poorest are covered at least in the states that have Medicaid."

Nevertheless, the common idea that almost all poor people are taken care of is untrue. Community health centers serve many Medicaid patients, but even they see over 7 million uninsured patients,[27] and the HHS/HRSA Community Health Centers program by no means covers all the disadvantaged areas. So the notion that Medicaid has solved the insurance problems of the poor is wrong.

Once in the public system, a patient can essentially just turn up, provide identification, and be treated. But even for these routes to health care coverage, there are possible gaps. Medicaid and CHIP are generally considered "safety net" programs. The analogy to the net protecting a high wire circus performer in case of a fall has, to say the least, several dangerous safety defects. In the first place, the administration of these programs is rigidly specific in what they cover, restricting the doctors' treatment options. Moreover, both the coverage details and the amount available for the programs are subject to state budgets. In addition, county politics can intrude. Counties are responsible for a portion of Medicaid payments from the states. Therefore, the specifics and amounts of coverage provided by SCHIP and Medicaid vary across the country, and with changes in the economy as well.[28] To illustrate, it has already been reported that many states have not improved coverage for children through the increased funding available from the ACA for CHIP.[29] These states have not been able to afford matching funds in their budgets so the federal money stays in Fort Knox and the kids lose.

Regardless of whether or not their state refused to expand Medicaid, the daunting problem for people who need it is that the near poor may be a bit too well off to qualify for Medicaid. They must further impoverish themselves in order to obtain coverage.[30] Of course if someone in the family gets sick, their medical bills can eat up their reserves and qualify them in short order. For states which expanded Medicaid under the ACA, the eligibility threshold is higher. For those with incomes above that, it may be possible to qualify for subsidies to obtain insurance on a state or federal exchange. Nevertheless, this unmet need of the near poor is a residual problem for millions in spite of the improved coverage provided by the ACA.

For Medicare patients, as with Medicaid, there are very specific details of coverage. A doctor's practice is bound by the administrative rules controlling what treatments are reimbursable. The majority of these coverage decisions are made nationally. On the other hand, much of the administration of Medicare is done by regional organizations. Previously called Fiscal Intermediaries, they have been reorganized, and are now called Contractors (MACs). These are private companies that have regional contracts with Medicare to pay Part A and some Part B bills (for example, bills from hospitals). Some exceptions and new treatments may be decided upon by the MAC if there has been no national coverage decision. This means that there is a patchwork quilt across the land of different medical coverage. This transfer of some of the responsibility away from the central national Medicare office is troublesome. In order to provide for patients equally across the country, a national coverage decision has ultimately been necessary to override the local policy. In my experience dealing with innovation in transplant drug treatments, for instance, it is not easy to convince the central Medicare office to enter into a national coverage decision in favor of a new treatment.

Medicare health and prescription drug plans may have copayment requirements like those for private insurance. These are particularly an issue for health savings accounts touted by the Administration from 2000 to 2008 and the "Medicare Advantage" plans. So to say that Medicare is a public plan is only partially correct. It is also a partially privatized public plan.[31]

Beyond dollars and cents, the human cost for those who do not have coverage for health care is an additional national burden. People without ready access to health care are more likely to miss work or to be at work impaired by illness, are less able to get education or compete in the job market, and probably are more likely to spread disease generally and in epidemics. Spillover to the more fortunate from inadequate health care for the poor is increasingly being emphasized. Even the well-to-do are safer if the rest of the public they rely upon to sustain their life-style can be counted upon to be healthy.[32]

In sum, the costs of insufficient coverage for so many Americans is a big but generally unacknowledged bill for the country in addition to the formal expenses of approximately $3.7 trillion quoted as the annual U.S. health care budget. These social costs aside, the savings are likely to be considerable from a national health program that minimizes more severe illnesses due to delayed or inadequate care for those who are too poor to get less expensive, timely care.

ADMINISTRATION, ADVERTISING AND PROFITS

Are there excessive profits in U.S. health care? To this point we have looked at the vast amounts of money spent on health care overall, including reimbursement for care and other less clinically necessary expenses. We now consider what costs might not be necessary for a doctor or hospital or drug company or health insurance company—or federal program—to spend on the actual care of patients. In later chapters we will look at details of hospital and professional work and reimbursement, and at drug and device costs and benefits.

Overall, much of the healthcare expense in the U.S. derives from the costs of arrangements and businesses surrounding but not intrinsic to actual patient care. Of course some costs are necessary. We must have administration to ensure accurate coverage, drug and device companies to provide the 21st century medical marvels, and a myriad of other businesses supporting hospitals and doctors providing care. It is revealing to address these separately from the intrinsic costs of the care givers.

The essence of health care is to have the doctor working with the patient to decide on diagnosis and treatment and then to make what is needed happen effectively. To support that good outcome requires payment for clinicians and administration to keep the shop running, to organize appointments and communications with all that implies, and to oversee the interactions with sources of funding. Costs to increase business profits beyond these straight-forward necessities are legitimate targets for savings.

America is a highly profit-driven society. This is evident in the business of health care. The returns on investment in drug and device companies, insurance companies, hemodialysis companies and hospital chains make these corporations the darlings of Wall Street. Dr. Lewin: "The big insurance companies are . . . looking to improve their margins of profit. That's what they are about, even the non-profit ones." Health insurance stocks soared in 2009 when the Senate bill for the Affordable Care Act emerged[33] and stock prices rose again after the King v. Burwell Supreme Court Decision that upheld subsidies for government exchanges. Health care remains a lucrative business.

Would reining these profits in somewhat with a national program that regulates reimbursement interfere with patient care? Let's look first at health insurance administrative costs and then at medical advertising. In these two examples it is hard to dispute that we can achieve important savings compared with spending in the U.S. now.

Health insurance administration costs are complex and controversial.[34] A major part of the argument swirls around the administration costs of health insurance companies as compared with the cost of running Medicare and other federal health care coverage. It is generally said that administrative costs account for 20% of the private insurance budget while similar costs for Medicare are only 3%. Since Medicare patients receive equally good care at a lower cost, this is considered by proponents of a national health program as evidence of the advantage of Medicare as an example of a single payer government program vs. private insurance. By this understanding, if we eliminate the administrative costs of private insurance in a national health program it will save many billions of dollars.

A measure of the cost of insurance company administration is given as the "medical loss ratio." This is an accepted accounting term for the fraction of money in premiums the insurance company receives that it actually spends for patient care. The slightly confusing label is because any money paid out for medical care is a loss to the company. How you view an insurance company's medical loss ratio depends on whether you are interested in service or profits. It is not a good clinical assessment of health plan performance.[35] The lower the ratio, the more the customer is paying for costs apart from actual health care. Since the insurance company has an incentive to lower the medical loss ratio because that raises profits, it is important to watch what is being said about profits within the industry. Generally they claim that profits represent 2–3% of premium income. This is misleading. What we want to know is how much of the premium dollar is paid out for actual health care. That low profit figure does not take into account the administrative costs, which are considerably larger. The medical loss ratio averages around 80% (although actually Congress found it as low as 74% for individual policies.[36] This accurately reflects the amount on the premium dollar—20 to 25%—that has been going to reimbursement for other than actual costs of care.[37]

The economic advantage for Medicare administration or some other national federal program was addressed in several of my interviews. Dr. Ida Hellander, with the PNHP: "Private insurers have overhead of about 14%, compared with Medicare less than 2% so that's a huge source of savings." Dr. Jo Ivey Boufford of the IOM, on a national health care program: "I think that it would save a lot of overhead costs . . . a fund saving mechanism for health care." Concurring were Cardiologist Dr. Lewin ("Medicare is much more efficient than private insurance.") and former Secretary Thompson ("Medicare is cheaper even than Medicaid and than private sector insurance.")

Obviously this argument that the costs for the public Medicare program are considerably cheaper than for private insurance is convincing to many. But it is disputed.

Dr. Rowe, former head of Aetna and Columbia University professor, presented me with the argument supporting the position of the health insurance business. Not surprisingly, Dr. Rowe's calculations contrast somewhat with the progressive understandings: "Well you get rid of insurance and you have single payer, you'll have a lot of savings. I was getting sued every day by everyone and I had lots of lawyers I was paying, OK? I was spending a lot of money on marketing—you wouldn't have to do any marketing because there would be no choice. Now about net savings: The way I understand it is the Medical Loss Ratio is 80%. So what's called the SG&A which is the cost of running the company, paying the pensions, paying the salaries, paying the health care insurance of the employees, keeping the lights on, paying the lawyers and all, that runs around 14%. So what's left is profit, which is around 6% and you pay tax on that so you're down to around 4%." Thus his reasoning brings you to only 6% profit, which after taxes is not too different from his 3% estimate for Medicare administrative expense.

That comparison by Dr. Rowe enumerating the amount of money that is used for things other than patient care left me skeptical about the degree to which it is possible to rationalize private insurance expenses, in view of the other claims I cited that Medicare is less expensive. For an authoritative opinion about the government side, I emailed my colleague Paul Eggers, PhD., who has spent a career analyzing Medicare data. I asked him for a comparison with private insurance administrative costs. As part of his answer, he emailed the question to about 50 of his associates, creating what proved to be a spectacular digital chain of opinions offered over a period of a few weeks. Various views and arguments were linked in, but he and several others concurred that the fraction spent on patient care is much greater (i.e. lower fraction of costs for administration) with Medicare. One of the participants who was particularly knowledgeable and clear was Rick Foster. He had been Chief Actuary for Medicare and Medicaid Services from 1995 to 2012. After considerable back and forth with many in the chain, Mr. Foster's opinion regarding my question about plain single payer administration was: "So, in the world you hypothesize, administrative costs would probably look something like Medicare's 1.4% rate, plus perhaps another 2% for utilization management (UM) and 1% for improved fraud and abuse detection. Note, however, that a centralized, national approach to UM would probably not be as effective as a more distributed, local approach. In that situation, medical claims costs for the national program would reflect somewhat higher-than-ideal utilization."

I think the 1.4% is the closest to the comparison with private insurance—utilization management is now largely a patient care issue for the medical team regardless of payer, and we will talk about how to restrict fraud and abuse inexpensively when we get to electronic medical records. But regardless, this discards much of the expensive activity cited by Dr. Rowe because it is unnecessary for the bare specifics of patient care.

Moreover, there are additional administrative costs for private health care coverage for hospitals and doctors: "We have 900 billing clerks at Duke (University Hospital, 900 beds). I'm not sure we have a nurse for (each) bed, but we have a billing clerk per bed . . . it's obscene." So stated health care economist Uwe Reinhardt, testifying before the U.S. Senate Finance Committee on November 19, 2008. The exact amount that we might save by not paying for administrative costs of insurance is controversial. Don McCanne of the Physicians for a National Health Program (PNHP) cited the estimate by Shannon Brownlee and Ezekiel Emanuel that it would boil down to a 5% savings,[38] but he noted that the $125 billion in savings which they come up with is, by far, a low-ball estimate.[39] Doctors will tell you that their costs for dealing with insurers must be close to the cost to the insurance company to produce the trouble in the first place. However the insurance companies frame their "medical loss ratio" administrative expenses, their calculations apply to their company's administration and surely do not include these additional irrelevant administrative costs to doctors and hospitals in the struggle over coverage. These costs end up as part of the country's health care costs since they are reflected in the bills from doctors and hospitals, it's just that they do not appear as administrative costs listed by the insurance company in their Medical Loss Ratio. In the chain of emails from CMS experts just described above, the costs of public or private insurance for doctors were recognized but not included in the calculation due to difficulty with the accuracy of estimating them. But the costs are there and are probably higher for the chaotic demands of private insurance than for Medicare and Medicaid.

The second cost for U.S. health care to consider in this chapter is medical advertising. It is a simple issue compared to the maze created by insurance administration: advertising medical care must be stopped.[40] The most powerful argument for this is simply that patient care choices must be made by patients when informed by professional expertise. Encouraging a patient to have some test or treatment when it is a correct choice should not require expensive exhortations in newspapers, magazines and on television, and if it is not a correct choice, no advertisement can make it so. Hiding behind the reminder to "Ask your doctor," doesn't cut it. With their eyes on the bottom line, administrators also manage to arrange news pieces on best hospitals or best doctors, not out of concern for your health but to attract your business. Most doctors and hospitals in the U.S. practice good medicine. Valid attempts to determine excellence generally require too narrow a restriction on what is being compared, and for whom, to be of much use to the average patient. Medical advertising is prohibited in Canada. In fact, the next time you see a smiling group of specialists being touted in an advertisement in the U.S., you might ask yourself, if they are so good why do they need to be advertising? Trusting advertisements for medical care is highly unlikely to add years to your life.

On occasion it might have the opposite impact. This raises the whole contentious issue of the excess use of medical care. If you get a test or treatment that is not warranted, it can involve potential complications that you can avoid by ignoring the advertisement for it. This is further reason that the expense of ads is an opportunity for savings.

The costs for advertising extend beyond pharmaceuticals, professionals and hospitals. We are all paying for the advertising costs in our premiums and other payments to insurance companies. The amount that we pay for insurance company advertising (because with private insurance, as Dr. Rowe tells his students, there is "choice") will be saved in a national system. And we will still have choice.

Large medical foundation and professional society educational meetings which are supported by the health care industry may provide informative information and display booths that can border on inappropriate sales pitches and need careful oversight. Public health advisories from responsible, medically sound, non-profit sources such as government agencies are not included in this condemnation and are not advertising in the usual sense. Public service announcements, encouraging people to get vaccinated for instance, or to stop drinking sugary sodas or stop smoking, are legitimate and constructive. No one is trying to get your business with these messages.

HEALTH CARE REFORM AND ITS COSTS

In summary, future health care reform to cover all Americans must incorporate restraints on costs. Whether or not Lawyer Charles Bond's fear of the bubble bursting is valid, and in disagreement with a couple of those who I interviewed, it seems to be common sense that too much is being spent for too little in return. To reiterate: extrapolating from present costs to calculate the expense of a single payer system that extends coverage to everyone and claiming that it will be too expensive is not justified. Medicare controls costs relatively better than private insurance but remains far from ideal. The galloping commoditization of medicine can be turned with a good hand on the reins. In recent years we have already begun to see cost control from sensitivity to needs and effectiveness of patient care. The simplified processes of a national health program as proposed will yield transparent data and substantial savings, even while providing care for every American.

CHAPTER THREE
DOCTORS AND HOSPITALS

Doctors are challenged as never before. Increasingly rapid advances in medicine have greatly expanded our ability to benefit patients. But these capacities mandate heightened attention to assessing quality and addressing the costs that accompany the changes. In this chapter we review medical practice in this evolving environment, including what has developed regarding the dominant role that doctors must play in costs and quality, and what problems need to be faced as a basis for our professional role in further reform.

About to become President of the American College of Surgeons in October, 2014, Dr. Andrew Warshaw had a broad perspective on American physicians. I first knew him during my training when he was a more senior resident and so one of my teachers. Later, during his many years as the Chairman of the Department of Surgery at the Massachusetts General Hospital, in addition to pursuing a career in gastrointestinal surgery he dealt with all aspects of the roles of doctors and others in medicine. He is now immersed in the national scene as one of the leaders of the College that oversees surgery practice, education, professionalism and health care policy in the U.S.

In our interview he stressed the problems and opportunities doctors face in new practice settings: "Number one, with the increasing number of physicians that are employed, the independent practitioners are a diminishing group and that changes how people think about a lot of this. The risk is now being assumed by organizations rather than individuals. The whole movement towards whether it is bundles, or individual episodes of care, or accountable care organizations puts the individual practitioner into risk-sharing and gain-sharing situations which change the attitudes towards the payer. The physicians say basically as long as there's enough money coming in and I get my share, I'd just as soon not have to worry too much about all of the processes involved with insurance." And also, from new attempts to regulate all of this: "The other factor is that physicians are being overwhelmed by regulatory conditions, requirements, quality measurements, all of the data that you have to keep and submit for the PQRS or something, the staff that you have to keep to make that happen and the misery of the electronic medical record at this point. All of that has so complicated the lives of physicians and has been such a time drain at the expense of patients that often—in one way or another—I would think that anything that simplifies life would be useful."

He also pointed out the difficulty with establishing care guidelines, pointing out that these will take a lot of work to define. Consensus on what is baseline or necessary will be subject to considerable debate. In surgery alone there will be the questions of cosmetic surgery, breast implants and bariatric surgery, for example.

Collegial and considerate but incisive in judgment, Dr. Warshaw supports the vision of a more organized and inclusive national health program for the U.S. but, perhaps understandably given the view from his experience, he feels that if it happens, it will take time, given the political and social realities.

GENERALISTS AND SPECIALISTS

Maybe that is true but the practice of medicine is evolving in the direction of reform. I have heard stories about a family relative who was a general practitioner early in the 20th century in the Midwest. According to the lore, he had aspirin pills available to give out in three different colors. I imagine him giving the patient two packages of pills and saying "Take one blue one and one pink one every four hours when your arthritis gets bad." He made a modest living although sometimes he was not paid. One rainy night there was a knock on the door, the doctor's wife answered. A man was standing there who explained that he had been treated by the doctor thirty years previously, had been unable to pay, but had now come to pay the fee, and he did. Another family story was about a payment that consisted of a turkey from a farm ("It tasted fishy, must have been eating tadpoles from the pond."). More recently, just a generation ago when health insurance first became common, an established psychiatrist described with a chuckle how he handled the new insurance forms beginning to appear: "I just draw a line down the pages, sign them, and send them in." Payments have changed a lot from those times but, as we shall see, how care givers are paid remains a judgment issue. In fewer than a hundred years we have come to MRI's, open heart surgery, deductibles, copayments . . . and professional service claim denials. In some ways, being a doctor has changed almost beyond recognition.

Not too long ago doctors were almost universally considered undisputed authorities. Too often in the past this status was not accompanied by very much specific medical or surgical control over the fate of patients. A great deal of the doctor's value lay in knowing what might happen to a patient, and to providing a source of strength and understanding. Of course doing something to help, however insufficient the available remedies, was part of it. But going along with this, whether the patient succumbed or regained their health was often not strongly impacted by the availability of a doctor's care.

Unlike the old days, it now matters very much whether people get medical care. Drugs are now effective and specific. Operations undreamed of before World War II are routinely successful. Imaging and laboratory testing provide pinpoint diagnoses of diseases that were previously vague or unnamed. As present advances in computer technology and molecular biology are exploited, these advances will be eclipsed by future developments. Ironically, the image and economic outlook of doctors has suffered almost in proportion to these technical improvements. This is partly the profession's fault. The American Medical Association has worked hard to prevent change to a fairer and more effective health system. Doctors resisted the development of electronic medical records for decades. The public's often guarded view of doctors in general (but rarely of their own doctor) may also come from changes in people's perspectives due to extensive social, financial, and communication changes in general during the 20th century. Regardless, this metamorphosis of the status of the medical profession needs to be recognized in efforts to improve American health care.

One way that the burgeoning availability of effective modern drugs, devices and procedures has revolutionized the field of medicine is by driving up the numbers of specialists. The AMA and the American College of Surgeons memberships are for all medical and surgical doctors but their members tend more to general medicine and surgery practices; specialists tend to join their specialty society and often do not join the AMA or ACS. The role of the physician in the old days has been usurped by modern technology and pharmacology, producing greater reimbursements to specialists. The huge loans burdening many medical school graduates adds to the appeal of the higher reimbursement of specialty practices. What balance between specialists and general practitioners will best serve patients and how to set education and reimbursement incentives to achieve this is disputed. Beyond our modern medical miracles, a need remains for the intrinsic strength and understanding in the doctor-patient relationship that has always been an aspect of the doctors' work. Of course specialists are real doctors, able to help their patients in a personal way as part of the care they give. The most extreme solution to the question of generalists vs. specialists was provided by a suggestion, made perhaps only partly in jest, in a free-wheeling discussion over a dinner I had with a surgery colleague: "Get rid of family practice!"

That position is too radical to be taken seriously. Perhaps the best rejoinder to it is the story of Mrs. H., a patient I heard about from her kidney doctor. Mrs. H. is very upset. She is on dialysis three times a week for kidney failure due to diabetes and high blood pressure. The dialysis has been going well although it is less reassuring recently because her kidney doctor is more rushed because of the increased time doctors must spend on paperwork. But Mrs. H is not upset about that. Her problem is all of the other difficulties. She has had heart bypass and requires a blood thinner, but she also has benign colon lesions that tend to bleed, but surgery to remove these is too risky. She needs regular blood tests, and an occasional transfusion, but can no longer get these during the time she spends on dialysis as she had in the past. This is because of billing restrictions and to avoid cost-shifting. As a result she must use up much of her remaining time on non-dialysis days for these other tests and the transfusions. The additional blood draws, that could be spared by doing testing and transfusions while she's on dialysis, are difficult and painful. Moreover, her several doctors and care locations all keep their own separate paper records. As her issues become more complex, it becomes unclear whether each care giver knows enough about what the others are doing. All of this is a result of a combination of well-intentioned requirements. They include quality rules (the dialysis unit cannot be responsible for her blood thinner), economically-required cost-shifting (the dialysis unit cannot charge for a blood transfusion) and legal issues (which doctor is legally responsible for what item). Even though she is in our End Stage Renal Disease entitlement program hers is a real case that illustrates the cruel circumstances that can befall a patient receiving the fragmented care provided in the U.S. Do patients care? They don't want this. A general practitioner with appropriate authority in the system that I propose could take this over and make it better from every angle. As treatment options and specialists proliferate, the family doctor's role is changing but remains important.

For general patient education, strength and understanding, but also as navigator, taking everything into account and charting the patient's course, the generalist will often remain necessary no matter how medical technology advances towards some highly technological domination of care that now exists only in science fiction. A general practice gerontologist Dr. Andy Lazris establishes a middle ground about general practice in his book *Curing Medicare*: "When people are young and healthy they develop more unusual and severe diseases that require specialists. In fact, young people who get sick rarely have to see primary care physicians. But when they are older and every organ begins to deteriorate simultaneously . . . a more palliative and holistic approach makes sense."[1]

Charting the patient's course brings up the gate keeping role, which presents its own problems. In the U.K., fiduciary responsibility for a defined population of patients ("capitated" reimbursement) has been given to the general practitioners with a cap on total funds available. To receive care, a patient must go through a "fundholding" primary care doctor, who retains more of the fund for themselves if costs are held down, creating a financial disincentive for referral to expensive specialists. The impact of this fund-holding process has been controversial. Britain abolished it in 1999 and then partly reintroduced it a few years later with as yet undetermined results.[2] With its control over referral practice, this assignment of risk could be considered the socialist extreme, compared with increasing shift of risk from the insurance companies to patients and providers in U.S. health care that Dr. Rowe described in Chapter 2. That is the opposite extreme represented by our market-based economy. The potential for interference with specialty care by generalists doing the fundholding in the U.K. is obvious. A complete opposite to fundholding is the attempt, also misdirected, at frugality from requiring cost sharing by patients with private insurance in the U.S. described in the previous chapter. Fundholding on the one hand and the sharing of financial risk by patients on the other each produces an unbalanced disincentive against correct choices of care by the doctor and patient. So the generalist can be important for an efficient coordination of options. But the decisions about care by doctors or patients cannot be hostage to their individual costs. Knowledge by the doctor and patient of cost implications of minimal vs. extreme treatments is hardly a mystery, and knowing their costs to the health care system can be a legitimate element in a patient's preference when confronted by care choices.[3] But I think that for optimal care there must be provisions to control hospital and physician costs in a more systematic, balanced way.

This is an issue as insurance companies increasingly transfer risk to practitioners and Medicare rewards institutional moves away from fee-for-service reimbursement. The advantages for a salaried practice doctor in a large group are more appealing to both specialists and general practitioners. Practice patterns may be stabilized, disruptive income fluctuations smoothed and inter-specialty interactions streamlined. These have the potential to improve care and save money. On the other hand, doctors are rightly fearful of an absence of a financial incentive to extra effort. There remains intrinsic professional satisfaction for a doctor to take the extra time to see the two unexpected additional patients that just showed up in the day's already busy clinic, or to get up in the middle of the night to go in and do an urgent operation that the patient needs but which might wait a few more hours until morning. But, although difficult to measure for quality review, for most people such dedication is naturally a little harder if one is going to make the same salary.

Even prior to the Affordable Care Act, the practice patterns of doctors have been moving from conventional reimbursement to jobs with a group or large institution. This is a trend that could facilitate the development of a national health care system. Two major options are evident: relinquishing one's private practice to work in a hospital setting, or the recent proliferation of doctors joining Accountable Care Organizations (ACOs), organized to serve as "medical homes" with specified cost and quality oversight qualifications. Both of these departures from old time fee-for-service billing have a potential impact on patient care. Properly run, particularly with the effective involvement of physicians and nurses at the top,[4] these settings provide an opportunity to balance incentives by encouraging what will be best for patients, set against the absence of the fee-for-service incentive just to do more.

The difference in the fiducial relationship when doctors become employees of a hospital or health insurance company is exemplified by the career of Dr. Jack Ostrich. Dr. Ostrich has an interesting history, having managed to get through college while performing as one of the Yale Whiffenpoofs, the a capella singers who spend most of their junior and senior years delighting audiences. He represents a bond that people often have for technical things plus a love of music. After graduation he took required classes in organic chemistry and biology in preparation for going to medical school. He landed in California in private practice. He told this story about working at Kaiser Permanente: "I was in private practice with two other guys in family practice when I first came to Sacramento in 1980 so I had a taste of that life as well when I went back to Kaiser in 1985 here in Sacramento because of the onerous nature of that practice. I mean I loved it, but it was just getting to be economically impossible, really, especially with the appearance of so-called managed care. The for-profit companies were signing you up as a provider and then not paying you very much to do your job. One of the problems when I was in private practice with the other two guys was that none of us had any business sense. My wife Mary had to go back to work. You'd send these things to the insurance company and you wouldn't hear from them for months. Then they'd tell you that you didn't fill out line 14 of subsection b and you'd have to do it all over again. One of the great advantages at Kaiser Permanente was that was all taken care of." I note the disturbing implication that a well-developed business sense is a desirable attribute in private practice.

This reinforces Dr. Warshaw's view that doctors can become fed up and amenable to leaving private practice and becoming employed. Hospitals have been widely successful in bringing doctors on staff. The obvious administrative impetus for the hospital is expanding and securing local referral territory, particularly when it expands their geographic scope to highly insured populations.[5] This "vertical integration" can be associated with higher prices.[6] Nevertheless, in the increasingly cost-conscious medical world, specialists are beginning to lose out to less costly care by general practitioners in the income produced for the hospital, according to Meritt Hawkins, a leading physician employment business. This is another example of how reimbursement impacts patient care. Time will tell what benefits and harm this increasing hospital employment trend may bring for doctors and their patients.

ORGANIZATION AND ADMINISTRATION OF CARE DELIVERY

The Centers for Medicare and Medicaid Services began encouraging the group practices that eventually became Accountable Care Organizations. These are extensions of the movement toward care management and even capitation in primary care medical homes. ACOs are typically larger and multi-specialty. They may include hospitals and they centralize the reimbursement for the organization of some version of capitation. Initial participants in the Medicare Pioneer ACO program did well with quality requirements but many of the first ACO's tended to opt out over time, leaving a few organizations that were more successful in meeting the quality and payment goals. Problems with payment levels and obstacles due to quality reporting requirements were principle causes for those that exited ACO status. The general history of alternative practice modes such as medical homes and ACOs and their impact on doctors has recently been described in great detail in the report of a Rand/AMA study.[7] Even with recent results in three Medicaid ACOs showing cost savings,[8] growth to more than seven million patients enrolled in ACOs predicted for 2015, and administrative leaders tending to be enthusiastic, the general physician work force remains uncertain about their role.

There is one thing for sure that doctors ought not to be doing: In the U.S, a major expensive and time-consuming role for doctors is filling out forms, making billing phone calls and writing letters to deal with the billing and quality issues raised by insurance companies. This is in order to convince the insurer to cover the care the doctor has proposed, or provided, for their patients. A recent study documented that doctors spend 43 minutes a day dealing with health plan administrative requirements. Primary care doctors suffer the greatest paperwork burden.[9] So of the 60+ hour weeks put in by family doctors[10] around four or five hours of it are spent not in patient care but in doing paper work. This is costly. The estimated national burden is over $23 billion a year[11]—falling most heavily on family doctors. Anybody who has ever filled out a bunch of medical forms for themselves or a loved one would cringe at having to do so for an hour a day, day after day. Moreover, with 20% of claims paid incorrectly by the largest insurers,[12] they are only giving you a C+ or B- for your efforts, even if it is ultimately confirmed on resubmission that you are filing a perfect paper each time.

Although I disagree with some of Dr. Richard "Buz" Cooper's statements in the interview, nevertheless regarding how doctors view these hassles he put it exactly right: "But regulating every transaction? Should doctors have to get permission to use a different dose of drug? That would be like requiring bank tellers to get permission before they cashed every check."

The other aspect of the administrative thorn in the doctor's side is the burden resulting from the recent evolution of the quality reporting system, as described by gerontologist Andy Lazris. His overall conclusion is that being penalized by the quality reporting process for failure to follow set numbers for every patient often harms their care.

The complexity of requirements by the Centers for Medicare and Medicaid Services are daunting. The rules for reimbursement by Medicare are sufficiently dense that rather than deal with it all directly, CMS gets help by contracting for help with regional quality improvement networks run by Quality Improvement Organizations (QIN-QIOs). Each doctor or practice, for every Eligible Professional (EP) which includes the team's nurse practitioners, must be using an Electronic Health Record (EMR) with which Meaningful Use (MU) is attested. To avoid a penalty for payments under the Medicare Physician Fee Schedule (MPFS), continuing Quality Management (CQM) must be reported in the Physicians Quality Reporting System (PQRS—the only easy acronym). As of 2015, this PQRS report will be ranked by completeness compared with the performance of the field and this used in the calculation for each doctor's claim under the MPFS using the Value-Based Payment Modifier (VM).

In other words, an EP has a diminished MPFS rate if they do not satisfy the MU requirement with their EHR that will lead to satisfactory CQM with the PQRS—and it is worse if you do not rank well on the VM. It's OK: the QIN-QIO is there to help. Oh—and you can keep up with how you are doing by registering for the Quality and Resource Use Report (QRUR). You can look it all up on line.

As a random example of what you get when you do look it up, take this snippet about QRUR from part way down the CMS topic list on Feedback Program/Value-Based Payment Modifier:

"HOW TO OBTAIN A QRUR"

You can access a Quality and Resource Use Report (QRUR) on behalf of a group or solo practitioner at https://portal.cms.gov. QRURs are provided for each Medicare-enrolled Taxpayer Identification Number (TIN). You or one person from your group will need to obtain an Individuals Authorized Access to the CMS Computer Services (IACS) account with the correct role first. The sections below ("Setting up an IACS account to access a group's QRUR" and "Setting up an IACS account to access a solo practitioner's QRUR") will tell you. . . .

This little extract is one third of one of 11 bullet points in a small part of the CMS requirements. Keeping track is increasingly important because soon failure in compliance could drop your Medicare reimbursement by as much as 9%: MU, 3%; PQRS, 2%,;plus PQRS/VM, 4%.

Even if this CMS quality assurance process promised improvement in care, this is not how doctors and their teams should be monitored. The worst thing is that this administrative exercise does not improve care. The actual guidelines to be followed are arguable, sometimes contradictory, and often not applicable to the different issues presented by a given patient. Dr. Lazris, whose practice is largely with elderly Medicare patients, stressed this:[13] ". . . The quality indicators stress when to test and treat rather than when not to. They are far too generic to be relevant to many of the older patients and force us to devote too much of our effort to documenting things."

Moreover, private payer quality stratification, actually created with an eye to limiting payments, is equally detrimental to patients as well as doctors. As just one example, we hear from Matthew Katz. He is the CEO of the Connecticut State Medical Society. In addition to the Connecticut State Medical Society being the local advocate for improving medical practice and being very active on behalf of patients, he is proud of the successful roll-out of the ACA Health Care Exchange in Connecticut (although the state was still owed millions by HHS when I talked with him). He also noted the help Connecticut provided Maryland when our ACA Exchange faltered. He told me of a six-member cardiology practice that receives quality rankings by insurers. The problem is that each insurer provides different rankings of the doctors within this practice, so as a patient your option of which doctor to see within this same practice is different depending on which insurance company will be paying the bill. Pamela Harztband and Jerome Groopman document the degree to which insurance company contracts with professionals increasingly control practice decisions and drug choices.[14] Participation in the restrictions of care due to the U.K. health care coverage system, resulting in interference with providing quality care to their patients, is a problem for many doctors.[15] Because reimbursement for insured patients is generally negotiated down with the care giver, doctors are in the uncomfortable position of billing uninsured patients at a higher rate than insured patients.[16]

You might think doctors would already be thinking up a better way. But presently they do not have much authority to be proactive. And they have little time left over for medical organizations or lobbying. Commonly, doctors see their patients being at the mercy of the insurance companies or the federal bureaucracy. But they limit their personal advocacy to the time and work needed to treat their patients. Doctors may provide input on their professional views through the AMA or other societies which then represent members on the national scene and it is understood that physician leadership is essential.[17,18] Of course, concern exists that doctors, as a powerful special interest group, must be kept in check regarding health care decision-making.[19] At any rate, to date these discussions have not had a lasting impact in any particular way. The AMA remains the dominant professional association, although at present only about 1/3 of the country's doctors are members. Moreover, the medical profession is not monolithic. Dr. Warshaw, in his American College of Surgeons role, on whether doctors can get together on health care reform and establish a national solution: "Such a big leap. The ACS and AMA have not quite been holding hands but holding fingers together. They have been going to the Hill together for a given mission but I don't see them collaborating yet on such a big picture. The AMA is a very big, very diverse, not very unified organization in the end." Nevertheless, I believe that the proposal in this book shows a way forward for doctors to be effective at the national level.

MEDICAL PRACTICE DECISIONS

Most practicing U.S. physicians will agree that there is overutilization—providing more care than is clearly indicated for the patient. In their commentary, *The Perfect Storm of Overutilization*,[20] Ezekiel Emanuel and Victor Fuchs described factors that drive overuse and called for policy changes to redirect incentives in the system that cause this. How much there is of this overuse and how much money could be saved by controlling it are reasonable questions. But there is no question that American patients suffer preventable harm due to this financial incentive–supported overutilization. Tests and treatments have risks and side effects. The issue discussed above about balancing incentives for physicians to encourage aggressive care without doing too much is critical as medical care moves from individual general practice to medical teams with more internal and government oversight. Overutilization has been subject to study and dispute for decades. It exploded into the public (and political—allegedly including President Obama's) consciousness with the widely discussed article *The Cost Conundrum*, by Dr. Atul Gawande.[21] He popularized the understanding driven by decades of work by Dr. Jack Wennberg[22] and others culminating in "The Dartmouth Atlas of Health Care."

As can be seen in Figure 4, there are large differences in the amount of care received by Medicare patients when comparing different regions across the country. It has been calculated that about half the variation in Medicare spending is due to clinically unjustified differences in health care utilization. Patients do not have poorer health or better health outcomes in areas of higher spending to justify the spending differences. Since the patients are all on Medicare, they do not have differences in out-of-pocket expenses that would prompt different levels of care. In addition, looking at hospitals rather than hospital referral regions, quality was not improved by increased intensity of spending,[23] and patient satisfaction is not higher in regions with higher spending for health care.[24] Moreover, similar geographic variations without apparent clinical correlation are found in commercial health care utilization.[25] These careful studies include calculations to show that differences in the severity of the ailments in different parts of the country cannot explain the differences in the amounts of care received. These variations must be due to different doctors' practice patterns. So this regional variability in the amount of care provided does not correlate with outcomes. Former Senate Majority Leader Tom Daschle neatly summarized the politician's view when I talked with him: "There are a lot of different reasons why we have overutilization but no one denies we have it. The question is how do you address it?"

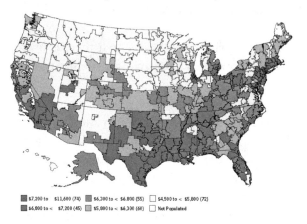

Figure 4. Variation in Medicare Spending per Capita in the United States, by Hospital Referral Region, 2003 (Percent in parentheses) Source: The Dartmouth Atlas of Health Care.

Nevertheless, arguments from a few who claim that overutilization is not a problem have appeared. Since this represents a major contention in economic philosophy as well as a threat to quality of care, the arguments need to be examined. A prime example is a reanalysis state by state from the Brookings Institute purporting to negate the conclusions in the Dartmouth Atlas.[26] The statistical analyses in this and other attempts to discredit the overutilization picture have been thoughtfully and forcefully discredited by Gretchen Nye.[27]

Digging further, I interviewed contrarian oncologist Dr. "Buz" Cooper, a strident critic of the interpretation of the findings indicating overutilization. He is a Senior Fellow in the Leonard Davis Institute of Health Economics at the University of Pennsylvania and Clinical Professor in the Medical College's Institute for Health and Society. He was formerly head of the Hematology-Oncology Section and later the Cancer Center at U. Penn and then Dean of the Medical College of Wisconsin in Milwaukee. He emphasizes that medical education and practice embrace continuing quality improvement. We can rely on that professionalism to review and adjust the use of tests and treatments as data become available. Therefore the interpretation that the government must be responsible for correction of overutilization is wrong. His view that the system is self-correcting and that doctors eventually get it right without needing regulation may be correct in some cases; perhaps the reduction in useless tonsillectomies and hysterectomies documented by Dr. Jack Wennberg[28] would have occurred in the absence of his pioneering work, although in my view even that claim of Dr. Cooper's does not hold up. But he strikes a nerve when he casually considers the eventual abandonment of a devastating medical misadventure as self-correcting: This was the temporary enthusiasm for autologous (from the patient's) bone marrow transplantation for breast cancer. This theoretically addressed the problem that maximum high-dose chemotherapy for breast cancer would cause fatal damage to the patient's bone marrow source of blood cells. The treatment was to remove bone marrow cells and treat them to kill cancer cells during an otherwise fatal high-dose chemotherapy of the patient. Then the patient's treated bone marrow cells were infused to reconstitute the bone marrow to save the patient who would have died without this bone marrow transplant. So far so good. But after starting out as a life-threatening experimental procedure, it became accepted as a standard procedure before it was shown to be safe and effective. These claims supporting this treatment were supported by legislatures and courts. And you can bet that the politicians were responding not to data but to public hopes and pressures. Understandable. But there was limited interest in, or funding for, clinical trials because of the conviction that this bone marrow transplant procedure was the right treatment. Data finally became clear. Dr. George Lundberg, quoted by Maggie Mahar: "The procedure was dangerous, debilitating and expensive. Between 15 and 20 percent of the patients died from the drugs used . . ." And this was not a flash in the pan. Mahar:[29] "Ultimately, the nation squandered roughly $3 billion while an estimated 4,000 to 9,000 women died, not from their cancer but from therapy." And nobody was cured. How Cooper can pass that off as an understandable temporary misjudgment that was self-correcting and not as evidence that objective oversight is needed is beyond me. This extravagant, frequently fatal experiment, however well-intentioned, is a perfect example of the need to have effective national oversight over clinical decision making. And it is not the only example.

Equally egregious was the recent response of orthopedists and interventional radiologists touting percutaneous vertebroplasty (injections of bone glue in the cervical spine for neck pain) when it was studied and debunked by outcomes data. A riot of disagreement ensued from the doctors involved, based on no real evidence. Although many practice advice recommendations for percutaneous vertebroplasty subsequently had language added to narrow the indications somewhat, it is still in common practice and Medicare and private payers now continue to reimburse for the procedure despite the knowledge that it is mostly useless. Katharine Wulff and colleagues noted the same problem that caused the useless, harmful breast cancer therapy, which was that the vertebroplasty treatment had become so entrenched in practice before evidence for it was obtained that when the treatment was proven wrong it was hard to get doctors to change.[30] This is further evidence against Dr. Cooper's claim that no oversight is needed.

Dr. Cooper holds that the findings of overutilization are really just measuring degrees of disease as a cause for the variation in cost and that therefore criticism of the huge spending on health care in the U.S. is not justifiable by those findings or correctable by government intervention. But Dr. Cooper's published evidence counter to the Dartmouth Atlas[31] uses the wrong statistics[32] and may instead actually confirm Dartmouth Atlas findings.[33] In summary, most experts are not swayed by Dr. Cooper's arguments against the data as showing overutilizaton.

In his defense, he went on to say that dealing with the minimum wage and the education system are important for establishing cost-efficient health care for poor people. In this he does underscore an important general truth that we will explore further in Chapter 6, Health, Education and Welfare.

Another resistance to the concept of overutilization (from a source conceptually opposite to Dr. Cooper's pessimism) is found in the position of the Physicians for a National Health Program. This is surprising and frustrating to me. The understandable PNHP position is that underuse is the most important issue because there are millions of Americans without health care coverage. But the PNHP downplays the problems of U.S. health care from overuse of procedures and treatment for patients with coverage.[34] This is puzzling because the problems of expense and quality of care caused by overuse are not inconsistent with the primary urgency to have everyone covered.

Beyond all of this, there is a large, significant but generally unrecognized insight demonstrating overuse. Dr. Nortin Hadler, whose views on how to structure the system we will see later, has written extensively about his "Efficacy Agenda"—which has gotten far too little attention. This involves taking a hard look at what really works in health care.[35] For instance, his rule is that you should only have tests and treatments that improve your likelihood of getting to age 85, since everyone is increasingly likely to die of something or other from then on, regardless.

This perspective is seconded by Dr. Jon Fielding, Dean of the UCLA School of Public Health: "One of the problems we have is that doctors have convinced patients that death is optional—It's not just doctors, it's the whole medical establishment." And gerontologist Dr. Lazris, most of whose patients are on Medicare, has written, "Tests and procedures, when not wisely ordered, are dangerous because they help perpetuate the illusion that we can reverse aging by looking hard enough. Not only is such magical thinking endemic in our society, but it is fully endorsed by Medicare itself."[36] So in the view of these experts, the presently understood levels of appropriate care that are not scored as overutilization often still represent too much care.

The simple powerful concepts just cited not only support the principle behind the Dartmouth Atlas, but actually demonstrate how inadequate the estimate of excess care in the Dartmouth Atlas is. The denominator of lowest care shown on the map in Figure 4 represents the lowest average amount of care in some regions in the U.S. today, against which larger amounts of care in other regions are compared. But that denominator reflects the misunderstanding that the lowest average amount of care observed now is the appropriate base level. If these experts are correct, then that denominator used to represent minimal care in the Dartmouth Atlas is not low enough. When calculated by setting the denominator at the more realistic, lower expectation of how much health care is beneficial, the statistics would establish even greater levels of overuse than is presently claimed.

MEDICAL INITIATIVES

The medical profession has already begun to act. Recent "PIVOT" (Prostate Cancer Intervention Versus Observation Trial) results show that resection is not better than observation for early prostate cancer—and help to define when the threat of disease progression is sufficient to warrant operation. General surgeons are using a data-based quality review called the National Surgical Quality Improvement Program (NSQIP) to monitor and improve their results. NSQIP has a display showing how much money the hospital will save by best practices in a variety of categories. Hospitals participating in the program have lowered their mortality and complication rates.[37] Moreover, the NSQIP information on the likelihood of complications or death can be shared with patients to include them as part of the clinical decision making.[38] Other initiatives include that of the American Board of Internal Medicine Foundation in partnership with Consumer Reports and joined by the American Colleges of Radiology, Cardiology and Gastroenterology to improve care decisions through a program called "Choosing Care Wisely." And the Bernard Lown Foundation plus the New America Foundation had a conference led by national authorities on "Avoiding Avoidable Care," co-hosted by the

Institute of Medicine. The Institute for Healthcare Improvement has had wide success in promoting system improvements for patients and doctors. The National Quality Forum has been defining best practices for a decade and these guidelines are widely used. Professional expertise on how to interpret misleading claims about drugs and procedures is provided in books by Dr. Lazris[39] and Dr. David Newman.[40] These institutional and academic advisories are all incremental and segmented and too often they present conflicting rules as described above, but they are the beginning of a general national answer to such questions as Tom Daschle's about how to address overuse.

A revealing coda recently appeared to the story of overutilization, which had been highlighted back in 2008 by Dr. Gawande's article *The Cost Conundrum*. Five years later, Dr. Gawande revisited the Texas area he had written about. In *Overkill*,[41] he describes reviewing the data with Dr. Jonathan Skinner of the Dartmouth Atlas. The spike of excessive care in McAllen had flattened, in keeping with the national data showing that health care inflation is the lowest it has been in fifty years. And this was not just a fluctuation of statistical noise. When he returned to McAllen he found that a lot had been going on. A variety of legal proceedings alleging incorrect care or billing, although involving only a few of the doctors, got the attention of all. With the light shining on them, referral arrangements, hospital admissions, tests and treatments all came into line as doctors worked together to become more mindful of their clinical decisions. To top it off, an Accountable Care Organization, WellMed, began to enroll doctors there to practice with a culture of focusing on patient needs, not of doing more. Initially angry at Gawande and those who had cooperated with him, the doctors then had moved on to see the wisdom of his observations and to do something about it.

One lesson in this is simply that costs in McAllen were brought down to the norm by restricting unnecessary care—another proof that the problem of overuse is real because it was shown to be correctable. A second lesson is that doctors, given the insights and appropriate culture, can make this improvement happen. Dr. Gawande's article mentioned no new laws or regulations. It was done by restoring professionalism.

Two major barriers to solving the problem of overutilization are resolved by the unifying national proposal in Chapter 7. The first, which is the technical issue of establishing a clinical decision process, will be found to be the easy part. The second, getting consensus on the control of overuse by using these precepts, is the hard part. Because overutilization fuels a lucrative part of the health care business, including highly expensive hospitals and some doctors who make over a million dollars a year, resistance to controlling overuse is more formidable. Both of these goals can be achieved if the medical profession takes responsibility for the national understanding of clinical aspects that only they can properly judge.

BEYOND FEE-FOR-SERVICE

The personal uncertainties that doctors feel about salaried work in a large organization might be a concern for a single payer system. The greatest fears are loss of autonomy and reduced income. Of course, we have these problems now. Between Medicare and private insurance, doctors are increasingly subject to unreasonable intrusion on their autonomy to practice. The single payer system supported by a practical electronic medical records system as I propose is a way that doctors can regain professional control and autonomy. And a concern about reimbursement decreasing must take into consideration that the baseline before reform is not reassuring. Physician incomes in the U.S. have not universally been keeping pace with the general economy.[42] Jack Ostrich notes that his general practice career on salary at Kaiser was "kind of like living in a single payer system anyway." When he saw patients he could concentrate on the medical issues: "When somebody came in they could be Medicaid, they could be Medicare, they could be private pay, they could have come off the street, it didn't matter to me. I was there and I had my schedule in front of me and I did my best to take care of them. The vast majority were people you saw again, you had a panel of your own and they came back to see you after being there 10 or 15 years. Occasionally someone would come in that you didn't know and there was no notification. It became all electronic probably in the late '90s and on the computer screen you didn't have any idea how it was being paid for. It was taken care of by the business office." It was easy to get appointments to specialists, the electronic medical records were very helpful, and although he tended to be more extensive in some workups than his colleagues, he didn't get hassled about it: "You wouldn't get a call from somebody saying hey you can't order an MRI or whatever. What they would do occasionally was every quarter or so you'd sit down with your department chief and they'd say well, Ostrich, you ordered 3 times more whatever test than your colleagues and I'd tell them <chuckle> it's the way I practice. There was never anybody who said no you can't do it or that they were going to assess your salary or something." He got his pay check every two weeks and felt that he and his specialist colleagues got about what similar doctors were being paid in the community. Similarly, Dr. Adam Owens, the Vice President of the Canadian Medical Association, in our interview reassuringly confirmed the freedom for Canadian doctors in their practice. Talking about their relatively limited health care bureaucracy there, he said that the rules are at a: "very broad level—not the specifics. Nobody gets into that here. Treatment depends on what the patient and the physician decide."

How does Kaiser make this work in the absence of fee for service reimbursement? Some insights from Dr. Jack Cochrane, Executive Director of the Permanente Foundation[43] "We began with the intention of taking care of the population. We integrate primary care and delivery. For our care to be value-based, we think of how many people we have to take care of, and then we figure how much it'll cost. We developed a culture that embraces data, acknowledgement, learning and improvement. We have a culture that measures and compares data across the board—it's very important. We put tools in place to measure what is important to delivering care. We reward transparency and find ways to improve. Doing the right thing will also be the best thing to make sure care is affordable." True, the mission of Kaiser Permanente does not include access for the indigent in general. Those termed "off the street," without insurance, in the quote by Dr. Ostrich, were usually there for followup of the emergency room care that hospitals are required to provide and after a visit or two would generally not reappear. Nevertheless, as an accurate depiction of practicing in a salaried position, this is reassuring. Here doctors are neither fundholders nor risk takers.

I have known Dr. Nortin Hadler from school days and he always seemed to be ahead of everyone else. He has had a long career in rheumatology and immunology at the University of North Carolina at Chapel Hill. In addition, he has taken the time to think about how to move best medical practices forward in the country for decades. He has published several books, most recently *Citizen Patient*. Regarding practices and payments for doctors, his "Efficacy Agenda" would have decisions based on ". . . clinical meaningfulness and personal values—what's the yield and who helps determine that—the critical question needs to be in fiduciary hands, not a single fiduciary hand. You need agencies like Medicare does with regions. Alvan Feinstein used the term clinimetrics for the clinical exercise of defining clinical utility. How about a clinimetrics unit—clinical epidemiologists with no conflicts of interest, pay them well to scan literature, conferences, get a notion of efficacy and superimpose on that wisdom and value to come up with an estimate of effectiveness and then cost-effectiveness. The principle is to refuse to underwrite interventions that help no one. If there's a meaningful degree of effectiveness, the intervention is underwritten. In between these judgments is room for debate but a need for compromise and for a determination. If separate clinimetric units undertake this exercise independently and simultaneously across the country—"comparative effectiveness research" becomes a natural experiment. Wielding dollars to support effectiveness and withholding when effectiveness is elusive is the moral high ground." In the system that I propose in this book, the fiscal threat would buttress compliance with Continuing Quality Improvement.

One of the single payer advocates I interviewed was Dr. Ida Hellander. She has been writing and working for health care reform for many years and is the Director of Health Policy and Programs for the Physicians for a National Health Program. She is an impassioned advocate for solving the problem of access to health care in the U.S., and has reassuringly straightforward answers to concerns about reform. Her take on the life of a doctor in a single payer system: "Most physicians have a certain number of hours they want to work and usually it's not more than 55 or 60 per week. Projections that utilization is going to skyrocket under single payer are not realistic because that would mean that every physician would have to work 100 hours or 150 hours a week. Physicians will work the same number of hours but they will see, on average, somewhat sicker and poorer patients. It is not necessary to put everybody on salary or to put everybody in big groups to control costs. Acknowledging that we have a limited number of doctor-hours puts a cap on what the budget is for clinical care." (I agree with her optimism that the national system will not have to manage doctors' incomes tightly, but the issue of overuse will require more attention than she allows for here.) Dr. Quentin Young, who appeared in the first chapter of this book, reinforced the PNHP view of reimbursement: "Pay them well . . . I believe you should support them and it works very well all over the world, in Canada and Europe, doctors in the advanced countries—they have a decent salary and they do very well."

DOCTORS' INCOMES

As a founder of modern economics, Adam Smith wrote in the mid-1700s "We trust our health to the physician; our fortune and sometimes our life and reputation to the lawyer and attorney. Such confidence could not safely be reposed in people of a very mean or low condition. Their reward must be such, therefore, as may give them that rank in the society which so important a trust requires. The long time and the great expense which must be laid out in their education, when combined with this circumstance, necessarily enhance still further the price of their labour."[44] This prescient portrayal summarizes the issues of professionalism and education cost for doctors today.[45]

To justify that trust, what do doctors do? What ought they to do? Those are not simple questions, and not always obvious in casual observation. When Dr. James Duderstadt, a PhD engineer and nuclear physicist, became President of the University of Michigan, he had traced a distinguished career working for the government, then eventually had become Dean of the College of Engineering at Michigan. He has also served in various roles in the National Science Foundation and other public and academic positions. He received the Vannevar Bush Award from the National Science Board in 2015. Since their health facility with its annual budget of $3 billion is part of the University of Michigan, he had responsibility for it as the President. As he told me: "The first time I got a tour of our medical care after becoming President, it became evident to me immediately that all of the health care was being done by the nurses. The physicians were simply diagnosticians." Of course in the OR suites, the cath labs, and around the screens in the X-ray reading rooms, there is more to it than on the regular hospital floors.

Regardless, I think the basic understanding, whether explicit or not, from Hippocrates, Aesculapius and Maimonides through to today, is that the fundamental thing that doctors do is to take responsibility. This is what they are being paid for regardless of the specialty or historical time period. That is a fundamental essence of the doctors' work.

But the essence of taking responsibility has been difficult to measure. Therefore, three decades ago, in an attempt to rein in costs, a study to quantify physician work was done: In 1980 I sat in a hall at Harvard as one of the physician advisors at a meeting to describe a new physician reimbursement system. Dr. William Hsiao of the Harvard School of Public Health had just completed a study that purported to establish an objective way to reimburse physician work, called the "Resource-Based Relative Value Scale." It established the concept that rational comparisons of fees could be made by deconstructing the amount of work involved into its components, then adding the different amounts for these components together for each service or procedure. Their sum is a measure of the work involved by this construct. The value calculated by the RBRVS for each item of care is used in a formula to calculate the actual amount to be reimbursed for it as a fraction relative to all others in the cumulative annual physician reimbursement budgeted by Medicare.

As a young academic surgeon looking forward to the intellectual satisfaction of instituting a rational approach, I found myself disappointed. The underlying experimental psychological principle was suspect, the data collection sessions were criticized by some as biased, and the validation of the statistical analysis was flawed.

Nevertheless, the juggernaut was in motion. In addition to setting

Medicare payments, it is now generally followed by private insurers, usually with incrementally higher reimbursement amounts.

The RBRVS has not been convincing to doctors. The general principle that procedures were more work than evaluation and management services was initially reinforced, possibly beyond reason, and certainly contrary to the intention of supporters of the Hsiao study. In addition to cost control, a major motive for the reimbursement of doctors through the Resource Based Relative Value Scale was to erase the divide between specialists' and generalists' incomes. Before too long it became clear that the RBRVS did not do this. Bodenheimer[46] points out that this was due both to the underlying political structure and the ascendance of procedures in comparison with general medical care in the years following the RBRVS. So adjustments were requested. In fact, the history of the RBRVS since has been one of arbitrary adjustments under pressure from various interest groups. This input is partly through the politically-driven AMA Relative Value Scale Update Committee that advises CMS, with each specialty group represented on this committee continually attempting to convince CMS that their services were undervalued, and represent relatively more work, in order to maximize their fees relative to other specialties. Over time the divide may be closing : a recent study, 30 years later, found that codes for specialists are not valued higher on average than the evaluation and management codes of general practice and internal medicine.[47]

If the amount doctors are paid is not to be left to the arbitrary whims of an imaginary market, then any national health system must include some way to guide reimbursement. After all the study and analysis, the RBRVS formula resulted in a rather prosaic emphasis on time and physical effort as strong determinants on the scale of a doctor's work. So one way to think about how much doctors should be paid might be to just look at time. As a basic reference point, this calculation could estimate a typical 60 hours a week at $100 an hour, 50 weeks a year, which would yield $300,000 (pre tax) in salary a year. According to a MedScape survey, in 2013 American general practitioners and pediatricians made about $180,000 year, orthopedics doctors were highest at $413,000, other specialists such as cardiology, urology and gastroenterology around $350,000. General surgeons averaged $295,000.

There is a fear that a national federal system of any sort will require devastating cuts in physician reimbursements. Dr. Joshua Cohen, who you will meet in more detail in Chapter 4, wielded this threat bluntly: "If you had a single payer system, doctors would become essentially salaried employees of the state, as in the VA. My sister is a doctor in the VA she chose it consciously and loves it, but she could earn close to double of what she earns at the VA in, say a different setting. That would happen across the United States. You would perhaps have salaries for doctors reduced by half, so it's not just a matter of the pharmaceutical company having to drop its price because of the monopsony. Because of this powerful leverage, this take or leave it negotiating stance of a large single payer, doctors and providers would lose some of their money but also some of their autonomy as well."

Doctors in the U.S. are paid more than other countries,[48] although far from the high range of reimbursement for business executives in general Of course, the problem in the U.S. seems to be that too often they are getting paid for doing too much for a given patient. This reinforces the point that it is overutilization—the unnecessary work that they are doing—that needs attention, not their reimbursement rates. Bringing overutilization under control would cancel out that aspect of these relatively larger salaries. And the great thing is that doctors will still have plenty to do. Actually, with expansion of coverage to everyone, the concern is the opposite: There may be too few doctors. So U.S. doctors can continue to work more, and make more, than their colleagues in other countries if they wish.

Of course this overview of measuring work based on time leaves intensity untouched, a concern that the RBRVS attempted to address. Would anyone figure that a half hour spent operating on your eye is worth only one sixth of a 3 hour operation on your hip? As with the doctor taking responsibility, the essence of that arbitrary issue defies direct academic study and cannot be quantified by legislation. We can only resort to Adam Smith.

In addition to time and intensity, another value to society of a doctor's work is how much it saves on other expenses of the untreated illness. Necessary assumptions about the cost of later care for more serious illness, future earnings, benefits to the family circle and the value of health vs. living with illness cloud any precise calculation. But there really are savings to be had from timely, effective care. The concept of value-based care or payment for performance ("P4P") is the administrator's way of codifying this, but will only be reasonable with better ways to measure these than we have today. Otherwise, as Dr. Donald Berwick, health care guru and recent Administrator for CMS, notes, it is doubtful that we will solve the problems in American medicine by paying doctors to try harder through P4P. Instead, given the right environment, doctors will want to do better. Talking about motivation to do a good job, Berwick observed:[49] ". . . when someone shows up and says, I'll pay you ten bucks more to do a good job, they feel . . . not incentivized. The feel insulted. And they ought to feel insulted."

Ken Terry describes a story that Dr. Michael Fleming, former President of the American Academy of Family Physicians, likes to tell his medical students.[50] A patient arrived in the emergency room having awakened with chest pain. Fortunately, it turned out not to be from coronary artery disease. Unfortunately, he was caught in the tentacles of an unthinking U.S. health care work-up. A CT scan and multiple other tests in the E.R. triggered a neck scan, which showed a calcified mass. An ENT surgeon therefore did an operation, only to make the diagnosis that it was a calcified carotid artery bulb – which he wisely left alone since the patient had no symptoms—and that would surely not have been causing chest pain. (That needless operation is the most unbelievable part of the story—an embarrassing failure both of imaging and surgical indications.) At any rate, the next "step" was a treadmill stress test which was confusingly, equivocally positive, so off to the cath lab. His heart cath was "cold normal." So he is a healthy guy. But now he has a few incisions here and there. And he still has chest pain. He finally turned up in Dr. Fleming's office, and during the exam "he raised his arm up and said, 'Oh, that's it.'" Dr. Fleming squeezed the muscle between the chest and the shoulder and the patient said that's where it hurts. As it happens, the patient had been working on a new power scaffolding at his job that did not go as high as the old one and it had made that muscle sore. That was the benign diagnosis. Ouch indeed!

His bills added up to $128,000—of which just $60 was for the visit to Dr. Fleming . . . the only medically useful care he received. Only in America. So here we see ineffective initial evaluations, perhaps by doctors pressed for time, unnecessary tests, and unnecessary surgery adding up to frightful endangerment and a lot of expense, all for naught. It is an extreme case and there may not be many such examples. But each separate instance of poor quality in this story happens over and over in the U.S. now. In the single payer system that I propose, patterns of repeated instances of this sort will be detected in the data by the Board of Health Security, allowing remediation. The culture that fosters these mistakes will yield to improvement by the medical profession if doctors will take it on.

In an effective national health plan, for the man in this story who awakened with chest pain, the initial evaluation and follow up would have been through a doctor or someone else on the medical team that the patient has seen before, rather than the patient ending up with an incomplete assessment by a harried emergency room doctor initially. As it was, his status of a man presumed to have active coronary artery disease was unquestioned, with no one taking the initiative to reassess the diagnosis and stop the cascade of mistakes. Given the inaccurate initial assessment which would have been done better with the coverage provided in the a properly run single payer system, the guidelines from the Board for persistent chest pain would not have included a neck scan with a subsequent operative detour for an asymptomatic neck mass. The next step after an equivocal stress test, if that test was indicated in the first place, would not necessarily be immediate heart catheterization. And the Health Security Board guidelines would include an independent reassessment by the angiography team before the catheterization, which would likely have forestalled immediate catheterization because this was by now a case of atypical chest pain without much evidence for coronary artery disease as the cause. In fact, at that point this clinically stable patient had already undergone an operation without evidence of any consequences of stress to the heart, for incorrect indications that would clearly violate reasonable guidelines by the Board. Moreover the guidelines would specify that, even if there had been an indication for an operation, it should have been deferred until the cardiac status was settled. No one was navigating.

This man finally received the correct diagnosis, at a cost of $60. By coming up with this in the first place, the single payer plan would likely have saved the country the remaining $127,940. At that rate, we could pay the general practice doctor and team even two or three times that $60 for his care and still be way ahead in quality and savings.

A final perspective on how much the country spends on doctors can be had from considering the degree of potential savings that might accrue from an opposite approach with a law that would cut doctors' incomes. Dr. Uwe Reinhardt notes that even cutting all physician payments by an unreasonable, badly demoralizing 20% would save only 2% ($30 Billion) from our national health care budget.[51] That sounds like a lot but of the $3 trillion annual U.S. health care bill, hundreds of billions of dollars in savings are reasonably available by other means: control of the costs of administration, overutilization and as we will see, costs for drugs, devices and diagnostics. Moreover, it is commonly noted that the work that doctors do governs about 85% of health care expenditures. That is where the money is. As illustrated by the benighted workup for chest pain just described, the goal for the country for savings as well as quality must be to incentivize physicians to optimize best clinical choices, not to arbitrarily cut professional payments from their present fee-for-service amounts.

Practice decisions are really a major part of quality, so, perhaps beyond Adam Smith, one can view payment for the work a doctor does in terms of some measure of quality. In Chapter 5 I describe a novel proposal for dealing with the issues of quality and the work done by doctors and nurses. I will show that in a single payer system there is a straight-forward path to solving this conundrum.

At the end of the interview with former Aetna chief Dr. Jack Rowe, perhaps reflecting my questions about the costs of insurance, he advised that I might also look into the costs of doctor's salaries here vs. in other countries. I allowed that I had (see above) and that although there were some differences it was not a huge issue . . .

Q: from me (to the savior of AETNA): ". . . it's nothing like, you might say <ahem> what the CEOs of insurance companies are paid."

A: <Quick pause> <Laughter> "That's fair!"

There has been some speculation about this, although probably reining in reimbursement for top health care CEOs somewhat would save the country at most a few billion dollars a year. Beyond the expense, the disparity of the high CEO pay for health care business is also harmful as a benchmark that irks doctors, but since this benchmark reflects the multi-million dollar annual salaries and benefits that top U.S. business executives in general are paid—this is a topic beyond the scope of this book aside from some observations about inequality in Chapter 6.

Of course there is a major professional responsibility for doctors to be reasonable. If the Medscape figure of $413,000 annual salary for orthopedists is accurate, there must be a considerable number making over a half a million dollars per year after taxes. I do not think absolute rules are necessary nor will they work. But a doctor making a million dollars every two years for treating patients is an issue, at least until we make sure that every American has great health care.

On the other hand, it is straightforward to censure uncivilized mendacity. Elizabeth Rosenthal in her New York Times series, *Paying Until it Hurts*, recently described a case of neck surgery in which, among the large medical bills, including from the surgeon, that the patient received, there was also one for $117,000 from an Assistant Surgeon whom the patient had not met and did not realize would be part of the surgery. In discussing how fiscal constraints might evolve in medicine and surgery, I asked Dr. Warshaw about that case. About to begin his year as President of the American College of Surgeons, he replied: "The public doesn't have any idea about the complexities of assistants and networks and physician oversight. What the public sees is not so much the question of the assistant but, you know: 'Those doctors are at it again,'— this is unbelievable and its shameful—it makes surgeons look awful."

The argument might be that this fee is what the market will bear, but surely it is time to consider some constraint. The market is rigged.

The cost and quality of a country's health care is often considered dependent on the number of doctors. Historically, relying on data showing greater expenses where there are more doctors, CMS has tried to discourage the number of doctors, and it may be that anti-competitive doctors and their associations have similarly tried to limit doctors as a guild might work to bolster reimbursements. Conversely, with the ACA generating increasing numbers of new paying patients, there may be shortages particularly in general practice, adding to the stresses already present for these doctors. In the U.S. recently we are seeing longer waiting times such as we typically ascribe to Canada and Europe.[52] An additional factor is the pressure for medical students who graduate with a huge debt to choose a highly paid specialty hoping for more control over their lives and finances. But regardless of their field, what doctors do is changing rapidly because of advances in tests and treatments and the structure of delivery of medical care. From all of this, Jim Duderstadt, musing about his responsibility to the University of Michigan Medical School, said: "I think it may be time for another Flexner Report . . . the basic character, the values of what you need to know and how you obtain that information are changing dramatically and so we need to think in a very fundamental way how we create the physicians and the health professionals more broadly." Not, I suspect, by accident, the University of Michigan Medical School has been one of the medical schools that has overhauled its curriculum, teaching students to collaborate in groups and how to communicate to peers and the public. The AMA is supporting 11 medical schools in a restructuring of training for the medical practice of the future. Specific scientific and clinical study are not discarded, but medical knowledge is too enormous to be learned thoroughly in a few years, and moreover by the time these students even finish their residencies and fellowships the field will have advanced with new things to know. So education for a clinical career must prepare a doctor for what he or she must learn about and adapt to in the future with as much rigor as it provides for the medical practice of today.

HOSPITALS

Although hospitals would ideally be nothing but an extension of the doctor's care, they represent an independent business with its own quality issues and costs and their special role in the social fabric. Rosenthal's reporting shows that in general the cost problem is not doctors' fees.[53] Hospital reimbursement is another thing. As she reports, the spread of charges for the same medical reason in the same hospital for patients with different payers is astounding.[54]

At the least it suggests that those hospital charges are not based upon calculations with a defensible rationale. Moreover the trend to acquisition of physician practices described above may have the potential to streamline care, but the hospitals' principle motivation is to expand their patient base. This increased market share provides increased power to negotiate with private insurance companies to increase revenues and profits. Of equal concern, many large hospitals are acquiring other smaller hospitals for the same market share-driven reasons. A classic case occurred in Boston. To avoid the insurance companies driving down rates by playing one off against the other, two large expensive Harvard hospitals merged: the Massachusetts General Hospital and the Brigham and Women's Hospital, forming Partners HealthCare. The power of this united front allowed the two hospitals to increase prices and when the Tufts Health Plan tried to refuse to pay these high prices, the Tufts plan had to capitulate to stay in business. On the other hand, when Partners recently tried a further major acquisition, it was halted by the state until an eventual compromise including a stay on price increases might be worked out. Although legally binding for now, no one expects such very profitable expansion not to continue in the long run under the present system.

Finally, a remarkable study of the 50 highest cost U.S. hospitals by Ge Bai and Gerry Anderson shows that nearly all are for-profit. Fully fifty percent of the hospitals with the highest Medicare charge to cost ratios are affiliated with Community Health Systems, and an additional 28% with the Hospital Corporation of America.[55] The map showing this distributed variability of costs by state is analogous for the hospitals to the Dartmouth Atlas for doctors' medicare charges discussed earlier in the chapter, and these data represent similar prospects for cost control.

The Physicians for a National Health Plan takes a stance against allowing for profit hospitals to participate in the single payer system. Although that might help oversight, large non-profit hospitals can realize bottom line 'gains' in the range of 50 to 100 million dollars per year (Dr. Duderstadt: "We call it gains rather than profits since it's a non-profit."). Non-profit hospitals, including many successful stellar academic institutions, have been just as vigorous as for-profit hospitals in expanding their reach by acquisitions.

Hospitals are under the same unrealistic pressures by Medicare as doctors to document quality. A good example is the rate of readmission. No one doubts that readmission can represent a failure to complete necessary care thoroughly before discharge. As such, a low readmission rate has been a standard measure of quality review by Medicare. But necessary care may take time, and when the number of hospital days allowed for the DRG (diagnosis related group) payment for a given condition is reached for a certain patient, there is financial pressure to discharge the patient. If the patient is discharged on time but is unprepared and further care after discharge is not effective so that the patient must come back in, the hospital has not lost money regarding the truncated length of stay (in this patient's case) due to observing the DRG restriction, but it loses on the readmission. And where is the patient's best interest in this? There is no question that incentives to streamline and improve hospital care may help early discharge and lower chances of readmission. Both are worthy goals and there are many reports of improvements in this. There is plenty of room for the review of hospital practices to encourage better care, and even decrease the need for hospitalization in the first place. Incentives to improve care in this way are appropriate. For instance, to save costs the American Hospital Association has described ways that hospitals must avoid nonbeneficial care such as antibiotic overuse and unnecessary scans.[56] That makes sense. As a doctor, I applaud these restraints, and suspect that both of these will also decrease hospitalization days and readmissions. But when medical issues require being in the hospital, there should not be a disincentive to the patient being there. This is an example of how reformed medical care in a single payer system can be better managed with physician oversight.

More generally, if the courageous trial of "payer agnosticism"[57] by Alta Med, a multi-site federally qualified community health center in California, is successful in treating patients equally and evaluating quality and outcomes regardless of payer, this initiative can be an example of how a national system might develop. For many years Maryland has had a waiver from Medicare that established the same hospital reimbursement rates from all payers, rather than the marked difference between Medicare and private insurance seen elsewhere. This has been run by a state Health Services Cost Review Commission to which all hospitals adhere. Pressure to increase the volume of services has recently caused a renegotiation by Medicare with Maryland that will hold prices down by focusing on the overall per capita expenditures for hospital services.[58] This is analogous to single payer for hospitals and there is a commitment to begin including doctors' practices in this initiative. Although certainly the opposite of a purely market-based approach, neither is it pure socialism. It represents a practical process that works and therefore contains lessons for delivery system reform needed for a national health plan. The coalescence of hospitals and doctors in the U.S. health care system will avoid the costs and harms of competitive behavior by hospitals and other providers only if it can be made to exist with continuity throughout the country. In that case, the ultimate, theoretical, novel result could be thought of as one big national ACO via a single payer system with optimized efficiency and no market competition among hospitals, payers or providers for increased profits.

NURSES

What about the nurses that Dr. Duderstadt had observed were doing all the work on the patient care floor of the hospital? There is little doubt that nurses will continue to be indispensable whatever health care system evolves. As improved outpatient followup and medical home organization expand, improving care and saving money, nurses will do much of the work. Institutional and national budgets have a responsibility to support nursing schools and salaries without which patients will not get the best care. And the increasing trend for nurses to obtain further education and become a licensed nurse practitioner is also likely to continue. Common ground must be found on how much medical responsibility is appropriate for someone without an M.D. degree as this field matures. On the other hand, general practitioner Dr. Ostrich recalls at Kaiser: ". . . back in the '90s I think all of a sudden nurse practitioners and physicians assistants started appearing in the clinics to help with the crush of patients and the doctors finally said you know this really is not helping very much. All we end up doing is kind of taking care of all the loose ends which they can't do professionally. So right now they are in some of the other clinics. I think they were much more useful there. In primary care when I left, for the last 10 years there were none. "More commonly, however, these advanced nursing roles are viewed as valuable. From my personal experience in doing organ transplants, the attention to details, the continuity, and the personal investment by the several nurses and nurse practitioners who are part of our transplant team are an irreplaceable addition to our team, both on the hospital floors and in the outpatient clinic. The American Association of Critical Care Nurses has established a hospital leadership model with regional leadership groups which developed initiatives that allowed them to decrease patients' length of stay in intensive care units and progressive care units and to achieve big decreases in falls, infections and bed sores. The value of expanded nursing practice was mentioned in their interviews by Dr. Lewin, and Senators Sanders and Daschle, all of whom have an eye toward an improved system. It would seem that a blend of general physicians and nurse specialists navigating the ship will be optimal.

IT'S THE MONEY

One thread that runs through the provision of care by doctors and hospitals is the accelerated pace of change, bringing remarkable new medical advances. For health care professionals, catching up with this pace of change in order to do our best by the patients will be an ongoing challenge. Beyond that, the more critical problem now is the unrestrained commoditization of medicine that has accompanied the clinical changes of the last couple of decades. That thread appears in all the considerations about health care reform. This spending must be reined in if every American is to have access to quality affordable care. The power of a national single payer health care system will provide for cost containment that incorporates the best interests of patients and doctors.

CHAPTER FOUR
DRUGS, DEVICES AND DIAGNOSTICS

U pon the advent of antibiotics in the 1940s, along with the breakthroughs of antisepsis, anesthesia, and diagnostic X-rays (the first clinical use, to view a skater's wrist fracture, amazingly only a week after Roentgen's initial report in 1895), the era of modern medicine had begun. These innovations produced wonderful improvements in patient care, and, particularly for antibiotics, caused fundamental changes in society.[1] But these advances did not greatly perturb the fundamentals of medical practice initially. Now they have.

This chapter reviews the impact on medical practice and policy of the astounding further progress in drugs, devices and diagnostics since those seminal beginnings.

Walking towards the Washington D.C. Convention Center on a sunny Sunday morning in September, I encountered serious people going my way with TCT ribbons holding their admissions badges for the TransCutaneousTherapy 1014 Conference run by the Cardiovascular Research Institute. Rounding the corner, the place was a hubbub of Dillons Buses circulating from local hotels and meeting attendees: 12,000 people whose jobs are fixing hearts and blood vessels "non-invasively" through catheters inserted in the groin or arm and directed to somewhere in the body, enabling treatment without open surgery. With large plenary presentations, numerous scientific sessions and 150 commercial exhibitors of the latest technology who help to fund it, this annual event is a quintessential big medical meeting, evincing all of the promise and potential cost of modern medicine today. Did you know that their magic includes "the world's smallest heart pump" that can be inserted via the groin in only minutes to support the left ventricle of a failing heart? I didn't, but it's promoted in an announcement right there with a picture in the *tct2014daily* guide to the conference.

I was there to interview Dr. Jack Lewin, among other things former Officer in the US Public Health Service including Director of the Navajo Nation Department of Health, later CEO of the American College of Cardiology and now the President and CEO of the Cardiovascular Research Institute, there with his outfit to oversee this meeting, He had agreed to provide his views to me on further health care reform.

He has been a strong proponent of the Affordable Care Act, although his thinking has evolved to addressing the needs and issues to accomplish further reform, as you will find in several of his opinions quoted in this book. In cardiology, innovative technology has been expanding the doctors' capabilities. This expansion has driven costs up: "Yes, doctors could exercise their own accountabilities and clearly fix a lot of problems in efficiency and variation in our systems," although he is pessimistic about that happening. On the other hand, he does see a possible way forward with a "value-based agenda that produces better outcomes at lower cost."

DEVICES

So what about the slick, shining displays of expensive new gadgets crowding the displays at his TransCutaneousTherapy congress? Technology per se is often not a separate cost line on the accounting for U.S. medical expenses, partly because in spite of the expense of some of these new gadgets, overall they account for only a few percent of annual expenditures. But of course the cost of the device is only the beginning. What really counts is what doctors do with them. Dr. Lewin notes that although doctors get paid 16% of Medicare spending, they control the other 84%. Increasingly that represents doctors employing new technology.

So for the average new radiology catheter or surgical instrument that comes along, the main issue is whether the doctor actually needs it. Only occasionally does a new tool save money for the hospital or the doctors' practice. A new surgical tool can make it so much easier to do something that it seems worth the additional cost. Otherwise there is little reason to buy it—unless it saves more lives. The percutaneous heart assist device mentioned above might prove its worth by saving lives: Gasping in the grip of acutely worsening congestive heart failure, if I were otherwise medically salvageable, I would figure that my chances were better if I have that gadget threaded into my heart to buy time than to have my chest pounded on to resuscitate me after cardiac arrest or my "chest cracked,"—the vernacular for a median sternotomy used in open heart surgery—for an unplanned emergency cardiac operation. One way or another, such devices that improve the risk spectrum have a relatively unchallenged path to wider use. Over time the cumulative cost of such important advances is felt mostly when it significantly increases the net number of high-end procedures that doctors are doing. The issue is when the reason for using it is not what it does for the patient but just that it's a new gadget. The reason to be cautious with devices is the same as with the problems described in the previous chapter regarding new treatments that become accepted practice before scientific evidence about their risks and benefits is obtained.

Take the laparoscope. For the past 30 years, laparoscopic surgery, the "Band-Aid operation," has been displacing conventional open surgery done through a larger incision by which the surgeon gains access. In place of the surgeon's hands, two or three tiny incisions are made through which a narrow fiber optic telescope hooked to a TV camera can be placed inside the abdomen, along with long handled instruments. The operation is performed by the surgeons manipulating the tools from the outside, viewed on the screen for all to see. This is clearly a remarkable advance, but with some limitations. Studies show earlier recoveries and less narcotic use for patients who underwent laparoscopic surgery compared with those recovering from the larger incisions of open procedures. Initially there was a higher incidence of complications and reoperations, for example in gall bladder removal. These problems have receded and seem to have largely been due to the learning curve when a new set of understandings and skills had to be achieved, similar to those that must be acquired in surgical training to avoid complications in conventional operations,[2] although the claim of fewer complications across the board remains in doubt. Also whether the laparoscopic approach improves patient survival is doubtful, although because it entails less operative and postoperative stress, it may increase the likelihood of a successful surgical procedure in marginal high risk patients. The main concern today is whether it is more expensive. A conventional open procedure does not require the costly apparatus, just the surgeon's direct approach using some routine instruments, and in many cases, conventional surgery requires a shorter time in the operating theater. Since laparoscopic surgery almost always replaces the open procedure that would be done otherwise, the cost attributable to the advent of laparoscopic surgery is the difference if its costs are higher than the open approach. As skills have matured, the benefits of laparoscopic surgery in properly selected cases by appropriately qualified surgeons have brought costs down to be equivalent with the open procedure.[3]

Much more controversial and distant from the gadget category is the Da Vinci robot machine for assisting laparoscopic surgery. To use this, the surgeon sits at a console and manipulates virtual tools which precisely reproduce the actions with actual tools in the patient. In this way, operations have been done globally by surgeons many miles away from the patient, limited only by electronic signal transmission time lag. Dr. James Breeden, President of the American College of Obstetrics and Gynecology, cautions: "At a price of more than $1.7 million per robot, $125,000 in annual maintenance costs, and up to $2,000 per surgery for the cost of single-use instruments, robotic surgery is the most expensive approach."[4] It was estimated that use of the Da Vinci adds 13% to the surgical cost. Even that price might be justified if using the Da Vinci helps patients. But there are no data showing that it makes outcomes better.[5] Because of the extensive hype from the manufacturers directly to the public, and the claims in advertisements by hospitals touting its availability to their competitive advantage, the Da Vinci is likely to remain in the armamentarium for special cases and will perhaps become less expensive over time. But it may never be shown to provide better outcomes than routine laparoscopic surgery.

Proton beam irradiation is designed to focus tissue damage from the radiation more precisely on the tumor, thereby sparing skin and other tissues in the path of the beam compared with conventional X-ray treatments for cancer. This new high-tech approach presents the same two challenges. The first is the cost. Medicare is paying $32,000 for proton beam therapy instead of $19,000 for the standard radiation therapy for prostate cancer, the commonest condition in which proton beam therapy is substituted. Since this is a common diagnosis in the U.S., annual revenues for it are around $50 million,[6] a good return on investment for the approximately one dozen centers that have made the investment. This is obviously good for business, but how about for the patients? There's the problem. In addition to the cost, the second challenge is that so far there is no evidence in the data confirming the theoretical advantage. Of course there is also the question of how many men really need the treatment at all. We will get to that in the next chapter. At present, proton beam irradiation treatment is, at best, only justified for occasional special pediatric or neurologic cases, at a small fraction of the cost that we are paying today.

We will soon have other devices challenging our management of benefits and costs. The robot will evolve and turn up in some form more frequently.

Well before "The Singularity" in about 2045, when some experts predict that computers will be smarter than the sum of all of mankind's intellect, we will see more robotic incursions into medicine. In fact, even now it is possible that you may find the doctor's robot (actually a sort of glorified mobile telehealth gadget at present) seeing you on its rounds, checking your wound, and so on.[7] It's OK, perhaps with an excellent bedside manner programmed in, studiously deferential but unfailingly accurate, it can soon develop a very good robot-patient relationship with you. . . . Or, my favorite, the "Huggable Bear" robot in use in Boston to cheer up children in the hospital.[8] As both of these are now console-controlled by a remote operator, they are not a robot in the way a Roomba (the little automatic vacuum cleaner) is—but just you wait.

DRUGS

For costs and quality, the pharmaceutical industry presents a numerical problem. There are too many drugs. Not to say that a major fraction of them aren't critically life-saving in the stamp of the original discoveries in the mid-20th century, but too many still make no difference to any patient. This is true for many over-the-counter varieties, obvious exceptions being help for allergies, for "heartburn" (a classic misnomer—after too much food and wine), for symptoms of a "cold" or simple skin infections. Although these may be oversold, they can help, don't hurt and are not extravagant. The big money is in prescription drugs.

The eminent physician Sir William Osler famously said: "The desire to take medicine is perhaps the greatest feature which distinguishes man from animals." Perhaps less well-known in his wonderfully rich legacy of aphorisms is the remedial perspective: "One of the first duties of the physician is to educate the masses not to take medicine."

Keep in mind that a good medical cure is generally better and more cost-effective than any procedural or operative solution (although it may take a little longer). You are hearing this from a surgeon, remembering all the stomach resections that I did for peptic ulcer disease well in the past. That was before the discovery that the cause for benign peptic ulcer disease is a bacterium, "Helicobacter pylori," that is easily treated with antibiotics. The hemigastrectomy plus vagotomy operation for this—a good operation in its time—and the interesting Grand Rounds presentations about its occasional complications are medical history now.

But the present extravagant pharmaceutical pricing situation in the U.S. does not serve the best interests of patients and taxpayers. What contributes to these high costs in the U.S.? The costs are not high because we use more prescription medicines in the U.S compared to other countries. Overall, the greater prescription pharmaceutical expense for medical care here is due to the higher cost per pill.[9] This is partly due to the cost of development of new drugs, which is an expensive, uncertain business, but is money well-spent by the drug companies. Nevertheless, much of the cost of pharmaceuticals seems to be attributable to marketing costs, not just technical production demands. Moreover, when marketing takes hold, the proliferation of various drugs beyond benefit for patients makes the whole cost of such pills a waste of money in the first place.

One way to save money and help patients will be to sharpen our indications for new drugs. An easy problem is "look-alike" drugs. Too much of the drug companies' resources go to make a drug designed to replace an older drug that is just as good but less profitable.[10] An example is the many second generation brand name antibiotics that have a spectrum of activity that mimics an earlier, truly blockbuster drug to no additional advantage. They are profitable if they are sufficiently different chemically to escape the patent protection of another company's drug, or when the patent of a brand name drug is about to expire. Federal incentives in a national health care program could steer drug companies to concentrate on truly new and more effective remedies.

Regarding marketing costs, we addressed the general problem of medical advertising and advocated the simple solution of getting rid of it in Chapter 2. But beyond that is another fundamental issue. As Osler knew, it is all too easy for people to think that they have a problem that requires a pill. In Chapter 2 we noted that preposterous "direct to consumer" public advertising must be restrained and, if allowed at all, made to serve the public's interests.[11] But there is more to it in the case of drugs. The pharmaceutical companies have generated a massive market for many drugs whose large scale use reasonable experts agree is not justified. From "Selling Sickness," by Ray Moynihan and Alan Cassels:[12]

"With promotional campaigns that exploit our deepest fears of death, decay, and disease, the $500 billion pharmaceutical industry is literally changing what it means to be human. Rightly rewarded for saving life and reducing suffering, the global drug giants are no longer content selling medicines only to the ill. Because as Wall Street knows well, there's a lot of money to be made telling healthy people they're sick."

The creation of this market this has been an explicit, aggressive strategy by drug companies. Moynihan and Cassels document this in conditions ranging from high cholesterol or high blood pressure through attention deficit disorder, osteoporosis and . . . "premenstrual dysphoric disorder." There are medical aspects to some, probably all, of these conditions. The problem is that the routine of prescribing an expensive medicine has become accepted by doctors and seems to be expected by the public far in excess of a reasonable likelihood of benefit. This is another obvious place where a national authoritative physician board could intervene effectively.

Generic drugs generally provide savings. Once a patent has expired, if the chemical structure can be reproduced by another manufacturer, it can go into business making and selling the drug at a lower price. To pass FDA approval, the manufacturer must prove the active agent of such generic pills is identical to the imitated proprietary drug, and it must follow FDA good manufacturing processes. Animal and clinical studies proving safety and efficacy, side effect profiles and other licensing requirements are satisfied by merely referring to the original brand name drug since the generic is chemically identical. The Veterans Administration National Formulary lists drugs by their chemical name, encouraging VA hospitals to buy generics at a savings.

Of course the pharmaceutical companies fight the claims that the generics are equivalent, but the requirements for generics, albeit fewer, are rigorous. There is good evidence of equal clinical effectiveness in most cases, and generic drugs may even improve adherence because of improved affordability[13] and can therefore be more effective. A drug company also may fight the incursion of a generic by paying the generic manufacturer to delay production. In recent years the prices of generic drugs have been rising closer to the brand name pills, to a point where the trend has attracted Congressional attention. There are fewer generics now and therefore less competition among them. Generics represent a segment of possible savings on drug costs but perhaps not by a huge amount.

Then there are the very effective new drugs at sky high prices. This is the most difficult area to evaluate in drug costs. Recently a drug was developed that cures Hepatitis C, at $83,000 per patient. Then the next similar anti-Hep C drug came along, priced at $94,000 for the course. I have highlighted these sticker shocks but other drug costs are not far behind. Nevertheless, it is not easy—Dr. Boufford, President of the NY Academy of Medicine, told me: "We're very concerned about treatment for Hep C for example because its currently ridiculously expensive but its curative so important to cover." Dr. Wells, National Institutes of Heath investigator and former surgery department chair: "One could argue that the costs of the drugs recently approved by the FDA for treatment of hepatitis C are a bargain, since the majority of patients are cured by a single treatment course." True, but the argument loses impact when you calculate the cost of treating all 4,000,000 folks in the U.S. who are Hep C positive at $90,000 apiece: $360 billion dollars, or just over one tenth of our total annual health care expenditures.

Also troubling are the myriad of anti-cancer drugs appearing at high prices although they may be of little additional value.[14] This is another example of having too many drugs. Presently the recommendation is often to keep trying one drug after another in patients with recurrent cancer. Oncologist Ray Drasga told me: "Right now the problem in the United States with oncologists is that a lot of patients are treated until they basically cannot move or they're dead. Economic incentives are to keep treating patients until they can't walk," because they can bill for patient care in the office but if they send the patient to hospice they can't bill any longer. Dr. Drasga does not follow that philosophy—he makes referrals to hospice when it's appropriate. For the national system, he favors the principle of limiting coverage to perhaps a few of the possible sequential treatments as the best thing for relapsing patients. For example, guidelines might pay for 3 lines of chemotherapy sequentially for lung cancer. Beyond that the patient would need to go into hospice.

My attempts to interview someone in the pharmaceutical industry directly were met with rebuffs, but I arranged to talk with Dr. Joshua Cohen, PhD., a Research Associate Professor at the Tufts Center for Drug Development. He studies public policy issues related to prescription drug reimbursement and market access. He lived in Europe for about twenty years. The Tufts Center has a relationship with the U.S. pharmaceutical industry, and perhaps he checked me out and was prepared for a more argumentative interview, not realizing that this project was a field trip for information-gathering. He talked easily and informatively about his comparative views of the drug industries in Europe and in the U.S. Although he has some appreciation for the approach to health care in European countries, he approves of the free market advantages of the ACA: "The industry folks, many of them, (not all, but many) are OK with it because it expands their base. They realize that there is still some underutilization in the system of appropriate pharmaceuticals and they want to have that part of the pie. I think at the same time there's still some concern about price controls down the road, but ACA doesn't include price controls. So far so good. I do see the industry now is waging a war it cannot win, and this has little to do with the ACA but it has to do more with the debate on prices raging as you know in oncologic circles. They won't be able to price the way they're used to. The reason I say it's a losing cause is that I don't think there are going to be price controls per se in the United States but I think there are going to be ways that payers in the private market and hospitals like

Sloan Kettering and M.D. Anderson are going to simply use their leverage and say, look, if your drug is only providing a marginal benefit and we have an alternative we're either not going to include your drug on the formulary or we're going to ask you to lower the price. That leverage is being used for the first time."

In our interview former Health and Human Services Secretary Tommy Thompson argued that the control of drug costs, constituting only 16% of U.S. health care spending (before the Hep C antibiotics), is not a major concern. But to decrease costs, we must accumulate fragments of savings in many parts of the health care economy. Notwithstanding the huge benefit that drugs provide, which has continued to expand and diversify since the first blessed antibiotics 80 years ago, there are savings to be had in regulating overpriced drugs, Dr. Cohen's faith in the free market's power to control prices notwithstanding.

Secretary Thompson's lack of concern was strongly disputed by others whom I interviewed, including Dr. Duderstadt: "The pharmaceutical industry is as much of a threat as a benefit in all this. We see it in the newspapers over the last month or so because the reluctance of the pharmaceutical industry to get involved in developing suitable vaccines for diseases like Ebola, because they're not chronic. So it's not meeting the public interest. Private industry is mainly interested in making profits and not necessarily in serving public needs. That's not their primary objective."

Note that the structure of the single payer system that we are considering in this book would allow someone to get more and more treatments of various drugs if they have the money for private coverage to do so and wanted, for instance, to continue to endure the miseries of chemotherapy until they are dead. It is just that, unlike now, payment for hopeless treatments will not be costing you and me anything in our taxes or other health expenses through the national public system, nor restricting access for the poor to effective treatments due to an excessive cost of U.S. medical care.

Medicare is prevented by law from negotiating the price of drugs. In the U.S. there is no general restraint on drug prices. There are a few exceptions: the VA, which is allowed to save money on pharmaceuticals by bargaining for price—with savings of 25% to 50% ; the "340b" drug pricing program for community health centers and federally-qualified indigent care hospitals and clinics; and the occasional occurrence of market competition. Recently, insurance companies have begun to try to negotiate with pharmaceutical companies as predicted by Dr. Cohen but this is not the coordinated effort that a national health program could make.

I interviewed a Canadian expert on the trade-offs of drug prices. I first heard of Dr. Andreas Laupacis on the radio. He is a former Chair of the joint provincial Canadian Expert Drug Advisory Committee. A few years back he discussed a difficult drug choice decision on the Canadian Broadcasting Corporation.[15] The Committee reviewed a drug for lung cancer that appeared to offer little improvement for the patients and was very expensive. Of course there was industry pressure to approve it. The Committee voted against putting it on the "formulary" that lists drugs that are acceptable for general use there. On the airplane home from Ottawa to Toronto, he felt comfortable with the decision. But that evening he happened to see a man interviewed on television who had been on the drug for two years and, as Dr. Laupacis said, "Looked pretty good." He said that night was the only time he really did not sleep, worried that the Committee that he chaired might have made a mistake. Later the manufacturer presented results from a scientifically solid study of that drug that his Committee had turned down and the results showed that it was not very effective. The Committee had made the right decision. Of course the Committee could always reassess any decision and if this more stringent study had been positive, they could have reversed their decision. It was not a federal or provincial decision per se, it was up to the doctors. At any rate, as Dr. Laupacis said, you have to deal with it rationally, but the responsibility takes its toll emotionally at times. The announcer ended the program saying that he sleeps better because people like Dr. Laupacis are working on these issues.

Dr. Laupacis runs a public web site in Canada, "Health Care Matters," in which people debate everything from policies on supply of test strips for diabetics to the latest pharmaceutical controversy. If we could ignite a national discussion of this sort in the U.S. it would be wonderful.

In Canada, drugs administered in the hospital are paid out of the global budget for doctors and physicians, but outpatient drugs are handled separately. Dr. Laupacis said the provinces have negotiated individually to restrain drug prices with unsatisfactory results: "For a long time we weren't negotiating at all, and then we were saying no to a bunch of drugs because of the ridiculously high prices, in view of the benefits, and some provinces, Ontario being one, started to actually negotiate prices." A pan-Canadian Pharmaceutical Alliance (pCPA) with all the provinces has formed to advise the provinces on the basis of extending access to drugs and how each province negotiates with the drug company. The price they end up with is a secret, which has pros and cons, but is understandable given the concern of the drug companies that they are just across the U.S. border.

I also asked Adam Owens, PhD, about this. Dr. Owens is Vice President for Health Policy and Research in the Canadian Medical Association and has 24 years of experience working on ethics, professional workforce issues, public health and health reform. The CMA is the Canadian counterpoint of the AMA, although it seems to operate with a more unified data-driven public health perspective than has been evident in the U.S., at least in the past. He commented on the incompleteness of drug coverage in Canada: "Provincial governments are working on it—the province of New Brunswick for example, has recently brought out a drug program for people who do not otherwise have coverage, and Quebec's had such a program for some time. I guess what's lacking at the moment is any kind of a concerted national will to address these things. I think—it's been not just our current government but the previous government . . . certainly in the case of prescription drugs there's a lot of worry about cost."

Interestingly, the provinces are chary of letting the Canadian federal government into their drug alliance process now that they have it underway, although that may be changing because the pCPA has formed a committee to consider a federal role. The lesson that I draw from the Canadian experience for the U.S. is that regardless of how states are involved in other ways in future health care reform, a national, not state-based, consensus law for federal negotiation of drug pricing is necessary for a single payer system.

But how to structure the argument on controlling drug prices remains unfocussed. In the U.S., with no market forces and sparse categorical regulation, drugs are priced with no rationale except what the companies think they can obtain. A good example is the fuss that has arisen over Sovaldi, one of the new Hep C cures. Supported by hedge funds, Giliad Sciences bought the rights to Sovaldi at an astounding cost and is now marketing it at its equally astonishing price, with no development costs to recoup—for Giliad, this is not about pharmaceuticals, it is high finance. The high cost per pill precludes treatment of many needy patients, while the profits go to the hedge funds. The only innovation to be inhibited by regulating this might be to curb the ingenious financial shenanigans.

Nevertheless, there is concern that drug cost control would suppress research and development. For instance, a study reported that a 10 percent increase real drug prices is associated with nearly a 6 percent increase in the growth of research and development.[16] The worst outcome from regulating drug prices would be the suppression of innovative new drug discovery. The argument of the pharmaceutical companies was given by Dr. Cohen: "Even though I'm actually someone who's sympathetic to a single payer model in some ways, I know there are issues of rationing. Sovaldi's a great example where the company really didn't do much of the development at all. But it clearly is exerting its market power. It's important to keep in mind that that is probably an exception to the rule. For the most part industry is still doing quite a bit of R&D. I'm sure everybody in industry would love a Gilead story because they wouldn't have to do all the scut work, but for the most part they're doing it and often times coming up empty-handed because there are so many failures, right, I mean Phase 1, and Phase 2, Phase 3 . . . so the industry is of course faced with these higher costs of development and, yes, there are these success stories that unfortunately for the industry, also breeds contempt among the public. The high price of a Sovaldi really turns people off. I'm critical of the high prices but I do see that there's still plenty of innovation going on here in the United States and we've seen this—I wouldn't call it a brain drain—but certainly a drain of research and development complexes from European companies coming to Boston over the last 15 years, to Cambridge, and the Research Triangle. Europe and Japan and other places are innovative but some of the cutting edge stuff, the orphan drugs, some of those cancer drugs I mentioned, this Hepatitis C drug, a lot of that is hitting the market here first and there's a reason for that."

On the most basic level it is clear that innovation will happen anyway, so the intense market activity may not be such a critical requirement. Behavioral psychologists note that humans exercise their ingenuity for its intrinsic rewards, not necessarily for monetary gain.[17] In fact, correcting the chronic underfunding of the NIH is probably a far better place for the country to put its money than in supporting greater gains of pharmaceutical stocks on the stock market. Many innovations that are part of medical advances used in the U.S. were developed in other countries.[18] Examples include hip or knee replacement for osteoarthritis (French technology) or deep-brain stimulus for mental disease (Canadian). Viagra originated in Pfizer Research in the UK (in the environment of the British National Health Service) when researchers studying how to improve blood flow to the heart noted a striking side effect. The two new drugs that revolutionized organ transplantation in the 1980s were developed and marketed by companies in Switzerland and Japan. And the recent fear of a global EBOLA epidemic, plus the need to control its continued smoldering presence in West Africa, have been met by very promising trial results for a new EBOLA vaccine—developed in Canada at the National Microbiology Laboratory in Winnipeg.

Moreover, the frequency of new innovative drugs may be decreasing recently[19] in spite of our highly commoditized U.S. drug market. This may be due to the need for new research directions, and also partly to the wasteful, harmful emphasis on seeking look-alike drugs. At any rate, a flagging rate of important new drugs would not support the hope that free unregulated profit taking as permitted now in the U.S. will necessarily increase innovation.

Dr. Cohen's take on this is more optimistic: "There are some breakthroughs in cystic fibrosis, there are even a few, I wouldn't call them breakthroughs yet but certainly better than we had before for multiple sclerosis, obviously the industry in HIV/Aids and that was back in the '90s but had some major breakthroughs, cardiovascular we see kind of a return to the trend that we had in the '80s and '90s, where the industry is beginning again to focus on cardiovascular and if you look at the incidence of heart disease and the fact that people are living longer lives with heart disease, these are things to keep in mind. There have been dry periods. We just experienced one from 2008 to 2012 in terms of the pipeline there weren't a lot of approvals but since 2012 I think we're seeing a spike in approvals, we're also seeing new indications and new formulations. You know I do some research in neglected diseases which are not typically found in the United States . . . well even here now we're seeing some. GFK (Gesellschaft für Konsumforschung) and others with malaria vaccines and dengue fever, a vaccine that I believe is about to be approved and for tuberculosis, the first drug in 50 years was approved. So I think there are enough counterexamples to calm the critics on that." So maybe the trend is reversing. Time will tell.

Dealing with orphan drugs is also illustrative. The problem of the cost of orphan drugs for rare illnesses is that the millions necessary for their development lead to a market of only an occasional patient, which prevents the drug company from recouping its development costs. Here the national consensus might be for a tight justification of innovation and development costs to be allowed, with reimbursement calculated to be spread out for several years of a few new patients a year, as a basis for calculating the allowable price for the national health program to pay. That price tag, still very high, might be acceptable to this rich country. But this brings up the general issue of development costs for any drug. The pharmaceutical industry claims it costs $1 trillion for development of each successful drug, partly because of amortizing costs for the number of false starts with possible remedies that do not prove out, as is generally deemed appropriate, and also for the extensive clinical testing that the FDA requires for validation. Others disagree with the way the costs are calculated by drug companies, and it appears that the true value for development costs is more in the range of $100 million. This includes the recognition that the basis for development of many drugs begins with an innovative discovery at the NIH or is otherwise funded publicly, before the pharmaceutical company enters the scene and incurs the routine costs of initiating manufacture. Given the estimate of $100,000,000 invested for one successfully developed drug to treat a common disease, if priced in the typical range at $100,000 for a treatment course, the company has recouped its losses after treating 1,000 patients, perhaps all in the first year of a 20-year patent protection. During the remainder of the patent years, the cost is more nearly all profit. Even if the development costs are closer to the industry estimate, it would not change the picture in principle. Of course if the drug company's stock is rising during this time—the common scenario—that can be balanced against the development costs as well. A national system as proposed in this book could use this prediction of eventual profits to negotiate a lower initial cost. In fact, right now the history for many drugs is that the pharmaceutical company may actually increase the price in subsequent years.

These illustrations about cost amortization are relevant to diseases to be treated that will continue to arise de novo year after year. But the treatment for Hepatitis C is different, which could help deal with the massive cost of treating it. Although not a certain cure for everyone, it seems that for practical purposes it will drop the incidence in the public to near zero once everyone has access to treatment. This results in a natural progression from a peak of use for the present number of patients that need treatment to an annual number of almost zero need for it before too long—there will be no one else to treat. The mathematical analysis of population incidence during and following an effective immunization campaign for some other epidemic would apply in principle. As with other infectious diseases, occasionally it might flare for a while at some focus due to an untreated patient but this could be quelled easily. And Hep C disease generally progresses slowly, with no liver effect or evidence of only mild liver damage for months or years before signs of more severe disease. During that early time, treatment would be curative but could be delayed. Not everyone would require immediate treatment to be saved. At some point there is generally progression to the development of chronic liver scarring called cirrhosis, at which point the Hep C virus could still be eradicated but the progression of chronic changes would continue to progress anyway, ending in death unless a liver transplant can be done. Once in the progressive cirrhosis phase, the only value to the patient for treatment against Hep C would be to prepare those patients who are candidates for liver transplantation to preclude infection in the new donated organ. The public health interest of treating everyone living with Hep C infection to prevent further spread is obvious, but given the financial reality, the public health need is less acute. Of the estimated 4 million Hep C positive patients, it might be possible to space out categories for treatment over 3 to 5 years. Patients who are the most recently infected and are least severely diseased, and those with severe cirrhosis who are not transplant candidates could be delayed in the queue. First to receive the drug would be those who will benefit because they are just starting to show progression toward more severe liver disease or who are about to be transplanted once their Hep C has been treated. Spreading out treatment for the country out over years would drop the annual cost by 60 to 80% and would be just as effective for each individual patient's needs. Within two to three years, the incidence of new cases would start to plummet, unlike other targets for expensive drugs in which new cases continually appear year after year. As this happens, residual patients with less urgent requirements could be accommodated. Although a realistic option in principle, this description is simplistic and there are clinical specifics that would require expert judgments to make this happen. It seems unlikely to be instituted quickly and accurately by legislation or regulation. But the professional board proposed in Figure 1, acting without political hindrance but with complete national electronic medical records, could initiate this recommendation very quickly and fairly, even as the details of follow-up and oversight evolved through monitoring the progress of the effort. Although I have not seen this said, the high prices charged by the drug companies for this pill may have resulted partly because they foresaw that their market would drop to the equivalent of an orphan disease in a few years, unlike most new drugs. Moreover, in the spirit of drug treatment instead of gastrectomy for ulcer, the several thousand dollars that a liver transplant costs shines a moderating perspective on the high cost per pharmacologic cure of Hep C. This probably would be true even if the cost of liver transplantation is also slated for some reduction. At any rate, this Hep C conundrum might be the most spectacular cost/quality example of the potential value of authoritative national oversight of clinical issues by a professional board in the single payer proposal in this book. This presumes universal access to tests and treatment. While millions of Americans remain without health care insurance, they will continue to harbor Hep C, endangering everyone.

DIAGNOSTIC TESTS

Tests are also a numerical challenge, but for a different reason than the issue of the many marginally useful or overused prescription drugs mentioned earlier. True, expensive machines for testing are not nearly as numerous as the huge and rapidly expanding number of drugs. The numerical problem with diagnostic tests is based instead the size of the population at risk for unnecessary, possibly harmful testing: everyone over about 45 years of age who is not about to die, in other words, a potential market of about 150 million people. Beyond the exquisite sensitivity of modern testing that provides for advanced diagnosis and treatment planning, this potential for unwarranted screening or unnecessary diagnostics is a huge opportunity for business to obtain big profits while potentially doing medical harm.

To counter skeptics about this view, I refer to junk mail just received inviting me to schedule screening that it claims is indicated for anyone with the risk factors listed, including being over 55 years of age. Ultrasound for carotid (neck) artery and abdominal aortic aneurysm (dilatation of the aorta that could rupture), EKG for atrial fibrillation (a common abnormal heart rhythm), peripheral artery disease screening, and osteoporosis risk assessment are all offered for a cost of $149, at a $181 savings! What the heck, I'm over 55, I'll do it all.

From the interviews with Drs. Hadler and Fielding, and the books by Drs. Newman and Lazris, all cited in Chapter 3, you may suspect the actual correct response to this letter: pitch it.

It is true that there is some agreement on having an abdominal ultrasound once, around the age of 55, to rule out an abdominal aortic aneurysm, although if you are reasonably trim you or your doctor can rule out a "triple A" by palpation of your abdomen. But carotid artery ultrasound is definitely not indicated in the absence of symptoms; if your feet feel healthy, don't worry about circulation; you or your doctor can diagnose likely atrial fibrillation if your pulse is irregular; and regarding osteoporosis, everyone who is older has osteoporosis and should be getting exercise and maybe extra Vitamin D, but the risk vs. benefit of other nostrums for osteoporosis does not recommend their indiscriminant use. So toss the ad in the wastebasket, stop worrying and save the $149 + $181.

Serious issues and judgments do exist for many of the diagnostic screening tests. Two of the most common controversies swirl around the PSA test for prostate cancer and mammography screening for breast cancer, which was already mentioned in Chapter 3 regarding overutilization.

Recently, the U.S. Preventive Services Task Force which is part of the Agency for Healthcare Research and Quality reported that routine mammograms were more harmful than beneficial and should no longer be recommended. The main reason was that the data show that mammograms do not help people live any longer. The point, which is a hard trade-off to grasp, is that the biology of the cancer cells determines how aggressive the cancer will be. Of course it is important for any real breast cancer to be treated when it is discovered—so, as with any part of the body, if you feel a new lump, call the doctor. But if you had a mammogram a few months earlier and the tumor had been discovered then, the likelihood of having been saved from dying with that cancer would only be marginally better, if at all.[20]

Moreover, there is risk to having a mammogram. One problem with mammograms is that they are far from being perfectly accurate. Statistics show that false positives, or the finding of "Ductal Carcinoma in Situ" that generally does not need immediate attention, cause trouble if many mammograms are done in normal women who are unlikely to have a true cancer. These findings can trigger more testing and often a biopsy and possibly irradiation. At some statistical point a woman is more likely to suffer or die from the unnecessary care due to those misleading findings than her risk of dying from an undetected cancer.

Finally, there is a small, finite risk because the mammogram itself uses radiation. You may wonder how serious that mammogram damage is? After all, millions of regular mammograms in American women have been done, and only a few of these women developed cancer eventually, and perhaps most of those cancers would have happened anyway. Remember that the last time you had a dental X-Ray they reassuringly put on that heavy lead apron with the thyroid shield around the base of your neck? It makes sense because any glandular tissue such as the thyroid is especially sensitive to cumulative radiation effects. What if they instead took off the shield, pointed the emitter down at your throat and Bzzt! got the thyroid gland? That is similar to what happens to the sensitive glandular breast tissue with every mammogram. The dosage per mammogram is minimal and so far the statistics do not convincingly show an increased cancer incidence except possibly for younger women and perhaps the one woman in 400 with a BCRA1 or 2 gene mutation. Still, common sense says that if the thyroid shield for dental Xrays is of any use, then mammogram frequency should be restrained.

The most important aspect of this is the public confusion and anxiety due to the rapid evolution of medical knowledge and the adversarial news articles that emerge. To quell the confusion, the Health Security Board proposed in this book will have the authority to publicly establish credible national guidelines, complete with rationale, for such controversies and to adjust policy expeditiously and creditably as the clinical science of a question evolves. None of this is happening today. An interim policy for informed consent shielding a woman from feeling guilty for either deciding to have or to defer routine mammography is probably the way the Health Security Board would decide this at present.

Similarly, there is the regular screening for prostate cancer. Modern advances in detection and treatment, including focused radiation and nerve sparing surgery to preserve potency, have improved survival and quality of life for men with prostate cancer. Although the prostate specific antigen (PSA) blood test has been part of that advance, it also presents the same general conundrum as mammography: Used indiscriminately, it may be as likely to cause harm from the response to a false positive as it is to save a life from detecting a cancer at just the right time. Otis Brawley, MD, a surgeon with the American Cancer Society says:[21] "What we all should be realizing is that we have to make a guess. While we know that screening finds cancer, we also know it finds cancer that doesn't need to be treated."

Another problem for U.S. medicine is the tendency to do tests—or worse, even to perform treatments—without sufficient clinical consideration of the specific patient. Cardiac testing is a huge culprit here—introduced in Chapter 3 by the story of the worker who had all sorts of thoughtless procedures done to him including cardiac testing for chest pain before the general practitioner found that the cause was simply the new scaffolding at work that was bruising his chest wall. One of the most common recent tests is the use of imaging with stress tests. About one third of these are not done for appropriate indications, at a cost of over $500 million.[22] But the fearsome part of that report is that this large overuse of cardiac testing was estimated to cause an additional 491 cases of cancer from the radiation used for imaging. That seems a bit high for common sense but if that finding holds, one would hope that there will quickly be a reassessment of when having the imaging added to the stress test is indicated. There are other examples of tests that are overused, but these prominent examples demonstrate the trend.

THE COMMODITIZATION OF MODERN MEDICINE

Part of the problem with devices is the cost to set up and run them. Given the intense commercial competition allowed for medical services in the U.S., it is understandable that hospitals feel pressure to acquire equipment that they can advertise, such as an MRI machine or a robotic Da Vinci surgery assistant. Of course doing more tests that go beyond proven benefits to people is too often encouraged in the absence of curtailing rules. This is part of the reason that many of the experts I interviewed noted that the general participation by U.S. companies producing medical equipment in the bloated U.S. health care economy leads to resistance to reform.

For instance, with health policy economist Dr. Anderson:

Q: "Is business pressed enough to do something about health care costs?"

A: "Other than companies contracting for roads or military work every company is in health care. 20% of GE's business is health care; with Microsoft, 20% of its business is in healthcare . . . etc."

And Dr. Schroeder: "These are all political decisions. No one's having an honest dialogue over those and you've got an industry which is almost 1/5 of the GDP with various components—the docs, the hospitals, the teaching hospitals, the device makers, big pharmaceutical companies, health insurance. These are companies that are very, very powerful. I think the cost problem is going to stay with us."

Lawyer Bond: ". . . the significant problem in American health care is the segmented interests that seed the greed cycle."

Much of the entrenched profitability for business all across America is from the new devices, drugs and diagnostics that are used with no central concern for the pros and cons.

Lest I be accused of bias by letting doctors off the hook regarding these criticisms about the incentives for volume in our fee-for-service system, take the question of annual physical exams. Dr. Ezekiel Emanuel recently wrote a clear, reasoned column describing the argument against the annual physical.[23] It produced a firestorm of frustrated disbelief in response, from patients and doctors alike. But Dr. Emanuel is right. Citing the Cochrane Collaboration, a bastion of probity recognized for its objective recommendations about health care based on available data, he points out that no one lives longer because of something found by the doctor in an asymptomatic apparently well individual, and, as with everything else in this chapter, false positives lead to dangerous tests and treatments best avoided by keeping oneself out of harm's way. If you have a lump, if you are sick, if you have a chronic illness that needs monitoring, of course you need to see the doctor. Growing children should see their doctor for a checkup at regular intervals in the early years. But for adults to have a "well baby" visit every year wastes time and money and produces some endangerment each time. It is an invitation for the medical business to transform you from a well person into a patient. When you are feeling fine, that comfortable feeling that all is well after a negative routine checkup by the doctor doesn't add any guarantees. The medical profession in other countries understands this and it is time that U.S. doctors embrace such good sense.

The regular checkup for cause is another thing. Whether just to get your flu shot, or for an interval assessment of hypertension or diabetes or some other known problem, keeping those preventive appointments do help to deal with known health issues. And breast self exam, occasional rectal examinations and stool blood tests and perhaps a few other targeted preventive recommendations are important—and where we need to focus our time and money.

It will get even easier if the diagnostic aid invented by college dropout billionaire Elizabeth Holmes is successful. The company that she founded, Theranos, will market her micro-scale blood testing involving only a painless prick instead of tubes of blood drawn, with testing that can be done inexpensively at the drug store instead of at a commercial laboratory. If it gets past the Food and Drug Admininstration, professional guidance against overuse must address this for it to be an overall benefit.

Everything discussed in this chapter is a medical advance and is good for some individuals in certain settings—mammograms, PSA testing, stress test, of course even routine blood tests and the physical exam when indicated. The system must leave the specifics of indications to the patient and doctor. And this will be a moving target given the rapid unpredictable but inevitable technological advances arising.

How should we evaluate all that evolving technology? The principles are simple. Is the advance in technology better for patients? And does it hold down costs?

The common thread is that doctors must take an increasingly active public surveillance role. If, with a modern national health program, we can overcome the unbridled commoditization that modern medical magic otherwise invites, it will save money and make us healthier. In the next chapter I will tell you why I believe that there is promise for this now.

CHAPTER FIVE
QUALITY, ELECTRONIC MEDICAL RECORDS AND THE HEALTH SECURITY BOARD

The idea of a single payer system raises concerns among both doctors and the public about what care will be provided. This may be one of the most important questions in health care reform. Yet the medical profession and policy makers alike have not explicitly addressed this problem successfully.

Due to budget demands of a federal system, will there to be too little care—even rationing? Or on the other hand, in the absence of insurance market restraints, will patients obtain too much care—the "moral hazard" fear? As shown in the previous chapters, we will save money, avoid unnecessary care and do the best by patients if we put professional judgment in charge of quality. But how? The novel answer envisioned in this chapter will be a cornerstone for a reformed U.S. health care system. It will require collegial physician involvement separated from political influence and necessitate state of the art electronic medical records. Moreover, coming to this conclusion reveals the advantages of a single payer system.

Dr. Peter Pronovost started as an anesthesiologist and critical care specialist at Johns Hopkins and soon incorporated into this a career of data driven patient care improvement. An initial target that he aimed at has come to be called CLABSI (Central Line Associated Blood Stream Infection). For monitoring and reliable access, acute care patients often have an intravenous line placed centrally in a vein at the base of the neck. These lines then end in the great central vein, the vena cava, near the heart. The rates of CLABSI were high—19 cases per 1000 hospital days at Hopkins at that time. They caused expensive morbidity and sometimes death, and if you asked doctors pre-Pronovost, they figured it was just one of those risks.

Peter Pronovost fixed that. He devised principles for a central line checklist protocol and after he got it going in the Hopkins Intensive Care Unit, CLABSI went down to near zero. This saved Hopkins $2,000,000.[1] In conjunction with the University of Michigan after a tortuous academic and political process, they finally applied his checklist principles there and the rates of infection also plummeted to near zero. These rules about setting up a central line protocol are now being used in all 50 states. One thing led to another and now, as CEO of the Armstrong Institute for Patient Safety and Quality, in addition to doing medical rounds during his regular stints in the intensive care unit, he oversees research, teaching, and implementation of safety protocols.[2]

At the interview he was smooth and youthful in appearance as always, but powerful and infectiously convincing with the force of his experience and commitment: "I focus on the outcome—what we want to achieve and then look at the policy options or the tools we have. . . ." Discussing his success with getting doctors to achieve a high degree of safety. "My journey on this took a lot of personal learning because like most doctors I wasn't exposed to social science. I didn't know about leading change or the sociology of teams and communities and tribes and motivating people and mobilizing people. We realized from the sociological literature that when you're dealing with professionals like physicians, things done to them rather than with them are highly resisted. I was, as you know, a practicing ICU doc on the receiving end of these decrees from management and regulators even while trying to design improvement processes. I got to see the world from both ends and I saw that top down stuff never works. What we did in our work was align everyone towards a common goal, then agreed on a standard measure. We shared our best practices for reducing infections. Then we got all the clinicians together and asked how do we implement those in your own work environment? The key was we created structures for peer learning . . . in other words, connecting clinicians horizontally was much more potent an intervention than vertical accountability."

As he describes in his book,[3] a major part of the "horizontal accountability" was the involvement of the nurses. Part of the protocol is that doctors agreed that nurses helping with the procedure were empowered to challenge the doctor placing the line if the protocol was not being followed exactly.

So, increasingly, anyone who is ever seriously ill in a hospital is better off because of Dr. Pronovost. And he is busily working to improve that degree of protection with more and more specific safety projects through the Armstrong Institute.

I believe that the principles that he has developed can be expanded to deal with the general issue of quality in medical care in our single payer system.

QUALITY

This chapter provides a novel proposal for a practical way to understand quality of medical care. In addition to its relevance for the involvement of doctors in the implementation of a national single payer system, this discussion illuminates the more general issue of quality. With our expanding technical capacities, it is important for ourselves as caregivers and others, including patients and the payer(s), to have a basis for an objective review of how we are doing. We have not yet had much success in getting a measureable handle on what doctors do. As discussed in Chapter 3, I think that the essence underlying the work that doctors do is that they take responsibility. You might extend that to say that doctors must take responsibility for quality care. But quality remains operationally defined in only a foggy way. Nevertheless, quality remained a common issue in the interviews.

To some degree, the confusion about separating costs and quality was evident. As Dr. Boufford, of the New York Academy of Medicine and the IOM put it: "You're moving from fee-for-service to value-based reimbursement. The key is how you define value-based, is it high quality or is it low cost? The triple aim is really about cost, quality and health result. So theoretically what people are talking about is some combination of that in value based payment. It's harder to do with exploding health premiums and exploding pharmacy costs."

Sen. Daschle emphasized transparency, but the costs are still intertwined, describing a: "Strong consensus between Republicans and Democrats on health cost, access and a reluctant but growing consensus that we have a serious quality problem. Also there is a general agreement on the causes: fee-for-service, lack of coordination especially with chronic illness, lack of transparency. . . ."

But Sen. Daschle clearly articulated the imprecision of quality as a criterion: "Until we get better transparency on both price and quality, it's going to be very hard to successfully deal with these many challenges. It's partly a function of payment because fee-for-service rewards volume. Partly it's a function of transparency and providing greater clarity with regard to judgment of quality, and partly it's a better definition of what quality actually looks like: maybe a successful response to circumstances medically, maybe a number of ways to judge it, so I think we still have a ways to go."

Both of the medical society CEO's that I interviewed were sensitized to the inappropriate ways that practice assessments confuse cost and quality, miss the point and complicate medical practice. Matthew Katz, of the Connecticut State Medical Society: "In many cases CMS, the federal government, has been unable to get out of its own way and so many of the guidelines have created more uncertainty and complexity. The quality guidelines and changes to payment methodologies have created huge hurdles, barriers and complexities for physicians." And from Gene Ransom, J.D., Maryland MedChi: "So the Care First medical home program is giving bonuses to primary care doctors which is terrific. My guys loved it. Over 5,000–6,000 doctors signed up for it and now they're getting bonuses for better health care. The problem is that they can't see how much money is being spent or what the savings are. They get a bonus at the end of the year, they're not really sure why, and when they get quality information from Care First it's only about cost. For example, they get a sheet where it has the cardiologist that has red green and yellow and it's based totally on how much they cost. So they may have a cardiologist on there who's retired or semiretired and they are in green. Well that doesn't help the doctor at all and they've got somebody in the red who's doing the most invasive, complex procedures, but he's the guy you really want to see . . . so in my mind it's not a good program because there's no transparency and you don't know what's going on."

And in line with his pessimism about cost savings, health economist Dr. Gerry Anderson sees no economic rationale for quality:

Q: "Are quality improvements possible?"
A: "There are lots of opportunities for improvements in quality: the list includes chronic conditions (too often, with no previous care), obesity, smoking, and the IOM report of 100,000 unnecessary hospital deaths a year,[4] BUT there is no economic incentive."

The triple aim for the country's health care is described in various ways but always has something to do with quality as one of the principle requirements for improving U.S. medicine. Attempts to measure quality objectively have included: items filled out on a checklist for a history and physical evaluation, numbers of hospital readmissions, or whether ePrescribing was used. All of these may be distantly relevant, but the failure of such administrative elements to be effective measures of whatever is meant by "quality" was described in Chapters 2 and 3. So quality is discussed frequently, but only in a general way without yielding compelling measureable data suitable for use in quality control.[5] That can be difficult for regulators. Dr. Grant Bagley, former Director of the Coverage and Analysis Group in the Health Care Financing Administration's Office of Clinical Standards and Quality Chief Medical Officer for HCFA (now Center for Medicare and Medicaid Services) recalls that they were considering the need to stipulate Quality in Medicare and it was suggested by someone at the meeting that since at HCFA they were lacking a consensus on "Quality," maybe it should be called "Value." Dr. Bagley, not fond of humbug, responded to that: "Huh! That'll fool 'em for sure!" But "Value" has stuck around anyway.

This idea of value as usually applied, a remnant of the obsolescent view of health care as a market, is even less satisfactory than the concept of quality. Value confuses the issue because lower cost can increase the rating received to the same degree as better care, however determined, will do, as noted by Dr. Boufford. It is particularly appealing to administrators who are thereby enabled to focus on costs, since costs are inherently measurable. As we have noted in Chapter 3, the intrusion of cost harms medical decision-making. The idea in this book is to minimize the need to consider cost because we can rely on the savings implicit in improving quality. Look at how the Pronovost central line revolution saved millions of dollars in just a couple of hospitals. The big savings provided by that safety achievement are but a drop in the ocean of possible economies in health care. It was not driven by a financial reward for value, it was driven by the innate satisfaction to be had from making things better. So the concept of value, although increasingly emphasized, does not help us to understand a doctor's quality of care any more than just looking at costs.[6] And it has not helped us with the fundamental issue of finding a useful alternative to the simple, critical but indefinable concept of quality as a way to assess care.

Moreover, an insidious unconscious harm in the concept of 'health care value' is that it perpetuates the commoditization of health care through viewing it like any other product for sale, rather than a necessary public good, such as education.

Dr. Pronovost told me: "I believe in America that quality of care ought to be improved, that we have to reduce the number of people suffering preventable harm, and the number of people being disrespected or feeling disrespected in their care."

Dr. Pronovost and his team are known particularly for their work to improve patient safety in the hospital. But I propose that addressing preventable harm plus promoting patient satisfaction can sum up the whole matter of identifiable, measurable quality. This new insight shows the way to a powerful new approach to viewing the doctor's responsibility.

The whole idea of what a doctor does for a patient can be subsumed in the concept of safety. Doctors work to protect patients from harm. They work to protect a patient from the disease the patient has and from errors in diagnosis or management. They work to protect their patients from accidents while under medical care, which must extend beyond a fall in a hospital to protection from an accident at home to the extent that best medication judgment and home care interventions by the team can help prevent the accident. They work to protect a patient from the patient's noncompliance. This resonates with their Hippocratic Oath in which doctors swear to first abstain from doing harm.

This concept goes beyond a restatement of the obvious. It relieves the confusion about quality and value and puts the issue into an operationally explicit mode. You can define the harms the patient is to be protected from, then measure success in this. Quality of care operationally defined as patient safety in the largest sense establishes a framework for measurement and improvement. I tell the medical students that health care is digital, it is either the right choice (or range of choices) or it is wrong. You cannot think about it like fabrics or wine or cars or the "Good, Better, Best" ratings of appliances in the old mail order catalogs. This understanding eliminates the vague uncharacterized concept of better or worse value or quality in health care and provides for an objective view.

As with any assessment of health care, other personal things that are desirable come to mind such as respect and compassion. A positive feeling about their health care improves patients' ability to be effective in working with the doctor's team. Moreover, since as taxpayers the country's citizens will be paying for the health care they receive in their single payer system, they deserve our efforts to monitor and improve their experience.

Of course the doctor cannot always arrange the best for the patient while administering medicines or doing an operation. And the doctor cannot always make every patient feel at ease or satisfied with their care or bolster them perfectly to be effective in carrying out the regimen decided upon. The system I propose can use administrative intermediaries, such as frequency of hospitalization, to the extent that these can be incorporated in a convincing, constructive way form the clinical data in the EMR. There will always be ways that doctors might try to improve their clinical effectiveness. That is why a continuing quality improvement process, not filling out forms to claim adherence to certain numbers, is recognized as the best way to make care better. And I think that Doctor Pronovost even has a prototype of how this can be adopted easily by every care giver, using a process pioneered in his Surgical Intensive Care Unit practice. But that must wait until we take a look at a critical but so far underprivileged ingredient necessary for modern health care: the electronic medical record.

ELECTRONIC MEDICAL RECORDS

Given the rapid progression now towards a useful national EMR system, it is time to consider how it might be best applied in a single payer program. Among the failures in U.S. health care, the biggest tragedy is the lack to date of an interactive universal electronic medical records (EMR) system. Not having complete, accurate information on what is happening to everyone in the country hinders getting things right for every aspect of health care. It will be necessary for a thriving national health program. For that reason, the absence of an EMR system is an overarching failure: it ranks above the greedy profit-taking of the U.S. health care business, the perfidy of the health insurance companies and the variably inadequate quality (protection from harm) that corrodes our medical care. A national electronic medical record system will provide a basis for dealing with all of these faults in U.S. health care. Wouldn't you think, given the vast, accurate and nimble electronic resources now available to anyone from grade school on, that we could have a way to look at health care? Wouldn't you think that from the billions of dollars our government has spent on EMR systems that we would have a world class national system? No. And no. The EMR companies have behaved selfishly and are not focused on doctors and patients. And the government, instead of directing the money towards a national solution, has largely provided for soaring profits to private contractors. There is plenty of blame to go around, including resistance from doctors and hospitals. But one of the most appalling insights from all of my interviews was the government's seditious role in this.

"He's in the room across the hall, behind the green elephant." When I was visiting Former HHS Secretary Tommy Thompson at the law offices of Aiken Gump in the Robert Strauss Building across from Dupont Circle in Washington D.C., I was bemused by the quiet, measured, controlled feeling of a major law firm. By contrast, around Dr. Pronovost's office at Hopkins the halls were busy with staff, patients and visitors of all sorts, making their way in one direction or another, some quickly and some leisurely, some with wheel chairs or with other evidence of disability—a tumultuous ocean of human variety. On the capacious Aiken Gump floor there were a few people of various sorts but any activity was tucked away.

And across the hall were two large green statues, a donkey about life-sized to the right, and an elephant, not so life-sized, to the left in front of the conference room where Secretary Thompson was indeed to be found, in bipartisan proximity to the conference hall behind the donkey next door. In addition to having previously had a major program to revamp welfare during his tenure as Wisconsin Governor, he served as Secretary of Health and Human Services for part of the Bush Presidency so he has had considerable experience in the health care reform arena. In the interview he had several opinions that I quote elsewhere in this book and was in general in favor of any possible way that health care problems could be eased. But the unforeseen crack of thunder came when, near the end of the interview, I thought to ask him about problems with electronic medical records, that being a particular concern of mine.

Secretary Thompson: "Jim, to answer that I have to tell you a story. George Bush and Karl Rove called me over to the White House in summer of 2004 to ask what ideas do you have in health care for the election? And I said A, B . . . D, E and F, several things. And the President looks at them. Karl Rove was there and said he liked some and some he didn't, and one of them was electronic medical records and I said 'I want to announce that we're going to have the electronic medical record system ready to go in 18 months.' And the President said (I was working on EMR at the time) 'What if we brought in like a czar, to the White House to focus on this, to use this as a campaign.' And Karl Rove was looking at it and said 'You just can't get it done in 18 months, Tommy. It's going to take 10 years.' I said 'No, you gotta push it.' And the President said the 'we're going up to Johns Hopkins, we're going to fly up and I want you to go with me, Tommy. We're going to announce an initiative on electronic medical records.' They didn't like my other ideas but they liked the electronic medical records. And so I went back to my office. I had argued vociferously that they not put a person in the White House because I was already working on it. I did not want to have to go to the oval office on this. I was moving down the path very rapidly to get an electronic medical record system and I was having the private sector and everybody involved. I still remember I went over the next morning and the President says, he called me T.T., 'T.T. you won one and lost one,' and I said 'Well . . . Hah! . . . What did I lose?' and he said 'we decided we can't have an electronic medical record in 18 months, were going to announce we're going to have an electronic medical record in 10 years.' And I said 'Mr. President, no one's going to even remember you saying that in 10 years. Eighteen months, we're going to put the pressure on and you'll be surprised how fast people react when you put a short time on it' and then he said 'We just can't do it, Tommy.' And I thought so it's going to be 10 years, and to this day nobody ever remembers that we went to Johns Hopkins and made that announcement. And I said 'What did I win?' and he said 'You won not having the person in the White House. But you're going to have to appoint somebody over in the Department of Health and Human Services to have it' and I said 'Well I don't consider that a win, I consider the fact that I'm doing it right now I don't need it.' But that's how Dr. Brailer arrived. I had to appoint someone and I appointed him and we were moving very rapidly when I left the Administration and Leavitt came in and then nothing really happened until President Obama came in and said 'We're going to have an electronic medical record,' then we moved very rapidly. And so, to this day I don't think anyone even remembers that we went to Johns Hopkins and said we were going to have an electronic medical record in 10 years. I agree with you that we have to put more emphasis on it and we need a ubiquitous electronic medical record, there have to be some consequences for people that don't use it."

Reading between the lines, this chilling revelation is that White House interference was a loss not only to the Secretary but to the many thousands of Americans who would have been saved from illness and death if they had been protected by a functioning records system that could have been developed years ago. And the winners? Big business benefitted. Certainly the medical-industrial complex must have had a hand in this. The absence of medical records and their consignment to market competition promoted profitability of health insurance misbehavior and prevented exposure of unnecessary health care business profits in the fog of confusion that has persisted and served the vast commoditization that is impeding U.S. health care.[7]

To bring the electronic details into clinical application, consider the data-driven success with difficult problems described by Dr. Gawande.[8] Dr. Jeffrey Bremer of Camden, N.J., realized that computer data analysis of local hospital records allowed him to identify "hot spots," a small fraction of people with atrocious health care access problems who were Emergency Room (ER) regulars and disproportionately expensive to the system. Dr. Brenner began addressing these with a medical team.

> In May, 2009, Brenner closed his regular medical practice to focus on the program full time. It remains unclear how the program will make ends meet. But he and his team appear to be having a major impact. The Camden Coalition has been able to measure its long-term effect on its first thirty-six super-utilizers. They averaged sixty-two hospital and ER visits per month before joining the program and thirty-seven visits after—a forty-per-cent reduction. Their hospital bills averaged $1.2 million per month before and just over half a million after—a fifty-six-per-cent reduction.

Similarly, a hospital in Boston saved 15% on costs as part of a new federal program for team management of difficult cases and one in Ocean City, a 25% savings. Equally important, it is clear that these difficult patients are made healthier. So there is hope that we can make improvements quickly with effective EMR support to identify problems and follow up on the interventions. A recent program that funds 53 interprofessional teams to provide local health care support for disadvantaged areas has been initiated[9] to provide an alternative to simply visiting the Emergency Room again. What is needed is often obvious to doctors and nurses once the information is available. When they are put in charge in this way, health improves and costs come down correspondingly.

We doctors, locked in our historic ways of practice, famous for illegible handwriting, saw no value in bothering to change our practices to use EMR and probably often distrusted new data systems as threatening loss of freedom in our practice, so we are also to blame. A major difficulty has been due to the misperception that EMR would consist simply of electronic equivalents of pages of handwritten notes, which admittedly would make them of little additional help. Dr. Bagley, quoted above, was frustrated when he was in HCFA because doctors resisted electronic records for decades—thwarting his interest in utilizing electronics in the 1970s and 1980s at the beginning of the computer era. But pressure on medicine to take on the functional advantages of the new technology increased with insights about their potential beyond mere word processing.

Engineer and big data computer user Dr. Duderstadt on electronic medical records: "I don't have enough experience other than my own experience in seeing how my own physicians take notes. . . . I don't know whether they're paying attention to what I'm saying or not so I do know that there's a whole issue—once we have this system in place, how do we make sure that it's working the way it should and that we use it the way we should. There's a learning curve and I would assume that going through a learning curve in a highly differentiated medical system on a national scale will also take time."

The first mistake revealed in the story by Secretary Thompson was opening up the process to private bidders rather than the common sense approach of putting a uniform national system in the hands of the federal government.[10] The precedent was there in the form of VISTA, the electronic records system throughout the Veterans Administration. But expanding that to national use was a road not taken, one suspects, because of medical business pressures even prior to the time of Secretary Thompson's story. After the Bush announcement, under Dr. Brailer each of the private companies developed their own system, very different from the next, preventing cross talk because of proprietary competition. Another mistake was that practicing doctors were only minimally involved in the construction of the software by these companies. The records were constructed to appeal mainly to administrators for use in billing. This left the doctors frustrated because of systems that were incompatible with their clinical needs. Added to these impediments, the Centers for Medicare and Medicaid Services, appropriately nervous about how little the EMR use was helping medical care, is requiring doctors to certify "meaningful use," as described in Chapter 3. This is supposed to support better evaluation of practice by doctors and extensions of interchange of records among practitioners. Actually, since the competition among companies selling EMR systems has caused them to block interchangeability of their products, doctors and hospitals are in an inexcusable bind with financial penalties for failure to comply. In 2009 a new federal government infusion of $19 billion into the EMR field ended up dominantly in private profits evidenced by a big boost in their performance on Wall Street, while doctors were left buying expensive but ineffective electronic records products and patients were seeing little, if any, benefit.[11]

In Chapter 3, the Meaningful Use (MU) issue was mentioned as part of the alphabet soup in which doctors are swimming, forced by CMS to try to stay afloat. The problems with this cannot be overemphasized.[12] A local general practitioner North of Baltimore estimated that as a result of the records rules by CMS, "I am doing 10% more work and seeing 10% fewer patients." The American College of Surgeons blog (American College of Surgeons/ACS Communities/General Surgery) is alive with stories of ridiculous administrative requirements superimposed on dysfunctional electronic medical records. When I asked Dr. Warshaw, recently President of the American College of

Surgeons, for technical information about electronic medical records, he demurred on the same generational grounds that I might, but said "You need to talk with Dr. Frank Opelka." Indeed, I found an inspiring departure from the above litany of hopelessness in my interview with Dr. Opelka, a gastrointestinal surgeon who has become Associate Medical Director of the American College of Surgeons Division of Advocacy and Health Policy and chairs the American Medical Association (AMA)–convened Physician Consortium for Performance Improvement (PCPI).

Dr. Opelka described the recent creation of a not-for-profit health services platform consortium[13] with ". . . a standard architecture, much like Android in your smartphone, upon which people can create applications that would leverage multiple different clinical data sources or nonclinical, even administrative, data sources, to optimize care. If you think of it as quality over cost, it's not just clinical informatics, it's economic informatics, financial informatics, geographic informatics. So with the data systems that I'm familiar with, we've connected state servers to insurance servers, to clinical servers to public health servers and Electronic Health Records servers to national registries. We have the ability to query that information and provide real time informatics back to the provider in a way that allows them to have leading and lagging indicators, predictive analytics, the ability to intervene before an event happens. It's basically taking the throttle, the governor, that's been on us by virtue of the electronic health records controlling the data flow and removing the Electronic Medical Records restriction from the equation."

And this is not theoretical, they actually have it working: ". . . we sat down with a bunch of different providers and they said well this is what I always want when I see this patient or this is what I always want when I see these patients. So that becomes basically an electronic summary page. It goes through the entire EHR and it summarizes everything that you want that's actionable so if this was a chronic disease patient, you'd say I want these 20 widgets to come up if the patient has any one of them and if they don't have it I don't want to see that widget. And if it's a cancer patient, it will look like this and if it's a congestive heart failure patient, it will look like that. So we built those so that when a patient hits the front desk and signs in, that system automatically queries and updates that page in microseconds—completes the analysis and update in about 1.4 seconds. You have it for the visit and then when the provider sees that patient, whether it's a pharmacist, a social worker, a nurse or a physician they can see that summary document and they have what they need on top of EPIC or bolted on to EPIC or Cerner or Allscripts [vendors for electronic medical records —JB]. So it's sitting there agnostic of the electronic health record but it's in an actionable format. That literally is the platform solution and what it does." This allowed a systematic way to care for patients in Louisiana[14] and similar systems are being built or are in use at, for instance, Intermountain, Kaiser, Mayo, and Harvard.[15] This solution to the present health care information technology snarl can provide a basis for a rational, functional use of EMR that will support doctors to provide improved care in a national system such as a single payer program.

In the meantime, an example of how the EMR might work in general is already in place in Maryland. It is called Chesapeake Regional Information System for our Patients (CRISP). It serves all hospitals in Maryland and Delaware plus some on the border with Pennsylvania. All the hospitals contribute to the expense of the system, and they have their admission data copied into a central CRISP platform. Practitioners can sign up at no cost. When a doctor in a hospital or in a private office sees a patient, any previous hospitalizations will be shown by CRISP, with some medical and demographic information. The physician can easily obtain some additional information, such as a discharge summary, by requesting it through CRISP and it will quickly arrive on the practitioner's computer as a .pdf file. This process provides an excellent clinical overview to facilitate the patient's care. In addition it has already shown its value in a public health study: In conjunction with the Maryland Department of Health and Mental Hygiene, CRISP allowed review of previous hospitalizations for Marylanders who died of a drug overdose, and found that the majority of them had had one or more previous hospitalizations for an overdose. They started a pilot project in which this history is checked by CRISP and the hospitals are notified to try to get these people into addiction services in time. Colorado is establishing a similar system records system in its Colorado Regional Health Information Organization, and this is designed to put the information directly into the doctor's EMR. These examples are valuable in their own right at present but they pale in comparison to the greatly expanded potential of a national EMR which they foretell.

THE HEALTH SECURITY BOARD

Now we refer back to Dr. Pronovost and the Surgical Intensive Care Unit (SICU). When I interviewed him, he touted EMERGE, a new electronic record system in the SICU that summarizes all of the things necessary to be in control of for these very sick patients: ". . . if you take a patient who's having surgery, they're at risk for a dozen harms. Every harm has a checklist that may have 5 or 10 items, every checklist may need to be done 3 or 4 times a day so when you add it up there's like 200 things that you and I should do as doctors, yet right now we have no feedback if we do those. And if you look at how many clicks it takes in the EMR it's literally hundreds to say—did I give DVT prophylaxis, I ordered it but did the nurse actually give it?—there are no visual displays. So we wrote this logical program that essentially you could say answers 4 questions. It makes visible who's at risk for any of those dozen harms, it tells me what therapy I should give because we took the time getting docs to get consensus to prevent those harms and it gives me a visual display of whether I've done it or not, so right now I could walk in the SICU and on a tablet there's a screen that shows every patient in the unit and if I'm missing any one of those 200 things there's a red box checked next to the name. So I take it around and I click on that red check and it tells me what harm it is or what thing is needed and then I can correct it. The only way we were able to do this is we flowed data out of the EMR into a platform that we built so it's easy to write for it." So this is analogous to the system described by Dr. Opelka. I visited the SICU (an all new facility since I retired from doing surgery—but I was rewarded with some familiar faces) and saw that it is simple to deal with but just as powerful as Dr. Pronovost claimed. It is another example of how medical record use can, indeed, be meaningful. Of course EMERGE in the SICU takes input from mechanical devices such as IV pumps, bed positioning, monitoring of EKG and blood gases and so on, in addition to medical records and orders. But it is absolutely applicable to simple oversight of the complexity of a patient's EMR data in any setting.

The national EMR will be based on a "platform" which receives all medical information, including doctors' and nurses' notes, lab values, test results and demographic information. The smartphone analogy described by Dr. Opelka for access to the platform makes this clear. (Whether one has, for instance, an Android or iPhone and whether your carrier is AT&T, Verizon, T-Mobile or some other service, you can dial up anyone else, who may be using any other phone or carrier and have a chat. If there are particular features you want on your smartphone you can download an app, which also will work for you to communicate to the variety of electronic devices and carriers as necessary.) In this way, the EMR platform will allow different doctors from various specialties to use inputs and outputs specific to their particular needs, "agnostic" of the brand of electronic health record or other technology, as described above by Dr. Opelka. Like Dr. Pronovost with EMERGE in the Hopkins SICU, the doctor working within his or her app sees what the status is of things that are important for the particular illness or care being provided. Rules for the computer to check on are established by doctors and nurses on the Health

Security Board and the individual doctor decides what they will see in their app on each of their patients. Possible harms (wrong medicine, side effects not tested for, compliance problem from prescriptions not filled) can be garnered and processed by the computer and warned against electronically. The computer summarizes the patient's information and the doctor does not have to check over 200 or 500 things, only the issues highlighted in red.

So now the doctor looks up from the screen and begins to discuss things with the patient. This startling departure from the usual opposite pattern in recent years for the patient-doctor relationship is the first on a list of advantages of this novel system. The increasing complaint both by patients (even if you are Jim Duderstadt, president of your medical system) and from doctors that the doctors are required by the rules to do too much on the computer during the patient visit is overcome. Billing does not depend on the physician certifying, for instance, that a complete "review of systems" (if found in the record to be normal recently) was redone to support a higher billing level. This improvement in the examining room is the first of five advantages of this novel system.

The second advantage is, therefore, the time saved for the doctor. The visit must include anything new that the computer might not know about, and discussion of any things in red to be corrected or followed up. The doctor must register any new issues, tests or plans in the EMR. But the professionalism of the doctor's work and the investment in the individual patient, each in their way threatened at present by billing and quality rules, are restored. And most of what happens is evident from input from the clinical decisions and results to the EMR so in most cases the doctor does not have to write or check more than a few explanatory phrases to complete the EMR record for the visit. The doctor is freed to practice medicine and helped by the technology to avoid omissions or mistakes.

A third advantage of this functional national EMR is another new opportunity for doctors: real, useful, convenient continuous quality improvement. As a corollary to the insight that quality can be recast as protection from harm in order to be measurable, this will allow doctors to be able to review how well they are succeeding in their actual care, not just on administrative items. Certain administrative flags, such as the number of hospitalizations, may continue to be used as justified by findings in the EMR but most of the information used will be data specific to each patient's clinical needs. Because the national EMR will contain information on all doctors for each of their patients, there can be automatic risk adjustments of the results for each doctor to correct for the severity of a patient's illness, the general health of their patients relative to the national population and other factors that can be calculated from the national data. Physicians' results will need to be compared to the results of their peers with proper risk correction in this way to be informative. Then each individual doctor can view their risk-adjusted successes and failures in comparison with national data from all doctors to get ideas on how they can improve their practice. My proposal will facilitate support through professional input by other doctors.

As a fourth advantage, the EMR for the national system will facilitate national continuous quality improvement of the country's medical system as a whole. Patients seeking a doctor must not be reassured just by ranking, but rather seek doctors that are review their results and work to improve in addition to how well they are already doing. This system will also optimize the use of national health care data for tracking and improving public health.[16]

The Health Security Board will be charged with determining standards to be followed in the EMR and when a problem is found it can determine the best next course. Statistics are probabilities, not certainties, so rather than condemnation or praise, these reviews must be considered as advisories for future action where indicated. As part of this, the performance of individual doctors may show up as outliers with lower performance, which the doctors may have noted on their own, and perhaps have already responded to with appropriate changes. Help may be found in outliers with better performance, which is a cornerstone of quality improvement. More serious penalties may be necessary when CQI is not effective. Of course, in some cases with good outcomes but differing practices there may be an appeal made by a doctor to consider whether their practice is beneficial. Such appeals to the Health Security Board will receive uncomplicated and authoritative consideration since professional expertise, not administrative rules, will be determinative. Moreover the Board will continually review data in the national EMR to identify possible research on ways to improve health care and to detect dangerous practices as soon as possible.

To continue regarding the fourth advantage, this oversight will be simplified by national electronic computational summaries, with rules checked and deviations prominently displayed in a manner similar to the way doctors will be following their individual patients. Such analyses of vast amounts of data are being done in computational biology, airline flight scheduling, and many other fields now.

A patient's status could be in the dashboard for every doctor who saw them recently, perhaps in the past 6 mos., with status only displayed if there is a "red" for a problem, and several doctors might get that for a patient they have in common. Eventually what was done, or should have been, will be evident in the data—and the relative need for involvement, relative success of different practitioners and so on could be used to point out the "blame or credit." The details of how to assimilate all of those issues will be straightforward bioinformatics problems with data, expeditiously updated as necessary, to be overseen authoritatively by the doctors' Health Security Board that I propose. Nearly all of this would be part of the CQI process, not resulting in penalties or rewards otherwise. Severe outliers requiring additional attention will be uncommon.

I think a group of practitioners in the form of the Health Security Board, armed with the reassuring responsibility to evolve the rules as indicated, will be able to manage that.

And there is a fifth advantage: billing—or whatever sign of involvement is to be used in group settings without fee-for-service billing—all will be done retrospectively by an appropriate app for extracting the information from the EMR. There will be no coverage determinations (everyone is covered, like the British students described by Sen. Sanders in Chapter 1) and there will be no forms to fill out or argue about with an administrator. Accurate clinical data will determine this just as it will allow retrospective monitoring of the doctor's practice and the national system.

This mechanism will provide an objective way for the system to deal with a doctor's work in terms of outcomes and system performance. There is no question that there is much more to medical practice that is not accessible objectively. Each doctor has their special way of doing things and each patient their special concerns and capabilities. So the underlying idea of quality can remain an additional item in the patient-doctor relationship. Certainly the structure that provides for access to effective care for everyone does not need to create a faceless homogeneity of impersonal medical care. I endeavored to do my operations and other patient care particularly well and I think, perhaps not inconsistently, that most of those whom I helped to train do as well or better. I presume that most doctors practice with such confidence as part of their professional commitment to do best by their patients. This underscores continuing attention to one's results and, occasionally, highlights mistakes. But to be meaningful, claims of better quality that appear by practitioners or institutions must bear up under the stark illumination of objective results. In Chapter 2 the absurdity of medical advertising was highlighted, which is germane here as well. But unfortunately the assessment of caregivers by the government and private carriers is hardly more solid than unsubstantiated advertising. CMS has tried to use center data for oversight, but generally with unconvincing results.

A small but powerfully relevant recent example of data misuse in the present that can be corrected through this national system was the indictment of small volume centers as having poorer outcomes by U.S. News and World Report. To the extent there is anything useful in the information, it can serve for continuing quality improvement. But the criterion of small volume certainly is far inferior to the process that I propose and it would be preposterous for smaller centers in general to cease most of their care because they do not do enough of it.[17] The American College of Surgeons Blog crackled with the unreality of, for instance, expecting general surgeons who do a large variety of small numbers of procedures in non-metropolis settings to cease doing all of the operations needed by their surrounding population except for one or two operations so they can "get enough practice" at those two.

In organ transplantation we began publishing risk-adjusted center-specific reports twenty five years ago and proposed a statistical method for dealing with results from small vs. large centers.[18] This was important for the public, for self assessment by the transplant field and for the agency funding most transplants, CMS. As a result of these principles for data assessment, transplant programs that were lower performers improved or, in a few cases, closed, nearly all without CMS decree. That is the way to analyze and utilize these data, not by brute force ranking on the basis of procedure volumes.

Proponents of private insurance rather than Medicare like to point to the potential for fraud and abuse in government programs, given the millions of dollars that CMS reports retrieving after successful prosecutions on occasion. Of course we do not know how many millions of dollars private insurance companies lose to fraud—they are not inclined to admit this since the news might tarnish their investment value. Regardless, the transparency of this EMR system can serve to minimize fraud and abuse in health care far more effectively than anything we have today.

Use of the platform containing all of the clinical data simplifies evolution of the rules as evidence accumulates: any information of clinical importance is already there so a new collection process is unnecessary. One merely reprograms an app to make the change to ask the relevant question.

Electronic security will be a primary concern. The public has concerns about the privacy of their data, but the Health Insurance Protection and Portability Act has severe penalties for misuse of patient data. The buying and selling of information now will end. A single national system may be less susceptible to a hack than the multiple places our health information resides now. In particular, patients may be worried about their insurance company finding something that compromises their coverage. But in the single payer system, since everyone is covered, regardless, there is no cause for such concern.

The critical driving principle is to change from reliance on administrative rules to assessments using outcomes and other clinically useful measures. Protection from harms is a way to frame positive outcomes that is measurable and actionable. The overall impact of this is that doctors will be expected to use the EMR to register only necessary, clinically relevant data. Continuing Quality (as protection from harm) Improvement, continuing quality oversight by the Health Security Board and billing will all be by apps extracting information from the clinically necessary EMR, rewarding doctors by freeing them to practice as professionals with unencumbered individualized consideration of each patient.

DOCTORS NEEDED

In previous chapters we have reviewed the powerful forces arrayed against meaningful health care reform. Proclamations by business leaders and academic pronouncements not withstanding, confusion and overwhelming commoditization remain. At present, public understanding, federal intervention and market-based business practices are all unable to break the stalemate. And doctors, increasingly beset by difficulties rather than solutions, have not had the national insight to free themselves and their patients. But now doctors are beginning to create the answer, not from governmental fiat but through innate professionalism. In this chapter we have described the inspiring possibility that a national electronic medical record system with professional oversight by the Health Security Board can take over responsibility of the nation's healthcare practices and by this simplify the system, make medical care measurable and effective, restrain overuse, improve the experience and outcomes of patients and establish rational cost control. This assumption of responsibility by doctors and nurses for the country's health is the only credible path to a national health program such as a single payer system. The exciting reality is that this is well underway. And as reviewed at the end of Chapter 7, there are additional glimmerings of hope in the form of political help now.

CHAPTER SIX
HEALTH, EDUCATION AND WELFARE

From talking with people about single payer, an important insight emerged. Health care reform cannot succeed without attention to the national social context. This was not a total surprise. As a doctor, I learned to consider personal issues with my patients in addition to technical clinical details. But regarding a national health program, the novel parallel understanding was brought home to me that just as poverty, lack of education, inequality, and racism are fundamental barriers that must be addressed if individual patients are to benefit from a single payer health care system, addressing these problems will be fundamental to the national reform effort to establish a health care program for the country.

As we shall see, this calls for a reformed national consciousness. Better education will help improve health care, but good health is necessary to succeed in education. These and other social supports are mutually necessary to a degree not generally acknowledged by reformers attempting to improve any one of them alone. And there are general principles that apply to all ways to strengthen our country's support networks. Dependence is not fostered by helping the poor. In fact, lasting improvements are a proven benefit of government support programs and these improvements also benefit friends and relatives of the recipients—and the rest of us as well. An effective national health care system will save money to be available for other social needs. Such investments in supporting a strong country are common sense, not socialism.

Our very rich society can afford this investment in the American Dream. Variation in health care and other supports jeopardizes the rights of states to be involved in a national system but these inconsistencies can be conquered. We can escape from racism. The residual reluctance must be overcome to clear the way for a new era of fairness and justice in America.

An insight that established the need for this chapter came in the interview with Dr. Jon Fielding. "People ask me what is the Number One thing to improve the health of our country. I say 'that's an easy question, ask me a hard question.' 'Why is that an easy question?' 'Its simple: increase the high school graduation rate.' The difference in life expectancy between somebody who doesn't graduate from high school and somebody who graduates from college is an average of 5 years for a male and 3 years for a female. Look at Annapolis vs. inner city Baltimore. [Prescient in this interview a year before the eruption in Baltimore discussed below.—JB] The average life expectancy is perhaps 10 years different. You have to look at conditions. If they don't have additional services when they need them and can't make a living wage, what prospect do people have? Or if they aren't health literate—one value of graduating from high school is they will be health literate." The speaker, Dr.Fielding, is a Professor of Health Policy and Management and Pediatrics at the UCLA Fielding School of Public Health. He also served formerly as Director of Public Health and Health Officer for Los Angeles County and Massachusetts Commissioner of Public Health and recently published *Public Health Practice*.[1] His impassioned declaration is a key to this chapter. In fact, it serves as a reminder about the reality of public services in the U.S. in general and their impact on everyone's health.

The point that education is so critical for access to health care was affirmed by the Institute of Medicine's Dr. Boufford, demurring on universal health care coverage as the most important initiative if government became concerned about people. When asked what she would pick as the first choice: "I'd probably pick good public education."

Concurring with this, Dr. "Buz" Cooper, oncologist and Dartmouth Atlas critic, also alluded to the interconnection of incomplete coverage for health care with other existing social inadequacies such as education.

Books about health care reform often end about where this chapter starts. Admittedly, the issues about medicine and the delivery of health care that we have reviewed to this point might seem sufficient without taking on the whole sociology of our country. Can't we leave that to someone else? No. In fact, in thinking and talking about health care reform, I am convinced that to get quality health care in place for everyone, the problem is not just the issue of a single payer concept, it is the context of it in the country. I propose that there is some common sense to be brought to our overall social and economic situation in this book, even if writings by others with more detailed academic understandings and approaches to controversies from other sources would be necessary for a more complete view in depth. Fortunately, Americans may now be poised to reconsider the underlying realities of social support in our country more fundamentally than we have for a long time. If so, improving the education level of disadvantaged citizens must be a leading goal.

EDUCATION

Deemed as a right for every child in the U.S., education has a favored status compared to health care. In modern times there have been no filibusters in Congress nor cases brought before the Supreme Court seeking to deny equal opportunity for education as a universal right. But that has been the strong presumption only since the passage of the Civil Rights Act, and the implementation of public schools is often still weaker in areas where minorities live. A problem for education is that it suffers more from uncertainty about process and goals than medicine, which has some clearer endpoints. That interferes with objectivity about solutions for education even when money and the best of intentions are in place. There are several other social support programs that are important for the success of universal health coverage including the Supplemental Nutrition Assistance Program, Aid to Families with Dependent Children and unemployment insurance. But the process of education shares with health care the attribute of personal service beyond the financial assistance provided by these other programs. Teachers, doctors and nurses are critical. The relationship of education to health was particularly stressed in the interviews I conducted. So education warrants special attention in this context.

Regarding Dr. Fielding's point about health literacy, an obvious impact of education in general on people's health—therefore on life expectancy—is that it widens the understanding of numerical/technical thinking, and the human experience in general. These perspectives make it easier to make sense of bodily functions and choices about health and medical care, so this education promotes participation by the patient. True, caring for oneself is severely compromised if one is nearly illiterate and has no understanding of measuring fluid and weight and has not been exposed to the simplest words in chemistry and biology. But there is much more to it. Education can provide a person with a sense of self-worth and purpose. This is as important as understanding pounds-to-kilograms conversions or knowing big words. You might observe that correlation does not imply causation and so whether someone graduates from high school is not important in health, it is just a marker for some other aspect of better health. Perhaps that is true to a degree. For instance, someone who has grown up preventably handicapped for some other reason, such as childhood hunger, is both less likely to have coverage for medical care and is less likely to make it through high school. But what I was being told is that it is all related. Working on all fronts is likely to improve efforts in each area. That is the point of this chapter.

There are parallels between improving education and improving health care. Religious and charter schools may help improve education in some cases.[2] Contrasting the principle of universal public education with the recent growth of charter schools promising special results might be seen as a parallel to comparing health care funded by the government with care paid for through private insurance. Dr. Peter Cookson has noted that there is no special advantage to charter schools although they sometimes work well.[3] The preponderance of the country's childhood education must be provided by the government. With deregulation in education that favors charter schools, too often commoditization intrudes. Interestingly, the situation with education, which is a federal right but is sometimes threatened by money budgeted to free enterprise charter schools, is a mirror image of health care, which has always been considered a free market function but is now increasingly provided by public programs that do the job better. Commoditization from the profit motive of charter schools that harms best choices for school children is similar to the impairment of health care choices by patients when cost is a consideration. Moreover, in some areas of the country, racial integration has been accompanied by "white flight" to private schools. For the future, as with health care, private schools can continue for those who can pay but taxes must provide the foundation for education for everyone if our country is to do its job. In fact, the issue of public funding even beyond high school is now being discussed. But our nation can be strong only if both education and health care are funded by taxation at a level that makes a high quality public service available to all.

I suspect that many doctors would recognize that the increasing attempts to supervise teachers through confounding administrative requirements and student testing look like our increasing troubles from rules and oversight in the practice of medicine. True, Dr. Cookson told me that regardless of public or private setting, what often makes the big difference in a school is the principal who is enthusiastic and engaged. Similarly, I have seen a huge boost in morale and performance in medical divisions upon the arrival of a director who is an enthusiastic, effective practitioner. Administration has a role. But multiple layers of complexity overseeing those actually doing the work must be streamlined—it is costly and counterproductive. Perhaps the remedies in education and medicine are parallel: Train them well, boost teachers' salaries and remove doctors' practice disincentives, and then let teachers teach and doctors practice in settings that will attract many administrators to come out from behind their desks and into the classrooms and clinics where they are needed![4] This introduces a theme about the structure of health care that is developed in the last chapter.

Efforts to improve education for the disadvantaged are complementary to health care reform, not in competition with it. In fact, imagine a national symbiosis in which high schools have a role not only in health literacy but in working actively with medical services to intervene early in avoidable metabolic handicap, challenges of teen sexuality and in addressing drug abuse, not as a crime but as a public health issue. All of these are partly medical problems with which doctors could use any help possible.

There is at least one other area that could share in this symbiosis: criminal justice. Fair access to the legal system is another problem of poverty. Richard Zorza described to me the similarity to health and education and lack of access to justice by poor people. Zorza is an award-winning access-to-justice expert who has worked in national self-represented litigation. He noted parallels between access to justice and access to health care, thus highlighting another way these multiple difficulties for the poor coexist. "As with health care, poorer states spend less [to support access to justice—JB] even though the need is greater. Poor people have more problems." A program that includes proactive self representation legal help for the students and their families in the educational setting could serve to bypass the sorts of legal problems—every clinician or teacher has seen them—that otherwise interfere with the patient following their clinical regimen or the student's ability to learn.

POVERTY

The worst problem for the poorest among us may be just that they are increasingly cordoned off and misunderstood by those in better circumstances. For background on the problems of the poor, I spoke with Arloc Sherman who is an expert in finding solutions for the reality of poverty. He is a Senior Fellow at the Center for Budget and Policy Priorities and has written extensively about parental employment and unemployment, welfare reform, barriers to employment, family structure, the depth of poverty, racial inequality, tax policy for low-income families, and the special challenges affecting rural areas. He has worked at the Children's Defense Fund and the Center for Law and Social Policy and wrote the book, *Wasting America's Future*. He told me: "Research has made clear that poor health can contribute to poverty and poverty can contribute to poor health. The incidence of disability is very high among the poor. It makes it hard for folks to get around, and there are increasing signs from research that growing up with inadequate nutrition and family income can damage infant health and produce lasting effects which are associated decades later with a constellation of health problems that are associated with lower work hours and lost working time because of ill health. So there's clearly a two-way street and solving either problem probably involves the other."

More than that, many do not understand that about half of poor people have a history of being above the poverty line and will likely be back in slightly better circumstances before long. Of course if the country gives them a little help, that move up will happen sooner and be more lasting. This is the answer to the complaint that social programs do not do any good. This "churn" around being near poor to poor, then rising again and being replaced by others who become less well off, shows that over a year or two a much greater total number of different people and families—well more than half the number in that status at any given time—qualify for and benefit from social support. And people who are poised insecurely in the lower middle class may sink due to financial problems with health care or other reasons, become poor but then qualify for help and work their way back up again. So the continued existence of a poor segment of society does not mean that no one is helped by the social programs that we have now. But Sherman notes that it is difficult: "In any given year 40% of the people who are below the poverty line annually won't be there two years later; they'll be above the poverty line. If you peg access to medical or health care subsidies by whether your income is above or below 40% of the poverty line, you know it means that you are going to create a lot of complications and awkward reconciliation every year for individuals and systems for whom that burden will be not trivial."

Moreover, he shows that the effect of the help, when available, is often lasting: "In the '60s and '70s we rolled out food stamp programs county by county. It was not introduced all at once but over a period of more than 10 years. As the kids grew up, those who were born into food stamp counties grew up with five to six per cent less heart disease, were less obese, showed lower signs of various metabolic disorders, and were 18% more likely to have finished high school in the same county compared to before food stamps arrived, or compared to neighboring counties where food stamps had not arrived."

The need to provide more than coverage for care was evident in my practice. The U.S. end stage renal disease program is part of Medicare and so provides coverage for care as an entitlement for essentially everyone in the country with this disease. As a surgeon taking care of kidney failure patients on dialysis to help with their "dialysis access," meaning doing the small operation to provide a site for necessary blood flow in and out of the machine, I have had an opportunity to see the impact of universal coverage that includes Americans from desperately poor circumstances who are nevertheless covered because they qualify as Americans with kidney failure. These patients are thankful for their care and survive because they try very hard to work with the team. I have been struck with the importance to them of their sense of self worth that stems from this commitment by society for their care, even if their education and other social supports have been inadequate. This rewarding experience has bolstered my conviction that a single payer national health care program will work. It shows that given the opportunity, the disadvantaged are able to benefit even from sophisticated health care. Nevertheless, it is too little, too late at present. If they had had more investment in their health, education and welfare from the start, many of them would not have developed renal failure from diabetes or high blood pressure, or certainly not as early in their lives. So although their success as patients in this universal care program would justify seeking a single payer system in isolation, absent help with other fundamental needs, the general status of their health is also an affirmation that only by addressing all of these societal needs together will any interventions work optimally.

In the "Moving to Opportunity" study,[5] scientifically derived data from a very convincing experiment showed that housing and the neighborhood characteristics were found to have a powerful influence on getting ahead. Beginning in the 1990s, thousands of families in public housing were randomized to either receive vouchers to move to a lower poverty area or not. The children were followed for over two decades. For those randomized to move to the better area, each year of living there contributed increasingly to their life earnings with a statistically remarkable consistent rise on that line. So the situation, not the people, were found overwhelmingly to be the determining factor.

As Arloc Sherman notes: "You would think, if you listen to some critics of government safety net programs, that the stronger those programs are, the less effort people devote to behaving responsibly and staying out of poverty. In that view, you'd expect that in times or places where more government benefits are available, surely there must be a lot more people who don't bother to work or who have huge numbers of children they can't support etc etc. But when you look, that's not really what you see. You see a lot of evidence to the contrary. In the U.S., the safety net has grown far stronger in the last half century but low-income families are actually having many fewer children. Family size has shrunk. Further, if you compare the U.S. with other wealthy industrial nations, almost all of them have more generous benefits, relative to their wealth and capacity to provide assistance; their safety nets are stronger than ours in the sense that they lift a larger share of their children above the relative poverty line (defined as half of median national income). So if more assistance leads to more irresponsible behavior, then you'd think that all those countries would have far more poverty, not counting government benefits. But it's not true. Before counting government benefits, most of those other countries have relative child poverty rates lower than our own."

INEQUALITY

Aside from medically certified personal handicaps, people normally differ in small ways that ensure some inequality across any society. In addition, the theory popularized by Thomas Piketty that differential of lower return from salaried work vs. a greater average return from investment income inexorably widens the gap between the poor and the rich has recently become fashionable. It is true that even for those with very high incomes, in addition to large salaries, a major part of their income is often from investments, reinforcing this trend to widen the gap. Wealthy believers in Piketty may find reassurance from being part of what is, if true, a law of nature by which we are all ruled. By this sense of a social order through a sort of divine right of the wealthy, they may feel no special personal responsibility for how to use their wealth. The converse argument would seem to be that the very rich ended up there by a happenstance of this economic effect and do not merit the distinction of having arrived at their wealth deservedly. By this, the wealthy cannot claim exemption from a special mandate to use their wealth responsibly. Naturally this is a reprise of similar very old arguments.

Nevertheless, no one can accumulate and enjoy wealth as a single inhabitant of a desert island. It takes a country. That is why in principle the country has an inherent right to some of the wealth of its citizens. The reasonable question becomes how much further health care reform will cost those with money, not whether it is the right thing to do. To calculate the budget needed to have a single payer system, it is necessary to ask how many poor people need coverage that are not covered now? If all issues are considered, it might extend to about half the population in trouble with inadequate access to health care—but that would be largely covered by the savings on those same people. It starts with the additional cost to the U.S. taxpayer of avoidable medical care that eventually must be provided to uninsured Americans. In recent years this has added up to about $36 billion over what it would cost if these people were getting timely, effective care instead.[6] But an additional part of the need is in the "churn" of those who are intermittently poor but then sometimes working, insured, and paying some taxes. Moreover, a significant expense for a single payer system will be to cover those who have low value insurance now when they get sick. These are not the very poor; rather they are working citizens paying for health care who become caught in the inadequate insurance net. Thus, many of those who need help with access to care are paying for it at least partly right now, but not getting it. Those funds, as much as $500 billion, redirected through taxation, can provide real protection for health care coverage. Additional savings from controlling overuse and excessive drug costs will add many billions of dollars more to the funds available for single payer coverage. The national expenses and savings may be too complex for precise calculations, but the offsets certainly cover a major portion of the cost of including all citizens under the umbrella of a national health care system.

Money to invest in the country's health care system if needed will come from two rich sources. One source is increased taxation (offset for the middle class by freedom from insurance premiums and copayments). The other source is the money saved by the medical profession itself through increased quality that decreases costs as described in previous chapters.

For the first point, looking just at health care reform, a narrow view is that not much additional tax revenue will be required even from the wealthy. There is reassurance about the comparatively moderate costs needed for the single payer proposal in this book. This shows how powerful the cost savings from an organized system of care with professional authority over treatment options will be. By reorganizing our chaotic national system with automatic coverage and an emphasis on quality, we will not have to spend much more to cover all of the disadvantaged middle class and poor than we in the U.S. are already spending on those with coverage at present. And the improvements in quality for the rest of Americans will decrease costs for businesses and for those who are well to do because of focused efficiency in care and avoidance of harm.

Regarding the interests of those who now have good health care coverage and may argue against helping to provide it for the less fortunate, the Nobel prize-winning economist Joseph Stiglitz has documented the ways in which our democracy is imperiled by egregious inequality from protecting the richest 1%.[7] Studies regarding medical care show this (See Chapter 2, ref. 32) and it is common sense that curbing inequality would extrapolate to an advantage for many aspects of safety and quality of life for everyone, rich or poor.

It is often unrecognized that improving health care has a particular budgetary advantage over other social needs. Unlike improving roads or education or public transportation, all of which could cost much more money, an optimized health care system will involve improving care in ways that will also save money.

On the other hand, the billions of dollars to be saved by reforming health care must be used for the other social needs—education for instance. This resolve to strengthen America in general will result in an incremental boost in health care excellence while abating other social problems. Owners of massive fortunes and big business in general must be convinced or forced to make some concessions because their taxes will be impacted by expenses for needs other than health care. Our country has generated so much wealth that we do not have to return to the tax rates after World War II, when the highest incomes were taxed at 90%, twice what they are now, and the corporate tax rate was 1.5 times that for individuals, compared to today's corporate tax rate of 25 cents for every dollar taxed from individual taxpayers.

The second major source for the single payer budget impacts a particular segment of the well-to-do. It falls to those whose profits from health care related businesses will be decreased by the improved national system. Drug and device companies will be faced with the negotiating wall of a single market in the national system, or with states negotiating within that context. Profit margins will be restrained by lower returns compared with our recently unconstrained pricing. No one wants to interfere with innovation, but as discussed in Chapter 4, a reasonable accommodation will not be more than marginally harmful to innovation because the overwhelming intellectual draw of inventing more exciting treatments will remain. Similarly, health insurance companies' risk free administration services will continue, with the 5% "at no risk" return described by Dr. Jack Rowe in Chapter 2. Added to that will be potential profits from supplemental insurance, although there will be reduced profits in this area because the present ways insurance companies profit from the taxpayer will no longer exist. There will be a fire wall between paying for private insurance and the public health care budget.

Some protection for health care businesses described earlier in the book exists for American business in general. Several times my interviewees cited the large fraction of health care business for many companies, expecting it to cause a huge resistance to reform. But if about 20% of U.S. business is invested in health care, much of that business will need to continue in any reformed system. And that huge sum, just under one fifth of the national GDP, is far more than is needed to fund health care and even the other social programs we are talking about. To be consistent with responsible patient-driven medical care, this huge portion of the GDP will be impacted only to a moderate degree. A reasonably modest reduction in those profits across the board is all that will be needed. The very massive financial involvement in health care in the U.S. is in fact a buffer for evolution of an appropriate system because the redirection of sufficient funds will be spread so much throughout the whole U.S. economy. IBM, GE, and others will notice some decreased profits and may shift their strategies a bit, but no one area of business needs to plunge on the stock market or fail because of reform. Most businesses are also likely to benefit financially from a rational cost-effective national health care system for their workers as the national economy is strengthened in other ways.

Big business is not blind to this. Dr. Hadler, proponent of the "Efficacy Agenda," states that "Corporate America is really hurting . . . so they are more than willing to decry the health care system but they can't say anything. If you say anything rational it sounds like rationing, as if you don't care about workers."

Of course part of the reason these insights are novel is because economists and health policy experts have not had necessary input from doctors. Even organized medicine and health policy experts who are medical doctors have failed to establish a firm front in favor of doctors assuming the responsibility for quality and cost control in our national health care system, thereby supplanting the government and private insurance industry. Without this new vision, experts interested in U.S. health care reform have had to extrapolate from our situation now to a future system that is about as bizarre and chaotic as we doctors and patients face today. Perhaps health policy expert Dr. Gerry Anderson cited in chapter 2 would be happy to relinquish his pessimism about cost control, but he needs reassurance that there is a way around his assessment of our present situation in which he sees no incentives to improve.

For doctors and nurses to lead in the struggle to establish a single payer system, the problem then boils down to overcoming resistance to thinking about socially desirable realities, whether they are education, climate change, infrastructure repair, legal justice, voters rights, campaign finance, or health care. This reluctance stems largely from an upper class that is unreasonably fearful of helping poor and middle class people. Even more unreasonable is this resistance voiced by less advantaged people who are likely to benefit by help from social supports themselves. Although admirable American self-reliance and individualism may contribute to that, there is little question but that these misconceptions are due largely to propaganda by rich corporate interests. This is not a new phenomenon. The classic book *Manufacturing Consent* by Noam Chomsky documented its insidious presence in the U.S. even three decades ago.[8] Contrary attempts by straight shooters in the discussion are shouted down—as has happened to the idea of single payer in previous decades until recently.[9]

In fact, given the reality of inequality, those that are more favored and successful financially and who wish to continue to live in the U.S. have by virtue of their station more responsibility than the average citizen to their country. Paying their fair share rather than escaping taxes, adjusting to a cap on certain income, agreeing to campaign finance reform and the enfranchisement of the general electorate: these are all things that are reasonable to expect of the rich and powerful in our country. Public social supports must trump the corporate welfare that is too powerful a part of the present U.S. economy. There is hope that tawdry protestations against these obvious truths will be increasingly exposed as just that and will be overcome.

In spite of his basic orientation toward unsullied free markets described in Chapter Two, Tufts Professor Dr. Joshua Cohen who had lived in Europe provided me with a compelling view of the European approach to a fair society: ". . . solidarity is basically the sense that we're all in it together and even if we are very wealthy or very poor for that matter, we as a society are in this together and health care is a social good." There is plenty of evidence from Europe to provide consolation to all taxpayers that this will provide a happier, healthier, safer and more attractive country in which to live. Dr. Cohen finds evidence in the impact of the ACA that without fanfare the United States is moving in this direction: "I look at some of the most controversial repeal bills that I've seen and I've actually reviewed them fairly carefully. They all basically include the provisions in the ACA that would help the vulnerable, the weak, the sick, et cetera. For instance, they no longer permit preexisting conditions to be something that payers can use to exclude or to raise premiums on patients. That's really moved the discussion along. . . . So again, even the bills most vehemently opposed to the ACA still say, well that's a good thing, that's a good thing, that other thing's good but we want to take out the rest."

Education, good transportation, adequate housing, freedom from hunger, a stable social setting, freedom from fear, hope for being able to get along in life—they all go together. When things are working well in a country, all of these goals are approachable for its people. When a country doesn't care in general, trying to fix one key element—such as health care—is doomed to fall short of its potential to help everyone. Moreover, the single payer proposal does not attempt to tear down the capitalist system. It merely asks that somewhat more of the country's wealth be used for the general good.

FEDERAL SIMPLICITY VS. A ROLE FOR STATES

As diagrammed in Figure 1, the simplicity of a single payer system as a straightforward national system is appealing given the confusing and expensive patchwork of health care delivery now. In addition, minimizing a role for states could avoid some political issues with health care delivery and bypass variable prospects for single payer support among the states that reflect all of the social support issues just discussed. Until recently, I had not questioned this simple approach to a national health program.

To think about simplicity, it is interesting to consider the size of legislation required for different health care systems. Start with the Patient Protection and Affordable Care Act ("Obamacare"). Its complicated measures were contrived to do as much good as possible while satisfying dozens of special interests. It weighed in at 2409 pages. Senator Bernie Sanders' single payer bill is only 189 pages long and the companion bill by John Conyers, continually reintroduced in the House for many Congresses, is 30 pages long. But the winner is . . . The Canada Health Act single payer law, this much feared monster of government meddling, at 14 pages. Moreover, since in bilingual Canada each page has a column in English and a corresponding column in French, a fair comparison with U.S. laws makes it actually only seven pages long in English.

The reason the Canadian law could be so short is that in essence it sets out just five broad requirements, the most important being universal access. Provinces complying with these five rules—and they all have complied—receive a major fraction of the cost of their health care budget annually from the Canadian federal budget. They provide the remainder of the cost from provincial coffers and each province administers their somewhat varied version of universal health care.

Of course there is a big difference between that and the prospect of the administrative complexity of 50 different versions of single payer if run separately by each state in the U.S. Among many practical details, a single payer state-by-state system here would require an understanding of how each state or region will reimburse the health care needed by a resident of another state or region, a common occurrence. In Canada, the province of residence is the payer unless the two provinces have a different agreement. Such issues would need to be worked out among the states in the U.S somewhat the way other interstate matters are dealt with. For differences affecting logistics and professional behavior, there might be advantages to having states involved in the administration of the national health program. The failures of single payer proposals for individual states such as Vermont or New York, and the defects in the generally effective Massachusetts law, are irrelevant to the prospects for a national system. It is unreasonable to expect any one state's single payer budget and administration to stay afloat in the stormy waters of commoditization of the U.S. system generally.

But one of the biggest problems in considering a partial responsibility for administration of the national system through the states is a monstrous difference in America that must be considered carefully. Racism is the one most worrisome peril lurking behind much of what is discussed in this chapter, which will be a particular concern if individual states have control. In the U.S., the terrible history of slavery and its aftermath seem to intrude in spite of best wishes and intentions, north and south. By the magnitude of its significance it distinguishes our country from any other developed nation. The resistance to dealing with the realities of social support mentioned above is partly based on racism: Self-serving conservatives disdain support for food stamps or health care subsidy because this assistance is—misguidedly—associated just with African Americans, and by doing so they win points among susceptible listeners. In one of the most somber and heartfelt of his many oped pieces in the New York Times, economist Paul Krugman wrote: "America is a much less racist nation than it used to be. . . . Yet racial hatred is still a potent force in our society."[10] The resistance by Republicans to the ACA's Medicaid expansion, particularly in southern states but elsewhere as well, surely reflects residual racial prejudice. Even after the failure of the third attempt to cripple the ACA through suits brought before the Supreme Court in June, 2015, numerous Congressional attempts to hamper it persist. In view of the outrageously bigoted response to President Obama's election by some congressmen, motives beyond mere stubbornness must include racism. A recent study showed that medical students in southern states were unaware their state had not expanded Medicaid.[11]

Topical and relevant to difficulties in health care delivery is the issue of police brutality against African Americans which again exploded into public consciousness due to the violent death of Freddy Gray in a Baltimore City Police van. Riots followed and soon thereafter came the hauntingly tragic shooting of nine black church members in Charlotte, S.C. Is it any wonder that a country that has widely tolerated such tragic reality for some of its citizens has problems assuring that everyone can get health care?

In the case of Baltimore, the disaster erupted in an area, Sandtown-Winchester, that was the legacy of discriminatory policies in the 1980s when financial help for housing of inner-city Baltmoreans steered European Americans north and African Americans west. In fact, that poor West Baltimore enclave has a subregion that has remained solidly lower middle class, with quiet, attractive streets, households with jobs, and a responsible, mostly African American citizenry. But the money ran out and without the same support, poor and poorer could not make it in the surrounding area, setting the stage for violent incidents. The impossibility of beneficial health care for everyone in that destitute area existed long before 2015. It was reported that the riots, although partly exposing pent up frustrated rage, were largely carried out by a small number of wild opportunists and the level of civilized restraint otherwise, even in that hard-pressed area, was notable. The greatest collateral damage may have been the drug store lootings, apparently yielding a supply of controlled substances equivalent to the illicit amount that usually reaches Baltimore in a year, so the increased frequency in West Baltimore of sporadic shootings over its distribution may continue for some time. Dan Rodricks, essayist for The Baltimore Sun and, until recently leaving, host of *Midday* on WYPR, did an in-depth series of interviews and commentaries on his radio program following the Baltimore tragedy. They were all the more powerful because his reporting had started in a way with a program about the situation in Sandtown-Winchester two weeks before the death of Freddie Gray. More recently, he has noted problems and the potential for decreasing housing discrimination in Baltimore,[12] which implicitly carries the sad reality that we still are struggling to get beyond racism.

In regard to the shootings in Charleston, S.C., there are indications that racist ideas and organizations barely beneath the surface contributed to the disastrous course the crazed young shooter took. Again, the forgiveness of the survivors and the African Americans in the city generally was remarkable.

Newspaper articles appeared on whether racism in either or both of these events was important;[13] the evidence, however strong, remains circumstantial. At any rate, these tragic circumstances, common in the U.S. today, demonstrate the complex needs that must be addressed for improving health care for the poor and the role of race in the problems of American society. Addressing these things, as much as the necessity of a single payer law, may be key to an effective national health program.

These distressing conditions raise concerns about ongoing housing segregation, gerrymandering and other ways of discrimination still evident in the country in general, not just in southern states. Part of the saving grace regarding health care for states in these difficult situations is exemplified by the position of doctors and hospitals that are in states that have deferred adoption of the expanded Medicaid option in the ACA: In general, regardless of the position of their state government, the caregivers have been for the expansion and were actively working for this politically. Probably partly due to the financial benefits, but certainly progressive in spite of any lingering reservations regardless of their basis, this strong advocacy by health care professionals for the right way to help more people get medical care is a sign of the way social and political resistance to reform can be overcome.

That the medical profession in each state can lobby for the good of its citizens, even granting some self-interest in it, provides reassurance for putting the administration of a single payer system partly in the hands of state governments in spite of problems with the history of race relations. A different argument, chilling but equally powerful, was articulated by Dr. Schroeder in defense of the moderating power of states in a national system: "As a liberal I worry about a scenario I haven't heard other people talk much about. Let's assume that Ted Cruz is the President, Jim Inhofe is the senate majority leader and somebody like that is in the House. They set the rules for a single payer program as to what gets covered—I'm not happy with that and it's conceivable that those kind of people might be in charge." If states are part of the single payer system, he reckons that they could exert a temporizing influence on the threat of radical revision at the national level.

Several of the people that I interviewed had been thinking about the details for a structure of a national U.S. health care system. No one offered a preference for a straight federal-to-doctor-patient system of payment. Perhaps that is an extension of the answer to the question at the beginning of the book. I did find that people were willing to talk about single payer, but they had not fully teased out the critical details enough to have any conviction how the money would actually flow in this system. What comment there was foresaw a role for states:

Dr. Hellander of PNHP: "I think [Senator Bernie] Sanders' bill is administered at the state level because he is a big advocate of community health centers and wants to keep his community-based health center model for Vermont. But he doesn't want to impose it on everybody else. What should be allocated to the states is some health planning role, but they shouldn't be setting fees or determining eligibility or any of the ground rules like that."

Senator Sanders, on his own behalf: "Roughly speaking, the Canadian model makes sense to me. I don't believe that what we want to do is necessarily a single payer system: you're not going to have this, this, this and this, but you will give some flexibility for states to move forward in their own direction. California is not Vermont. They want to do things a little differently. So long as all people have health care and you have a whole lot of parameters in there, I think you can give flexibility to have it administered at the state-wide level. You don't want a national bureaucracy, you want people to be able to walk into the legislature and say, you know, I think that acupuncture should be funded and why aren't you doing that or this. You want to empower people in the process."

Gene Ransom, CEO of Maryland MedChi, as his lawyer self: "What I find to be very interesting is in states like Massachusetts or Maryland, where there's been a lot of state government involvement, I think those states wish there had been a little bit less and then the states where there's not . . . I'm good friends with the CEO from Oklahoma and he says we can't even get Medicaid expansion, we can't talk about it, we need to do this, it's so stupid, so their frustration is there's not enough involvement. So it's one of those things that depend on what the state is and that's kind of how we are as a country—different states. It's funny because we did give up the Articles of Confederation, then went with a more federalized government. But we never lost that individuality and you can see it in health care too."

Former Wisconsin Governor, as well as former HHS Secretary, Tommy Thompson, asked about the role for states vs. the federal government: "I think you have to have both because I think the laboratories of democracy are really at the state level. I look back to when I was governor. I started with the welfare reform movement that would never have started, would never have happened, if it had not been for me trying it. And I started Badgercare which was probably and still is probably the best health care system in America helping poor people. So that was a state function and we know John Engler, Mike Leavitt and other people had innovative programs. I think it's good to have such give and take: allowing states to try things differently. Sometimes the Federal government is just too big to try an experimental program. I like to see the states have a role to play and I think they could play a bigger role and a better role if they were given the flexibility and opportunity to do so."

From having been Senate Majority Leader and then been powerfully important in the election of President Obama after leaving Congress, Sen. Daschle arguably had the most seasoned, authoritative perspective overall. He leaned towards agreement with my preferences: "A national system is so much better. A typical worker moves seven times in his or her life . . . there's a value in having consistency throughout the entire country. The reality is unfortunately that we have built up many aspects of a federalist model that will be hard to turn around. It's not all bad. I do think that states have been innovative—Vermont, Oregon until the exchange, Maryland, California early—and twenty years ago, Tennessee. So I think the innovative opportunity that it gives some states is a good thing, but my general feeling is that we're better off with as much of a national system as we can get."

For the economic impact of a national health program, Dr. Sherry Glied has written about the tradeoffs between national and subnational budgets, discussing the "single-payerness" of the health systems in different countries.[14] She details pros and cons to consider regarding whether states or other subnational regions will have a role in the (otherwise) single payer budget. The big difference, she confirmed, is not between these details of budgeting but between the much better performance of the other countries' systems compared with the U.S.

The last word clinching the case against my preference for a pure national single payer system that would bypass the states was provided by the nurse and former Robert Wood Johnson Fellow, Liana Orsolini, PhD: "I know that when I was a health policy fellow and working on the Administrative side in the Dept. of Health and Human Services, I noticed that pervasive to every issue was this tension between federalism and state's rights. It permeated everything. Even if all sides agreed on the principle of the issue, there was always an underlying state vs. federal rights conflict." She recognized the problems that we noted above: "You look at Medicaid controlled by states, and we had several states that because of politics refused Medicaid expansion, vs. Medicare which is run at the federal level in [the Department of] Health and Human Services. So if you're a Medicare beneficiary in California, you get the same access to care as if you're a Medicare beneficiary in Texas or Maine. Because of that variation, I would say it's a no-brainer that it should be administered at the federal level." In spite of that good sense, the insurmountable tension over states' rights that she described, given the inconclusive arguments for leaving the states out, seems to settle it. From these thoughtful discussions, it is clear that however appealing a simple federal process unblemished by states' involvement may seem, the U.S. is not going to completely bypass the states in implementing a single payer system.

Nevertheless, in the name of simplicity, it is instructive to note the duplication of boards and committees in both the Conyers House bill and Sanders bill in the Senate. If we can learn anything from Canada, we can note that administrative processes do not need to duplicate complex administrative structures for national oversight if they are relegated to the states. It must be one or the other. Overall, administration based on states or regions appears to be appropriate for financial and logistic administration. But for the critical generation and monitoring of clinical requirements, a national process must dominate. True, the incidence of disease varies geographically, with a wrist fracture from a slip on the ice more common in Vermont and Coccidioido-mycosis ("Valley Fever from a fungus of hot arid climates) is more likely in southern California. But the Health Security Board recommendations for evaluation and treatment of the patient for each individual case will be the same everywhere, regardless of the home state of the patient or where the illness occurred because for each human body, each individual diagnosis does not vary with geography, nor should tests and treatments. This is another novel concept for health economists and policy experts. Much in medical diagnosis and treatment is either right or wrong, as described in Chapter 5. Removing the fuzzy issues of value and quality means that no state or regional program can hide behind this fog. If a program is not doing its best by the precepts of the Health Security Board, it is not a matter of poorer quality as a darker shade of gray—it is a matter of doing it wrong and then correcting or reassessing the clinical rule. There is no need to delegate issues of clinical practice to judgments of the individual states.

SOCIAL PHILOSOPHY

Reforming a nation's health and its health care delivery system involves as-pects from much of life in general. Carrying this big picture forward: where are we headed, and can't we move faster? The tension between nature's invest-ment in the survival of a population and the human need to provide for each member of a species—from a nearly drowned bat to every individual per-son—is eloquently put by J.W. Krutch;[15] and impatience with delay due to the "white moderate . . . who is more devoted to 'order' than to justice," sharpens the majestic prose of Rev. Martin Luther King, Jr.[16] Although some inequality of wealth and success is a statistical, economic and biological certainty, it is also our socio-biological destiny to have in mind the best for each individual.

There is no clear rationale for the contempt that groups who differ a little in culture or appearance may display against each other, characterized by Dr. Sigmund Freud as "the narcissism of small differences."[17] U.S. racism seems to be merely a particularly savage, prolonged and ubiquitous case of the general capacity for ethnic discord that is apparently a common human trait, not related to anything specific about the prejudice of European Americans against African Americans.

Barriers are being overcome in the underpinnings of race distinctions in the U.S. But racial framing by whites which, at the least harmful, produces subtle discrimination against blacks, is a reality all over the country.[18] And, although race is often found to be a statistically noticeable factor in results of medical studies, in my books on U.S. health care reform, a stack that is taller than I am, there is very little about the enormity of racism as an underlying current.[19]

The biological sciences provide no refuge for racial strife.[20] When I was in college (before the big Civil Rights marches), I was bemused noting famed geneticist G.G. Simpson's accurate reflection on spurious allusions to the superficial closeness of different human races to monkeys: Apes have white skin, straight hair and thin lips. And Dr. Francis Collins at the National Institutes of Health, once he and Dr. Craig Venter had sequenced the complete human genome, reportedly declared over cocktails to his predominately white colleagues: "There are no perfect human specimens. We are all flawed mutants."[21] So much for white supremacy. There is no hard-wired block in the path to a societal unlearning of the racism that has caused so much misery and still infects all of us to some degree. We can hope that education and social understanding will reverse it.

Regarding health care reform, my proposal involves responsible capitalism, not socialism. In chapter after chapter, we have seen the difficulty caused by unnecessary commoditization of health care in our country. This must be recognized and corrected. But this does not imply a socialist revolution. Just as, on the one hand, the overwhelming rule of an absolute monarch, warlord or dictator has lost out historically both in Asia and Europe, history similarly shows that real socialism with all property and production owned by the people as a whole is clearly not the future of mankind. For the 21st century, the only model for successful government will be a democracy with capitalism and individual freedoms, but with regulations that support and protect individual citizens from being harmed by misdirected power and wealth.

CHAPTER SEVEN
ACCESS FOR EVERY AMERICAN

N ow to bring the issues together and propose an updated single payer solution for the problems in U.S. health care. In this chapter I summarize the results of the interviews particularly on the single payer idea and then provide a more realistic model for the single payer structure envisioned earlier in the book. Finally, although this book will remain relevant for the years it will take for our country to have complete effective health care reform, the immediate political situation is noted with a discussion of presently practical possibilities for single payer reform, given our political realities in 2016.

RESULTS FROM THE INTERVIEWS

I begin with listings of the responses that I received about single payer in each interview, with groups categorized as either "Yes," "Measured" or "No." When I first began thinking about the problem of health care reform, it was from the point of view that doctors must be in charge of the clinical issues in order to have sound, efficient national health care. Initially I was not concerned with how to make it work best beyond that. The need for single payer to maximize the system's benefits has become clear to me over time. Perhaps many of the people I interviewed have followed the same path, given the views expressed in the many "Yes" quotes below.

So here are the quotes from the interviews that were relevant specifically to single payer, starting with the positives, next the measured intermediate group, and then those whose views are definitely against the option of single payer.

Yes, approval of single payer either by that term or by federal reform that would produce a national health program of that sort even if the term single payer was not included, although many in this category expressed pessimism about it politically:

Anderson: Single payer would be fine but it is too impossible.

Boufford: With the ACA, the country has gone on the record to say that people ought to have a way to pay for health care. That's the first time we've joined the international community in that regard so you don't want to lose the basics by trying to transform something into a radical conversation—that would be my sense.

Daschle I'm supportive of single payer. I don't think it's likely we're going to see it for the forseeable future.

Drasga: It will work because it's been proven to be effective in multiple different countries around the world, a testament in itself. It insures everyone and saves money.

Duderstadt: Like it or not, I think within 10 years we're going to have a system that's a little like Switzerland's or Canada's. It could be universal health care as a government responsibility augmented by the capacity to pay for what you're not getting with the public good. . . . Even with all its bureaucracy, I would trust a public organization to handle that much more than I would a commercial organization."

Fielding: The USA sticks out—we are totally uncompetitive because the huge fraction of GDP [going to health care—JB] is robbing us from doing other things. I am very much for the government determined global budget.

It needs a political process—one thing is sure: we don't need more money.

Hadler: Single payer is a buzzword. Affordability and "paying" is not the primary question. Structure everything around effectiveness—I don't care who pays for it, or how much it costs, it doesn't matter; if it's not effective don't do it. As I explain in *Citizen Patient* [One of the books by Hadler—JB]—we are stuck tweaking this monstrosity—we missed the opportunity for an efficient, rational, ethical scheme by 80 years . . . we should have tried for a compromise in 1945, but didn't, now we must do the best we can piecemeal.

Hellander: You say "the ideal health system." No country has the ideal system but around the world you see lots that would be good for us. There has to be redistribution, progressive financing from very high income—part of affordability. You can use the single payer data base to identify the outliers who are overusing certain imaging tests or other services and give them feedback compared to others within their specialty. You absolutely don't want to turn single payer into government managed care.

Laupacis: Certainly Alberta [Canadian Province—JB] is the most conservative. Even a pretty conservative government like in Alberta would not think it should go too far in terms of privatizing health care because there would be a backlash." (Moreover, since the interview he later noted that: "Albertans elected an NDP government, which is the most left-leaning party in Canada." Moreover the Conservatives were routed in the national election in October, 2015.)

Lewin: We'd have only one ultimate payer, that would be the government funding everything through tax revenues and we have Medicare for all as a single payer model, but the actual implementation of it would be delegated to competing private insurance companies that would provide different versions of that even though it's all going to be commonly funded from the U.S. We're heading for a single payer.

Orsolini: So do I believe in the single payer system? Yes, for many different reasons. My mother loves her Medicare and that's a single payer system for people 65 and above. Although many veterans have had problems accessing their single payer system, the veterans I worked with at the San Francisco VA Medical Center loved their single payer system, so we know in pockets it does work very well.

Ostrich: I've always been inclined to be fond of the single payer system. They bitch and moan about government interference and that sort of thing. Frankly I'm a Medicare recipient now and it works well, there's no hassle, a little copay here and there. . . .

Owens: Basically [I have] two views—one is great admiration for the integrated systems you have whether its Intermountain, Kaiser—Canadians spend gobs of money going down to the U.S. to visit these places [to learn about their administration—JB], the work of the Institute for Healthcare Improvement—[I have] great admiration for that. The second is that there's been a lot of concern that there have been a number of Americans that can't afford health insurance and that's a concern because our system is universal up here."

Pronovost: So we need a health care system that achieves our policy goals. The question is what's the insurance mechanism and I assume you mean government-funded insurance. One benefit is you can coordinate national policy measures, right now every insurer I know has 20 or 30 or 40 different measures. Two, it's an awful lot easier to create national standards. If you look at health care as an industry, we are pretty grossly under-standardized compared to aviation and nuclear energy. Like most people I think we ought to insure our citizens—we're wealthy enough to, we ought to have high quality care, and we ought to get rid of the waste in the health care system.

Ransom: We should either go to straight free market or we should make it straight single payer and this in between gives us all the inefficiencies that you have without having a free market and you have all the cost problems as well. You get the worst of both worlds and I think it's horrible. I think we should pick one or the other and go, and I don't think we're going to pick free market.

Sanders: I happen to believe that health care is a right for all people. The question is how do you provide good quality health care to all people in the most cost effective way? Clearly the system we have now is so complicated, so dysfunctional, it ends up being extremely expensive so we have a system where 29 million people are uninsured, many more are paying high deductibles and copayments and the cost of that is almost twice as much as any other country. That's why I believe in the single payer system.

Schroeder: I think there is a huge, unmet role for physicians to make the moral argument for coverage, whether or not that's linked explicitly to single payer or to single payer as one of the options, but it's a moral crime that a significant portion of the U.S. population doesn't have coverage.

Sherman: It would save a lot of trouble for the reasons of income fluidity if nothing else. But beyond that I would be getting beyond my depth.

Warshaw: The principle of single payer is very attractive in principle. It would reduce the complexities of figuring out which payer you're dealing with and what the different regulations are for that payer and what the requirements are with very different payment schemes. So I think the concept or the principle is very attractive but the risk of a single payer system is that the government will be so dominant as to potentially be oppressive to doctors.

Wells: My personal opinion is that sooner or later we are going to come to [that] (single payer). I don't see any other way to cover health care for the people of the United States.

Young: Conservative doctors have been more victims of the system, but now have shifted over to willingness to accept national health insurance and now the public supports single payer.

Zorza: It's hard to make an argument against single payer but it's hard to have any faith that we will move towards it in this country. Having grown up in the English system where the absence of guaranteed access to medical care was a huge fear in the Depression, I inherited this deep sense that it's a right, it should be a right, and if it's a right its usually simplest to administer through some kind of quasi-administrative system which doesn't mean you necessarily have it managed the way the UK system is.

Measured approval by recognizing the need to cover everyone but against a single payer system to do it:

Boling: It should be how could we provide financial help to those people who want or need health insurance but who either can't get it through an employer or can't afford it on their own. If it's handled at the state level in conjunction with private insurance carriers with some kind of subsidy mechanism for different levels of policies in terms of types of coverage—these people can get the benefit. They would have the same access to doctors, hospitals, diagnostic centers, that I do. So if you use the private sector resources, but you find a way to design an insurance product that can be affordable with subsidy, I think that could get us a long way. . . .

Bond: Single payer is a really easy thing to say. That is its principle advantage. If, however, you were to kick any sector of the economy and say you were going to unify it, it would be an enormous task, much less one that represents nearly 1 in 5 dollars of GDP. It is a question whether it would be prudent to engage in that social reorganization which would be the largest social reorganization since the industrial revolution. There's no adequate incentive in the end to make a single effort and that's a great example of why if we were to say single payer tomorrow it might be implemented sometime in the lifetime of our great, great grandchildren.

Cohen: Historically, if we go way back there have been many attempts in the House of Representatives and presidents and the senate to produce some form of universal access or at least attempts to achieve that. Thus far all attempts had failed in the past. One thing about the Affordable Care Act: it has succeeded to a degree in attempting to include as many individuals as possible who were previously un- or underinsured. So that is a starting point, really, for any discussion, whether it be a discussion on the liberal or conservative side. I believe that both sides do agree that universal or at least near universal access is important. I think that both sides have very different views on the means towards that. I don't say a single payer system's bad, I just don't think it fits quite in the American framework of having these very very powerful stakeholders.

Thompson: I've been involved in health care so long, Jim, that every system has pros and cons to it. I can remember going to Europe and speaking at the European Community and various independent states and they were talking to me about going from their government to a private competitive system like the United States. They didn't think that they or their country or citizens were ready yet to go to a private competitive system like America but they wanted to hear about it, they were considering it. I think that single payer has some strong positives, namely that its one that all citizens, if you do it right, you're going to have access to it, which to me is a laudable goal and something that everybody should strive for is to give everybody good health. But then I harken back to my days as a Secretary and listening to the controversies and it always comes back to who's going to pay for it, how you're going to pay for it, we can't afford what we've got, so how would you be able to expand the health care system with the costs we have in America. And so it's in the details, the devil's always in the details. But I don't think you can say that single payer is better than the private system and I don't think you can say the private system is better than single payer system.

No, not for a single payer system:

Cooper: US voters will not be willing to sustain cross subsidies at the level that a single payer system will require. Therefore, getting to the goal incrementally will probably be wise. So there are lots of ideals that, as an idealist, it's fun to talk about. But that's the problem with single payer talk in America today. It diverts attention from the practical to the ideal. And it targets one particular policy approach, while allowing broader efforts that address poverty and health inequality to languish.

Katz: Single payer if it's a Medicare-based payer won't work as we've experienced so many problems with Medicare and the variability of rules regulations and requirements for cost. And quality—being paid on that, and the constant changes year to year as to what constitutes quality, what constitutes cost savings. Single payer provides very little opportunity for physicians and other practitioners to individually or collectively negotiate. Having fewer entities determining what constitutes quality and how physicians should be paid doesn't seem to be the right approach—it may provide universal coverage but it doesn't mean universal access and it doesn't mean the availability of the services.

Opelka: I think transforming the current system in terms of its total means of financing and not into so much a single payer structure but what will probably be a limited number of real payers going down the road. I remember talking to someone recently in Denver who is doing an all payer claims database and they have over a 1,000 different contracts that are being managed across the state of Colorado. So if there were 6, 8 or 10 different payers I think you'd find the right amount of competition from the payer side such that you'd get the kinds of service you need from the claims management service side of things and at the same time you could have an economy of scale. I'm not a single payer person but I'm not for 1,000 different management team contracts, there's some point in between.

Rowe: I would say with respect to a landscape analysis that says is there any momentum towards single payer, that is toward exclusion of the commercial payers—the traditional single payer the government will take over like the NHS—I think it's quite clear that all the evidence is against that. First of all, individuals who tried to get a public option included in the exchanges which could then morph into a single payer—

that was unsuccessful even in 2008 and in the current political environment would not even be discussed. Single payer is dead at this point. You
walk into the United States Senate and the guy on the other side of the
table is going to say Senator, you don't need to change the system, you've
just been correcting health insurance, Senator. You're going to take this
political fight on? You wanted to bend the curve? The curve is bending,
Senator. That would be the argument.

In summary, and with the reminder again that this was a field trip, not a scientific poll, so I advise against yielding to the misleading temptation even to
calculate simple fractions from these numbers, here is what was found in the
30 interviews: 22 were in favor of single payer or an equivalent national system,
4 expressed a measured, intermediate view, and 4 were declaredly against it.

Moreover, it seems plausible to me that the thinking of the four people
interviewed who were open to system improvement but said they were not in
favor of single payer might, upon further reflection, yield to an acceptance of a
single payer system. Nevertheless, these intermediate opinions do not belong
in the "Yes" tally. A criterion for them to be in the "Measured" group is that
it seems likely that they may become convinced of the need for a single payer
system when they read this book. For academic completeness, one might ask
about the possibility of an opposite shift from the "Yes" group. The answer is
that it would be extremely unlikely that any will change and shift to the "No"
category. Why would they? Lastly, the motives and likely future thinking for
the final four who were definitely against single payer are more difficult to guess.

THE UPDATED SINGLE PAYER SYSTEM

With this affirmation that people are willing to take it seriously and often are
in favor of it in principle, I remain convinced that a single payer system will be
best for the country. Although specific features of the structure that I propose
here would be helpful in any proposed reforms, it is hard to imagine any other
approach but single payer that will utilize them to best advantage. Nevertheless, the concerns reviewed in previous chapters and the eight intermediate
or opposed opinions quoted above warrant thoughtful concern about the
structural details that will be most convincing and effective. Figure 5 shows
my new proposal for the single payer national health care program based on
all of these considerations, revised from the initial simple concept in Figure
1 in Chapter 1. The principles listed there are unchanged. The general overall
national structure is the same. The proposal for an interprofessional Health

Security Board for the country remains just as important since cost control will be an integral part of its responsibility for quality. This plan is a response to the major problem that neither private insurance nor the programs of the Centers for Medicare and Medicaid Services have been effective in clinically accurate cost containment. Note that a place for supplemental care as shown in Figure 1 is retained, but with details omitted in Figure 5 for simplicity.

One big revision is that, although the legislation and overall foundation of the system will be federal, the states will be part of the administration of the funding stream. These will provide for care through regional fiduciaries as described most clearly by Hadler, which might be one large state or a set of smaller states. They would work within their joint federal/state global budgets to fund the care that is deemed by the Health Security Board to be necessary for Essential Care. The fiduciaries will play a major role in determining administration and reimbursements. But the Health Security Board will determine the details of Essential Care for the nation.

The other major structural change from Figure 1 is that doctors and nurses will be unfettered to practice from day to day as professionals, free from intrusion by the reimbursement system. The care documented in the electronic medical record will be used for retrospective analysis of individual practices and national outcomes. Derived from the interprofessional Health Security Board as well as from FDA and CDC regulations as now, the rules will constitute good medical practice, relying on the professionalism of doctors and nurses to be followed, rather than a set of complex administrative requirements for doctors to obey at the point of service that only interfere and fail to accurately capture the breadth and depth of good medical care. Clinical oversight using electronic medical records will be performed by each medical team for its own Continuing Quality Improvement and by the Health Security Board for the oversight of care that is being provided and for improvement of the national system as the data indicate. The majority of this activity will be simplified electronically by the dashboards described in Chapter 5 which will highlight clinically necessary issues. If questions are raised about individual practice patterns, physicians will be expected to respond with justification or an effective continuing quality improvement plan. In the absence of issues in Electronic Medical Reference data noted by the Board, no other agency or federal involvement—or interference—with the doctors' practice will be necessary. The description by Dr. Ostrich in Chapter 3 of the experience of a practitioner in Kaiser is a model for the role of a doctor in the single payer plan proposed. Administrative demands on government and the medical community are simplified and these processes will be transparent, providing for government and public review and input.

ESSENTIAL CARE FOR EVERYONE

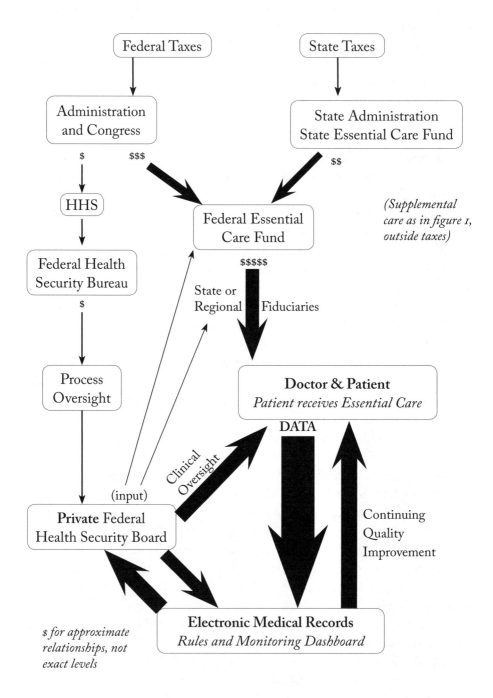

Figure 5. Single Payer Health Security with the Data Hub

TRACKING PRIVATE IDENTITIES

In order to follow each American in the national Electronic Medical Record system, a faultless unique identification will be needed. Whether it is simply an individually distinct alphanumeric string or includes other information, this identifier must be kept securely private. Social Security Numbers commonly are used as identifiers in various ways and this is a hacking risk since discovery in one database can compromise one's identity in others. Moreover, the Health Insurance Portability and Accountability Act forbids use of the Social Security Number as a national health records identifier.

A national EMR might use a different identifier as National Health Record Number (NHR#). This could be assigned around the time of birth or at registration of new adult citizens. Perhaps iris scanning could be used as a confirmatory identification. To support social programs, India has begun to do iris scanning of all of its nearly 1.3 billion citizens. People would be allowed to opt out of having the iris scanned for the U.S. system, although that could complicate things for them occasionally. The scan information and the NHR# would be on close hold in the national database to be used for confirmation when necessary. Simple demographic information available publicly, including date of birth and current phone number and email address will be used for routine clinical interactions, and data referred centrally to be linked to the NHR# and iris scan. No number or scan information would be retained except centrally. The only private identifying information transmitted outside of the database would be the iris scan when needed occasionally, which would be instantaneously wiped away securely after the transmission. The database could have a field for the social security number in case someone wanted it associated with their EMR, but there would be no need for that and it would threaten their security from electronic theft. No one would need to know their own NHR#. It would not be used for anything else.

In addition there would be a National Caregiver Record, with numbers and iris scans required for all users for routine clinical care or for studies and oversight. To guard against intrusion the national system would automatically monitor for unexplained access not justified by clinical activity or registered analysis by NCR#. This would allow rapid detection of any data breach.

THE DOCTORS' NATIONAL ROLE

Enlarging upon the description in Chapter 1, doctors will be a key ingredient in this public-private partnership amongst the Department of Health and

Human Services, the caregivers, the patients and the public. They will be organized in the Health Security Board to oversee the health care choices that doctors and their patients make. Although doctors' expertise will be a principle feature, the composition of the interprofessional Board of Essential Health Care will be widely derived: physicians, nurses, paramedical personnel, hospital administrators and the lay public may be included. The Federal Health Security Bureau in HHS will be needed for administrative support and federal oversight of the Board. But this Board and its direct administration will not be federal entities. Rather, they will constitute a "quasi-governmental" system deemed by the federal bureau to have the responsibility to carry out these technical functions and clinical decisions. Reimbursement cannot be a principle responsibility of the professionals on the Board of Essential Health Care, although this body may provide input regarding what is best for patients. The federal bureau will be in charge of administering the health care system with two exceptions. First, the government will not run the details of choosing care—that will be up to the board. And second, "market forces" will be allowed in supplemental care, with federal oversight only to prevent medical harms or interference with the essential health care system.

Professional and community members will be chosen from volunteers. Physicians will need to be in active medical practice to ensure that they will be authoritative and up to date. In order to attract appropriate doctors and others to volunteer, it will be necessary to minimize the impact on their careers, incomes, and retirement programs. Board members, particularly the physicians but some others as well, will need support from colleagues or other employees to help deal with decreased income and interruption of continuity in their practice or other jobs.

Two or three years of continuous service would be nearly impossible for practicing physicians, and probably difficult for some other desirable public members, so intermittent active participation for part of a year would be more practical. The term could be for a few months a year for several years, with other members on for the alternate periods. Some administrative continuity would be necessary, but encouraging a sense of "interchangeability" regarding Board functions will foster objectivity. After all, the decisions must be driven by data, not political preference. An arrangement would be needed for reimbursement of Board members for the time they would be away from their jobs.

Mandatory turnover every few years in these positions will be important with terms staggered to provide some continuity. Turnover would avoid the problem of individuals, particularly doctors, however well-intentioned, adopting service on the board as a career. Moreover, I think that it will be key for the physician board members not to completely forego their ongoing medical practice. Although service on this Health Security Board will be a heavy responsibility, the work will not be as hard as patient care which typically requires physicians to work a stressful 60 to 80 hours a week. It would be a bit of a break, at least for the doctors and nurses, and likely also for other board members. And it would be helping patients just as surely as one-on-one patient care responsibilities or any other role in society.

Who will choose these doctors and other board members? Of course the major specialty societies and interested industries would like to control appointments to try to influence policies. When I describe this board and its powers to other doctors, they nervously raise this question in spite of the protections just specified. Actually, it is not as critical a question as one might think. Medical leadership will need to exercise responsibility in the selection process to prevent bias in the board. The board cannot be composed according to political points of view. Its members must be clear that their principle commitment is to what is best for patients, not to other stakeholders. Surveillance by the public and professional societies for conflicts of interest by members of the board must be strong and continuous. There will be an extraordinary public interest in the board activities which will protect the board members from partisan misbehavior: with a transparent process it will be clear that there is little chance of violating this trust undetected.

THE INNOVATION OF THE HEALTH SECURITY BOARD

The novel proposal for oversight by the medical profession in the form of a doctor's board was not usually brought up in my interviews. Notably, no one was against the concept of doctors taking more national responsibility. As with despair about the failure of constructive public and political initiatives, some expressed skepticism about the likelihood of effective physician involvement. But no one felt that doctors have to be kept out of this. To the contrary, the views of several would favor oversight by the medical profession:

Dr. Duderstadt is Chair of the National Research Council which includes responsibility for the Institute for Medicine—which is soon being renamed the National Academy of Medicine. At its recent meeting on "Dying in America" that had "very serious financial implications" he noted that "once again those studies also suggested to me that the health care providers—physicians, nurses and so forth, frequently are not at the table when many of these policy decisions are made." Dr. Hadler, noting the pervasive profit-driven disincentives: "If doctors could, they would practice according to their consciences." Although this is not a prominent feature of the platform of the Physicians for a National Health Program, Dr. Hellander agrees with my concept of "doctors being involved and within that system at a national level to dictate the practices to the extent that a range of options that are appropriate needs to be described and something that's inappropriate needs to be made clear." Connecticut State Medical Society CEO Katz: "Everyone agrees physicians have to be involved." Dr. Lewin, as in Chapter 4: "Yes, doctors could exercise their own accountabilities and clearly fix a lot of problems in efficiency and variation in our system but that isn't going to happen because there's something flawed in our human nature." Dr. Opelka, whose focus is agnostic regarding the political structure, still agrees on the way the Doctors Board would function: "Readmissions, repeat office visits, inefficient follow-ups for asthmatics: The only way we can make heads or tails out of this global payment is to optimize the clinical care and the only way we can optimize clinical care is to get control of the clinical data." The Maryland MedChi CEO Ransom: "Doctors were excluded in Hillary care—so for clinical decisions that need to have much more organized authoritative national input than we've ever done before, doctors need to be independent in a politically protected way and in charge of the issues of determining what quality is and overseeing it."

During our interview Dr. Hadler had mentioned the problem described by Katharine Wulff and colleagues discussed in chapter 3 in which percutaneous vertebroplasty was found in two small randomized trials to be ineffective (and it carries some risks) and yet Medicare and private insurers continue to reimburse for it. Their analysis points out the need to "support a national structure for generating and assessing evidence." But this has not been easy. The Congressional attack, nearly destroying what is now the Agency for Healthcare Research and Quality in 1990, because the AHRQ published similar negative data on surgery for back pain, and similar attacks on evidence against universal screening for breast cancer in women are part of the background. In their article, Wulff et al recommend a strengthening of the Affordable Care Act Patient-Centered Outcomes Research Institute (PCORI) as a solution.[1] But that is not enough; although touted as valuable by Dr. Cohen and others, the PCORI is hampered from having any real effect by the ACA legislation that created it. This is why we must have a professional, authoritative national Health Security Board, protected from routine lobbying and Congressional interference, as I propose. American medicine must recognize the requirement to make and follow its own evidence-based rules with transparency but without political tampering. And politicians and the public must understand the benefit of this professional control.

Most national proposals for health care reform have not included an important role for physicians. A review of concepts about the proposed role of practicing doctors in health care reform is revealing. Some years ago the Conyers single-payer bill (HR. 676) first appeared. It mentions physicians mostly for description or definitions. It does call for a National Board of Universal Quality and Access that would oversee the reformed medical system. It specifies that the membership of this Board must include one health care professional. Similarly, the more recent Wyden-Bennett "Healthy Americans Act" (S. 334), which proposes to enlarge coverage mentions physicians only marginally. It calls for an HHS Secretarial Healthy America Advisory Committee to make recommendations on updates. The Sanders Bill (S. 915), Senate companion to the McDermott Bill (H.R. 1200 "The American Health Security Act") or, conceptually, the Conyers Bill, recognizes the need to set and oversee standards more directly with the American Health Security Standards Board and the American Health Security Quality Council to review practices that are outliers in outcomes data that may represent poor quality.[2] But these are federal entities like PCORI, inevitably politicized, not the independent, protected, interprofessional Health Security Board responsible for dealing with clinical practice shown in Figure 5.

In addition, it is remarkable that proposals in the many excellent, scholarly books on U.S. health care reform include very little involvement for physicians. Several are generally oriented towards systems based on conventional insurance and patient choice.[3] Three other notable books, by Daschle, Relman and Halvorson, respectively, come closer to the insight that doctors can be part of the solution.[4] In addition, there is a recent excellent video by Paul Hochfeld, *Health, Money and Fear*, describing the problems of U.S. health care. Screened at the 2008 Boston Film Festival, it has appealing interviews with many physician contributors including some of the authorities mentioned in this book. It provides powerful reasoning that leads to the conclusion that we need a single-payer system. But neither how standards of care would be determined nor a role for doctors, both critical for a national health program, are discussed in any detail in any of these works. As a practicing doctor, I find it particularly interesting that the three books that realistically consider the importance of physicians, by Jill Quadagno; Donald Barlett and James Steele; and Maggie Mahar, are not by doctors or even health economists.[5]

PROSPECTS FOR A NATIONAL SINGLE PAYER SYSTEM

I asked Sen. Tom Daschle how ugly the political climate might it become if we were headed to a rapid change with some doctors' high reimbursements dropping and drug and insurance company businesses diminishing. He smiled calmly: "First of all, I just don't think we will even get there. What happens in health is that we take this a piece at a time and we go through all the transformational effects that that particular legislative accomplishment entails—Medicaid, Medicare in 65, CHIP, the prescription drug program in 2003, these were all incremental steps that have had transformational effects [along with the ACA now—JB]. I don't see one happening now for quite a while just because I think we're going to have to digest what we have done and let it play out for awhile."

This view is reinforced by the opinion of some in the interviews that we will see a gradual progression of states taking it up here and there and eventually coalescing into a national single payer system. That would take a while and be difficult for each state to do in isolation.

There is some urgency. Moving forward with reform is important to every citizen. The single payer system is not just a proposal to help America's poor get health care. In the first place, it represents protection for anyone who has health insurance now but who may suffer a reversal through death, divorce, loss of a job, business failure . . . or merely severe illness. At present, any but the richest Americans may suddenly be looking at the world as a poor person with no health insurance. Moreover, quality—operationally viewed here partly as protection of one's health from harm—is important for everyone, rich and poor. Communities with better access to health care are more generally healthy. The reason is underscored in Chapter 4, describing the ongoing danger to all until equal access to health care for everyone ensures that there is no longer an untested, untreated reserve of Hepatitis C in our uninsured U.S. citizens. We can do much more to provide for everyone in this way and we will remain in harm's way until then.

The reservation about practicality even from those who see the advantages of single payer care is perhaps the most telling, though not unexpected, aspect of my interview-driven "field trip." Yes, I found that people are usually willing to talk about single payer and they are generally in favor of it, but it was also clear that many do not think of it as achievable soon. Some pessimism is appropriate in view of the U.S. history of tax breaks and regulation abatement for business and the wealthy being substituted for continuation of programs to help workers and the poor, an ongoing policy deterioration since Ronald Reagan's Presidency.[6] On the other hand, continued general denial of the possibility of enacting single payer reinforces that pessimism in a thoughtless, circular way.

Perhaps there is room to hope for a more rapid transition to health care for everyone. Many I interviewed see it as inevitable. Note in this regard, even the comments by Dr. Cohen in Chapter 6 on retention of some social good in anti-ACA conservative legislation. And, notwithstanding the success of some conservative retractions of social programs in the U.S., on average during the recent history of the U.S. and the world there has been a surge of increasing social civility. Cruel punishments and vicious bigotry are vanishing; voting rights and sufferance are expanding. A nearly unbelievable but convincing argument that violence in general is lessening over the course of human history, required reading for this topic, is made in *The Better Angels of our Nature. Why Violence is Decreasing*, by social psychologist Dr. Steven Pinker.[7] In the U.S., in spite of continuing attempts to stamp out public support, many helpful programs remain. The Civil Rights Act of 1964 represented a striking new national resolve. Lynchings of African Americans were once at the rate of hundreds per year in the U.S. with anti-lynching bills repeatedly blocked by Congress. Lynchings have disappeared and in 2005 we had a belated resolution finally passed by Congress, apologizing for that history. A century ago in America, small children were put to work as "breakers" sorting slate out of coal: that is inconceivable now.

Certainly, as alluded to by Sen. Daschle, health care in the U.S. has undergone big advances: Medicare and Medicaid, the State Children's Health Insurance Program, the Health Insurance Protection and Portability Act, Medicare Part D and the Patient Protection and Affordable Care Act, in particular. The End Stage Renal Disease program, based on kidney failure representing a disability, is an entitlement program taking care of some very poor people effectively. As with care for other chronic illnesses, this program is expensive. But its existence cuts across financial and racial barriers and provides care to everyone, not just the disadvantaged.

Other federal programs and social services such as food stamps, workmen's compensation and the Occupational Safety and Health Act, unemployment assistance, school lunch programs, Head Start and its congeners have all been fought and variously harmed but continue to illustrate underlying social resolve. Probably none of these came easily but they have all had strong, lasting, beneficial impacts on society.

Finally, to be practical, there are two recent major influences which can have quick and powerful impacts on health care reform in our country, constructively, and without ugliness. If we do make progress, these will be important forces.

The first is the semi-spontaneous evolution of advances in medical delivery. As described in earlier chapters, hospitals and doctors are improving medical care processes with better teamwork, more individual attention to all issues that interfere with each patient's health, restraint on unnecessary care, increased exploitation of electronic assistance in many ways, and, at least in some areas, incrementally diminishing the remaining fraction of uninsured citizens. Costs are not rising as before, quality is measurably better, and it seems that doctors are increasingly ready for a more national approach if it is designed to help patients and the medical profession. This has largely evolved without specific legislation. Doctors control medical care in any situation, and doctors have a powerful political advantage because just about everyone trusts their doctor. It may come down to medical progress, socially and technically, representing a politically irresistible force toward more complete, effective reform exerted at the political level. If doctors and nurses can push for expansion of these advances with an increasingly convincing and effective momentum, the Congress and the White House, almost regardless of partisan politics, will have to give way and provide for it.

The second promising influence is the changing political climate. Although clouds persist in the form of social intransigence and powerful obstruction by wealthy special interests, surprising recent progressivism has proven to be a sustainable popular presence. The Occupy Wall Street movement was a heralded early harbinger. And the force of Sen. Elizabeth Warren's populist offensive against business as usual for banks and Wall Street, showing these financial giants to be operating to the detriment of everyone else, has been welcomed far and wide. She is having a strong influence in behalf of lessening the problems discussed in the previous chapter that will be important for improving the nation's health. Campaign finance reform and an end to extreme gerrymandering are at least being recognized more publicly as necessary for the integrity of the country. And now we have a champion to elect to be President. The candidacy of Senator Bernie Sanders is off to an excellent start financially and by popular acclaim.[8] The quotes in this book from him, although from my interview before he had announced his candidacy, offer you an introduction to his views on health care reform.

Sen. Sanders recently published a summary of his political beliefs[9] that was well-aligned with the issues in Chapter 6, asking questions such as: "Why are we so far behind so many other countries when it comes to meeting the needs of working families and the American middle class? Why doesn't every American have access to healthcare as a basic right? Why can't every American who is qualified get a higher education, regardless of family income?" and so on. He gets my vote. His remarkable wide appeal and his common sense approach relying on the need for change that he senses in the air will be a strong force for a national health care program.

By these wonderful developments, the country may be in for important health care modernization soon. This can be achieved through a single payer health care system for all. We need to keep talking.

APPENDIX
THE OP-EDS

THE NEXT STEP FOR REFORM

To reduce costs, doctors should be in charge of determining standards for health care

THE BALTIMORE SUN **APRIL 04, 2010** BY JAMES BURDICK

The enthusiastic reception to President Obama as he has toured the country to publicize the health care reform bill is richly deserved. This historic law will help many Americans. In addition, even with the ink barely dry, he has already extended the vision. In a speech touting the bill in Iowa, President Obama promised care for everyone, which this law does not achieve. He talked of reining in the insurance companies, who will still continue to successfully wriggle out of restraints in this law. He committed to even more resounding reform for all Americans.

But the president will need some help in fulfilling these promises.

As a doctor, I am convinced that the country can have cost control and a doctor for every family. But we cannot do it with the present health insurance model. Even with "Obamacare," insurance companies and the fear of malpractice remain in control, regardless of what reforms are being touted. We need a professional process to define appropriate care that can move the decisions patients and doctors make out of insurance interference and into clinical reality. We have a proven example. Organ transplantation, my specialty, has a board of doctors and others that makes national policy for transplant hospitals and doctors. It is a public-private partnership, independent but man-dated and overseen by the federal government. This model could apply to American health care more broadly.

Imagine American doctors being put back in charge of defining standards for health care and establishing incentives to observe these practices nationally. That would allow the country to achieve the cost-cutting reform that Americans want, based on professional expertise, not insurance company profits or a "government takeover."

Quality would be improved for everyone, since doctors are now hard-pressed to keep up with the profusion of standards from various sources. Professionalism notwithstanding, in arguable cases it is in the doctor's narrow self interest to go ahead and do an invasive heart study if the patient wants it—and their insurance will pay. Best practices need to be provided in a man-ageable, authoritative way. For example, Dr. Robert Brook, professor of med-icine and health policy at UCLA, has called for national implementation of the Rand UCLA Appropriateness Method, a proven professional guide for care decisions.

Care based on clinical criteria would control expensive, dangerous overuse. It could free the Congress to establish regulated insurance or single-payer funding, which would control costs by removing insurance profits and expen-sive administration. With part of the savings—about $500 billion a year—we could extend care to every American. There would be no premiums to pay, no jitters about employer health insurance contributions or insurance that doesn't pay when you get sick, and taxes would not have to go up. People could continue with the doctors they have now. Putting doctors in charge of national practice would solve the complex health care puzzle posed by a need to control costs, ensure quality and provide for everyone.

For the national program, Congress could create a board made up of phy-sicians, plus other professional and public representatives. Many such federal public-private partnerships exist. The law creating this new board would have built-in federal oversight but would establish the board as a semi-indepen-dent entity, responsible for establishing and overseeing best practices for es-sential care because clinical decisions need professional authority. Cases when doctors do not follow the guidelines would be reviewed by the board. But with doctors making the rules and deciding on the validity of deviations, and federal oversight ensuring transparency and accountability, best interests of all would be served.

Board decisions would become national standards unless the government intervened in some instance. By law, the board's work would be transparent and therefore protected from medically irrelevant influence. An electronic health records system would provide accurate data for easily monitoring national practices without a vast bureaucracy. Uniform clinical practices would help control lawsuits. Within a year or two we could have national guidelines for the most common and expensive conditions. Standards would be based on data plus clinical expertise and would allow decisions for each individual patient's care. Private insurance for supplemental care could co-exist. This is how we can go beyond even the public option, minimize costs and have quality care for everyone. This is the help President Obama needs to fulfill his promises.

Doctors excel at taking responsibility for each patient. It is time for doctors to join together to take responsibility for care of all Americans.

MAKE REFORM BIPARTISAN

THE BALTIMORE SUN **OCTOBER 25, 2010** BY JAMES BURDICK

Politics can be bad for your health—literally. As a doctor, I feel that patients' needs must trump political party. But instead of benefiting from bipartisanship, health care has become highly politicized. Traditional party positions are being contradicted by belligerence that threatens patient care.

That is not to say that the Patient Protection and Affordable Care Act is perfect. But this law represents the first successful reform of health care in more than four decades. Now, in their worry over bogus issues such as big government and unconstitutionality, many Republicans and Democrats alike have overlooked the real values in the law: things like increased coverage, cost controls and flexibility for doctors (not government) to help make these reforms succeed.

One thing is sure: If Congress votes to repeal the law—or withholds funding when President Barack Obama vetoes the repeal—it would not only be immoral; the effect of such craven negativity would be to leave Republicans wide open for a rout in 2012, given the country's increasing health care distress. The October AP-GfK Poll shows that a majority of Americans now want the law left as is or made stronger.

Democrats are partly guilty because they compromised so much that the insurance companies instead of the physicians have retained control over patient care. Many Democratic candidates have been reticent to proudly proclaim the new law's advantages.

Despite the poisonous pre-election rhetoric surrounding the health care law, bipartisanship on this issue is still possible. After all, ordinary Americans of all parties recognize the disastrous health care situation America faces and the need for reform. And most doctors, whether Republicans or Democrats, would like to transfer medical decision-making from the insurance companies and the government to physicians.

Bipartisanship, after all, is part of America's history. In their goal to "form a more perfect union," the Founding Fathers recognized the uproarious divisions among the colonies. Our strength now is largely due to the sprit of compromise with which those early states united.

Today, appropriate federal support for health care must be recognized by both parties as a cost of doing business for our country. The 2009 GOP platform on health care proposes: insurability regardless of pre-existing conditions, prevention of unjust policy cancellations and maintaining dependents longer on their parents' policies. All of these Republican measures are in our new law. And the formal role that I propose for doctors—a novel idea not yet tainted by party dogmas—can provide an additional basis for restoring bipartisanship to support a spare, effective federal health care system.

If a new day of bipartisanship were to dawn, what might both parties contribute to a constructive vision for the nation's health?

It is said that we cannot have all three of the basics for health care reform: high quality, cost control and access for everyone. But that is not so. If we improve quality, it will save money, and we can extend health care to everyone with the savings.

Quality is based on clinical criteria. We can have high-quality care if doctors are given a formal national responsibility for it. The new law allows doctors to do this, and it will work. The U.S. organ transplant system has been run successfully for two decades by medical authorities, under a federal law. That model can be extended to our entire health care system. This will only happen with bipartisan support.

Take accountable care organizations (ACOs), which allow medical professionals to organize efficient quality care. Testing, consultation and follow-through on recommendations are streamlined. Mistakes and malpractice vulnerability are minimized by ACOs. They can save money.

Cost savings will also come from stopping the dispensing of unneeded "care" even if private insurance or Medicare will pay for it. Since all procedures carry risks, such overutilization is not only expensive but dangerous. Additional savings will come from the control of illegitimate insurance denials, which are dangerous for patients and waste expensive time for both the insurance companies and the doctors who fight them.

Previously, Congress tried to control costs by a law that restricted increases in doctor-controlled Medicare spending. But in recent years Congress has forbidden Medicare to make the necessary cuts, and now this "sustainable growth rate" law would dictate a 30 percent cut in that Medicare reimbursement this January. This would make it impossible for many doctors' offices to see Medicare patients. Decisions made by doctors in charge of care based on clinical criteria can save that money without hurting patients.

All of these are improvement opportunities that would best be achieved by doctors with the qualifications to judge the clinical details. The flexibility in the new law allows for professional expertise to provide quality improvement with authoritative national guidelines that doctors will follow.

Who was the president when the public-private national transplant system that is a model for physician involvement was passed? Ronald Reagan. Regardless of the party in control, putting patients first will serve everybody's constituents. Based on that common interest in what's best for patients, dare we hope for a new bipartisanship?

Copyright © 2010, The Baltimore Sun

YES, IT'S CONSTITUTIONAL

THE BALTIMORE SUN   **DECEMBER 31, 2010**   BY JAMES BURDICK

The first salvo from the forces aligned to bring down the Obama health care plan has been fired. Your health may land in the lap of the Supreme Court as it adjudicates the constitutionality of the Patient Protection and Affordable Care Act. Leaving aside the legal language and overheated rhetoric, where will that leave us?

As a doctor, I am thinking of the central focus: the frightened patient, perhaps in pain from a new illness, conferring with the doctor. Would the Founding Fathers have meant for the Constitution to allow access to care for any American who needs it? If not, America would have a problem—because, rest assured, the doctor is going to provide that care to the extent that he or she can possibly manage. That is the reality.

I am no fan of the "individual mandate" requiring everyone to have health insurance or face a penalty. But the U.S. has just made a major, realizable gain in funding and access for health care for the first time in 40 years, and we must not let it slip away. We must have the mandate to encourage everyone to buy in, because the principle of insurance is to spread the risk widely. It is fair (and, you would think, constitutional), because almost everyone will need medical care sooner or later. They do not really have a choice. In the health insurance-based system that we still have in the U.S., the payment of premiums is the only fair and effective way to have insurance when we become ill.

If the mandate is ruled unconstitutional, probably most people will still choose to get insurance. But the risk of the reform law without the mandate is that too many healthy people might forgo insurance with no fear of refusal for preexisting conditions, violating the principle of insurance. Premiums will then become too expensive, and this will quickly land Congress in big trouble.

If the mandate is upheld, there will still be problems. Again, if you get sick, you could obtain insurance with no fear of refusal. So there is an incentive to pay the lower mandate penalty and not get insurance. After all, with coinsurance for hospitalization rising rapidly, patients face potential bankruptcy in spite of their insurance. And the mandate forces the public to support insurance industry profits to the tune of 15 to 25 cents on the dollar, which is the range that is deemed to be acceptable for the "medical loss ratios."

No, constitutionality is not the problem. The argument over mandates is most important because it reveals the failure of American health insurance, although the insurance industry was given a pass by this law.

Nevertheless, the new law has given Americans the dream that some day everyone will be able to afford to go to the doctor, and this reform can bring us closer to that. So we need this law now. But we can do better in the future. How?

Let's return to that patient with his or her doctor. The most relevant question is: Does the patient have effective, affordable health care coverage? One out of three Americans has no insurance or dangerously inadequate coverage. America needs a national program that covers everyone, no questions asked. It needs to be free of excessive administrative costs and to be able to prevent costly, dangerous overutilization—that is, tests and treatments that are not going to help the patient and may be harmful. Instead of being sidelined, doctors must be given national responsibility to define and improve quality by establishing care guidelines based on clinical criteria. We should dispense with rules generated by insurance companies and federal agencies, which are not the way to decide medical details.

The beauty of this is that quality saves money. Insurance can be reined in or replaced by a federal fund, ending the excessive cost of insurance administration. Overutilization can be stopped if doctors are given the authority. The net cost to the taxpayer goes down, and mandates become irrelevant if everyone is covered through federal revenues. Then we can afford care for everyone. After all, we are paying for a lot of people without insurance now; Families USA says that care for the uninsured is costing us more than $100 billion a year. This is partly because such patients typically do not receive timely, efficient medical attention.

The conservative agenda is, paradoxically, bringing the country closer to the realization of the need for more fundamental reform. Doctors take responsibility for each of their patients. It is time for doctors to take on a national responsibility for ensuring that all Americans get the right care.

Copyright © 2010, The Baltimore Sun

UNIVERSAL HEALTH CARE ON THE HORIZON

Supreme Court ruling upholding Affordable Care Act puts the United States on the road toward eventually covering everyone

THE BALTIMORE SUN   **JULY 12, 2012**   BY JAMES BURDICK

U.S. Chief Justice John G. Roberts Jr.and the Supreme Court have not only upheld the Affordable Care Act, they struck down a barrier to universal health care for Americans. Looking forward from the Supreme Court's decision, by defining the cost of expanding coverage as a tax, the court has moved our thinking toward universal health care as a proper cost of the country's well-being.

The Obama administration's defense of the individual mandate in the Affordable Care Act as a tax was widely second-guessed. Analysts saw it as a weak argument compared to the Commerce Clause justification. But framing the mandate as a tax was resoundingly successful for a couple of reasons. It probably won the day partly because defending the mandate only under the Commerce Clause—a nemesis to conservatives—would have been less compelling to this court. Taxation, on the other hand, is a foundation of federal power and hard to argue against. JusticeAnthony M. Kennedy implied as much (even though in the end he voted against upholding the Affordable Care Act), calling it the correct power, and Chief Justice Roberts, with his allegiance to process, was compelled to agree and therefore voted against gutting the ACA.

The success of this defense on the basis of the power of taxation contains great promise. It sets the stage for a national system covering health care for all.

The ACA does not get us there. But future legislation might specify more complete coverage for Americans' health care, and pay for this through a fund raised by taxation. It would be hard for a future Supreme Court, no matter how conservative, to be persuaded to take on a constitutional challenge to a law based on taxation that would provide a doctor for every American family, given this Supreme Court decision. So it is just a matter of time.

Of course, not everyone is in agreement yet. Since the Supreme Court did not uphold the requirement that states increase their Medicaid participation, some governors are dragging their heels. But what a deal they are turning down: complete federal funding initially, and 90 percent or more from Washington after that. It is hard to imagine even a particularly obstinate state holding out against participating for long as its citizens face the hardships of lack of insurance coverage while those in surrounding states are cared for, thanks to this federal commitment. Its bureaucrats will know full well that the cost down the road to a nonparticipating state from the loss of jobs and expense of unnecessary tests and treatments from failing to support timely, quality care will surpass the cost to the state of the expanded Medicaid program. Dogmatic bluster will eventually have to yield, moving us closer to universal coverage.

Beyond its specific provisions, the ACA produced momentum for reform. In fact, even if President Barack Obama were to lose in November, naysayers' hopes for the reversal of humane health care reform will not be realized.

Of course, the Supreme Court did not provide the money to expand coverage. But Americans now pay twice as much in insurance premiums and taxes for health care as is necessary for them to get quality health care. The money is there. Spending it wisely, with dedication to quality, will provide savings even given the challenge of coverage for all.

Actually, and despite criticism that the ACA does little to reduce costs, this law ultimately saves taxpayers' money. Cutting overutilization is a major goal. Unnecessary tests and treatments can harm patients and are a huge reason for our bloated costs. Quality care is not the excess care contained in a "Cadillac" health plan; quality is precisely the clinically correct test or treatment chosen by the doctor and patient together—no more and no less.

American medicine is already heading in this new direction. Informed patient choice, as championed by Dr. Donald Berwick, former Medicare and Medicaid administrator, and Dr. Jack Wennberg of the Dartmouth Atlas of Health Care, will improve quality and save money. To quote Dr. Christine Cassel, president of the American Board of Internal Medicine Foundation: "Rationing is not necessary if you just don't do the things that don't help."

Yes, there are special interests against reform. But health insurance companies have been grudgingly making some concessions to improve coverage. The American Medical Association reports that private insurer error rates in reimbursement to doctors and hospitals have now been cut from 19 percent to 10 percent, which saved the country $8 billion last year. Drug companies are taking on a greater role in achieving savings from generics. The majority of doctors favor reform, and the AMA recommends that everyone have coverage, as do many other professional organizations.

All of these developments recognize the value, and the inevitability, of progress toward an improved national system. The Supreme Court decision has cleared the way.

MEDICAL ADVERTISING HURTS HEALTH CARE

Commercial messages divert resources, encourage unnecessary procedures

THE BALTIMORE SUN   **APRIL 8, 2013**   BY JAMES BURDICK

You do not have to look far to understand why U.S. health care is so expensive and uneven in quality. A recurrent offender advertises walk-in ultrasound testing of blood vessels and whatever other asymptomatic part you may choose to pay for. Worried older folks can feel lucky that it appears that Medicare would reimburse for the tests. But in fact, the whole course of tests and treatments encouraged by these ads will not improve your life expectancy—and could even have some chance of decreasing it.

Shouldn't we read these solicitations as symptoms of a very readily eliminated illness that plagues our health care system? An asymptomatic 65-year-old found to have an arterial abnormality in this mobile horror chamber is almost certain to succumb, eventually, to something else. That is, of course, unless you are told of it, go to your doctor scared, and your doctor injudiciously arranges an angiogram or a procedure. And so this harmfully profiteering practice of persuasion keeps our country's medical wheels turning.

It is worth wondering: If this test is medically indicated, why has the doctor not already ordered it? And if the testing is done and produced a normal result, the question of how often to get rechecked could arise.

One person in the ad tells of having a narrowing of the carotid artery (one of the two main arteries in the neck that go to the brain) discovered and therefore having an operation to correct it. That is very bad news for both patients seeking quality care and a country looking to control health costs. That expensive operation carries a risk of stroke and is only done in selected cases, almost never on someone totally asymptomatic (apparently the case with this patient). Money was wasted and the patient needlessly endangered.

This is not an argument for denial. Another smiling patient in that offensive advertisement is said to have had an aortic aneurysm found and repaired, which certainly could have saved his life. Not said was how urgent the aortic abnormality was, or whether cofactors such as obesity, hypertension or cardiac disease, which commonly coexist with aneurysms, might have tipped off the family doctor that the test was needed. Yet, even if a panel of doctors were to recommend that every adult have their aorta imaged to rule out the rare spontaneous aneurysm, responsible doctors surely would not recommend imaging the carotid artery in a patient without symptoms.

Is this advertising really so bad? Everybody takes ads with a grain of salt these days—right?

No. This is harmful profiteering. In "Selling Sickness," Ray Moynihan and Alan Cassels state: "With promotional campaigns that exploit our deepest fears of death, decay and disease, the $500 billion pharmaceutical industry is changing what it means to be human. . . . Because as Wall Street knows well, there's a lot of money to be made telling healthy people they're sick." The creation of this market for well people has been an explicit, aggressive strategy by drug companies. They document this in conditions ranging from high cholesterol or high blood pressure to attention deficit disorder, osteoporosis and "premenstrual dysphoric disorder."

There may be medical aspects to these conditions. The problem is that the routine of prescribing an expensive medicine with possible side effects, or doing a serious, risky operation, has become accepted by doctors and is expected by the public far in excess of a reasonable likelihood of benefit.

Moreover, these ads are expensive. The country can little afford the money spent by profitable hospitals, clinics and testing facilities to drive up their market share through advertisements. That money is needed by our health care system to extend coverage that will keep people healthy and protected from medical bankruptcy, and to help the nation's finances.

Other developed countries prohibit such medical advertising. There are good, responsible medical newsletters in the U.S. that help people think about their options realistically (although we could do better). Media fests about testing and treatment controversies highlight our lack of an authoritative national process for determining optimal care and publicizing that information.

Nevertheless, preying on people's weaknesses and fears to try to influence how they choose their medical care is ridiculous, harmful and expensive. It is time to stop it.

RX FOR ELECTRONIC RECORDS

The switch to digitizing medical information has been botched, but it's not beyond repair

THE BALTIMORE SUN   **JUNE 17, 2013**   BY JAMES F. BURDICK

A critical opportunity to improve U.S. health care finally lies within reach. In 2004, then-President George Bush announced the goal to have a national electronic health records (EHR) system in place in 10 years. Tragically, EHR development had become bogged down, dominated by dozens of contractors profiting from a competition to sell EHR services. But at last this initiative may succeed, which will have more profound benefits for our health care than has generally been appreciated.

Information is a cornerstone of medical care. As a doctor, I believe in the healing hand of a caring bedside manner, and I believe in the commitment I made to meticulous surgical skill. But I am well aware that today, more than ever, a critical part of improving the quality of patient care requires having the facts at hand for the medical team. The long delay in getting the national health records system functioning is frustrating because the potential advantages for patient care and for cost control have been deferred.

Using an effective EHR system, doctors and other health professionals will have patients' medical histories easily available. As medical knowledge advances beyond the doctor's capacity to review it during office hours, EHR will enable physicians to have indications and contraindications for their patients' care readily at hand. Billing from EHR can decrease doctors' administrative demands. A recent analysis by the business consultants McKinsey and Company found that big data could help save up to $450 billion annually in health care costs. An effective national EHR will connect the country's accountable care organizations (multi-specialty patient care teams), hospitals and doctors, decreasing the barriers that now impede national reform.

Doctors often distrust EHR, finding it inefficient and costly. But that is because of the ill-conceived private contracting strategy. Sadly, with dozens of businesses vying for the market, doctors were stuck with expensive, time-consuming attempts to guess which proprietary system to purchase. The Centers for Medicare and Medicaid Services (CMS) attempted to encourage EHR implementation with financial incentives for doctors to show "meaningful use" of their systems. But in practice, this amounted to a financial penalty for the doctors if they had guessed wrong in choosing a system that had left them, in spite of their best efforts, with the equivalent of a car without tires or a road on which to drive it. According to a recent survey by Black Book Rankings of health care information technology, up to 17 percent of physician practices plan to ditch their current EHR system. Recently, hospitals with EHR programs from EHRMagic Inc., were stranded when this company's products were decertified. Earlier this year, Marilyn Tavenner, the newly confirmed administrator of CMS, announced a pause in EHR implementation to assess problems thus far.

Meanwhile, the monstrous commoditization of the health records effort has been expanding rapidly. The Center for Responsive Politics documented the profits from $19 billion in federal grants enjoyed by big health care information technology companies from their highly funded lobbying for advantage in the 2009 economic stimulus bill. As The New York Times reported: "With money pouring in, top EHR executives are enjoying Wall Street-style paydays." Ironically, the Affordable Care Act still leaves about 30 million Americans without health care coverage.

EHR implementation can be accomplished much more effectively. The U.S. Department of Health and Human Services might establish a basic national system to serve essential needs common to all medical interactions—including billing and data collection—and distribute it to doctors. Done free or with a reasonable user fee, it would likely be less expensive than the present multibillion-dollar profit-taking. The many institutions and practices that want extras specific to their needs could purchase them independently.

Fortunately, doctors, hospitals and reimbursement systems are evolving toward more sensible, efficient practices. The American College of Surgeons and other surgical and anesthesia associations recently called for advancing interoperability in health information exchange. Dr. Steven J. Stack, chairman of the American Medical Association's board of trustees, told officials at a federal hearing that the government needs to act quickly to improve the usability of electronic health records if the technology's touted benefits are to be realized. HHS estimates that over 50 percent of doctors are now using EHRs.

These national trends exemplify an underlying reason for hope for medical reform in general: an almost spontaneous evolution of important elements is under way. It appears that we are finally poised at the tipping point of this innovation process and can soon have an effective national EHR system.

GETTING SERIOUS ABOUT A SINGLE PAYER SYSTEM

Now that Obamacare has shown the country can accept health care reform, it's time for real reform

THE BALTIMORE SUN   **MAY 1, 2014**   BY JAMES F. BURDICK

A single payer system—where the government pays for health costs—is now recognized by many in the U.S. as the best solution for our health care problems. It was taken "off the table" in 2009 by Sen. Max Baucus, A Montana Democrat who reportedly received more money from the pharmaceutical and health insurance industries than any other Congressman. But now the flood of single payer advocacy cannot be turned off by vested business interests. It is time to progress from the stereotype of single payer to having a serious discussion about it.

Ironically, even after its recent success in covering millions more Americans, the problems with the Affordable Care Act serve to illuminate the advantages of single payer. The public, although confused by the divisive rhetoric around health care reform, is coming to realize that the complexity of the law and the pursuit of insurance company profits are major problems for the ACA. Back in 2009, a majority of Americans favored a single payer-like system. The country may now lose patience with the protracted process of ACA implementation, with Republicans yapping at its heels, until 2020 when the final provision closing the Medicare prescription drug doughnut hole fully kicks in.

The 30-page H.R. 676, the single payer bill of Rep. John Conyers Jr., a Michigan Democrat, shows how simple it is to cover everyone. It provides savings through quality care—including protection from harmful overuse and efficient, timely management of chronic disease—as well as savings through national monopsony buying power and freedom from insurance business profits.

But if this bill, regularly reintroduced since 2003, is now to be taken seriously, it needs improvement. Most importantly, the proposed federal board governing both payment and care decisions lacks clinical authority and is too politicized. Instead, doctors must be granted, and must accept, responsibility for a national, private, transparent, interprofessional and data-driven mechanism to define quality options for care choices. This will free us from the snarl of various quality guidelines and protect our patients from irrelevant insurance and government interference while providing authoritative relief from over-utilization. This key improvement in the bill is also needed because coverage decisions must be removed from states, as proven by their politicized Medicaid problems.

Most politicians and health policy experts with national reputations remain silent. Some may have too great a stake in the ACA to join in the single payer adventure right away. But the country did just pass this valuable law. Even recognizing the tight political maneuvering required, this attests that the political potential for major change to our health care system is there. Luminaries who have asserted the wisdom of single payer include political commentator Bill Maher, former U.S. Secretary of State Colin Powell, Nobel-prize winning economist Paul Krugman, Sen. Bernie Sanders of the Vermont Progressive Party and former U.S. Labor Secretary Robert Reich. With even conservative columnist Ross Douthat alluding to the unspeakable in the April 5th New York Times "(ahem, single payer)" and a number of states trying to establish it on their own, supporting single payer nationally no longer appears out of reach.

There is considerable professional activity already underway with efforts that will fit the needs of a successful single payer system. These include defending against overuse by the "Choosing Care Wisely" and "Avoiding Avoidable Care" initiatives, plus the National Surgical Quality Improvement Program and the nationally successful program to abolish central line infections spearheaded by Johns Hopkins Hospital's Dr. Peter Pronovost, which are all examples of doctors and hospitals working together to share data and improve care. Placing the patient first through use of medical homes and Affordable Care Organizations is often led by doctors. In an attempt to rule out Wall Street domination, doctors and hospitals are establishing insurance plans for their patients on their own. These patient-centered programs will be more successful in a single payer context. For coordination of all of these care advisories, the American College of Physicians has recommended a national doctors board to determine core benefits.

The paper by Drs. Ray Drasga and Lawrence Einhorn, both of Indiana, in the Journal of Oncology Practice from January showing how their cancer patients would benefit from single payer is a beacon for all of medicine. Other prominent doctors recently supporting it include Dr. Nancy Snyderman of NBC and Dr. James Mitchison of The American College of Emergency Physicians. The Physicians for a National Health Program promoting single payer is now 18,000 members strong. American nurses strongly support single payer. Polls confirm that individual doctors support a national plan to provide health care to all Americans, as do the American College of Physicians and the American Medical Association.

This medical advocacy will reassure the public. Soon candidates who wish to be seen as working for all Americans will support single payer, or they will have some explaining to do.

SINGLE PAYER CRITICISM OFTEN UNTRUTHFUL

Criticism of a single payer health care system often contains misinformation.

THE BALTIMORE SUN   **FEBRUARY 10, 2015**   BY JAMES BURDICK

After discouraging election results, Vermont Gov. Peter Shumlin abandoned his effort to establish a single payer health system. This is bad news not only for the Green Mountain State but for all Americans. Governor Shumlin had been one of the only major U.S. office holders with the backbone to advocate this remedy for our ailing health care system.

The single payer system is already working well in Canada. The Canadian Medical Association strongly supports the system and is working to improve it. But some enemies of reform here are using Canadian stats and the Shumlin setback to decry the single payer system.

Arch-conservative Sally Pipes, president of the Pacific Research Institute and a prominent foe of single payer, claims that Vermont dodged a bullet. In the National Review, Ms. Pipes noted that "78 percent of Canadians over 45 are worried that they won't be able to access care when they need it."

So what? It is the rare Canadian who wants to cancel his or her health care system.

In fact, the 78 percent number she cites is from a Canadian Medical Association report, advising a change in funding strategy. The report is an endorsement of continuing the system by improving it. Of course any national system needs updating and other tinkering to keep it running smoothly. But we do not even have a functioning system in the U.S. to evaluate.

Ms. Pipes has joined other naysayers of health care reform in pointing to lengthy waiting times for care in Canada. Americans need to be aware that this is harmful propaganda. Yes, Canadians have to wait a few months for some elective procedures. They recognize this and are working on it. But Canadians typically find that if they get sick they will be well taken care of without a big bill afterward.

The truth about such comparisons with the U.S. was highlighted when a Canadian newspaper responded with indignation to Sen. Mitch McConnell's claim that the U.S. health care system was superior to Canada's because of the waiting times. A spokesperson for the Republican senator's home state of Kentucky, asked by an Ontario newspaper reporter what waiting times were typical in the U.S., admitted to not knowing what these were but said "anyway, they can always go to an E.R."

A country's waiting times represent averages for all citizens. In the U.S., our citizens without insurance would have to be included in our averages for comparison with other countries that do have national health coverage. In effect, the skewed comparison with other countries would be so distorted as to be meaningless.

This sort of disinformation is common in the health care debate: Statistics are applied manipulatively, leading to grossly incorrect generalizations being used to criticize "universal" health care systems. This is not civic discourse. It is nothing but a big lie.

But let's look further ahead. Given the extensive benefits for many from the Affordable Care Act, how do business interests vested in the status quo argue that more comprehensive reform is not the answer? For that big lie, proponents of the status quo say we must blame the ACA. In truth, the political impediments that prevented more complete legislation in 2010 are the cause of the trouble we've had.

With the ACA we made a good start, but there is much more to be done in order to enable our health care system to work for everyone. It is critical to recognize and neutralize malicious misinformation directed against further health care reform. The real fix lies in the prospect of a single payer system along the lines of the Vermont legislation.

Although moving directly to a national system such as single payer would be the most prompt and effective next step, the present political climate provides little hope for this. Perhaps gradual coalescence of state programs would work. After all, gradual provincial participation is the way the federal Canadian health care system grew to maturity. Efforts such as those in Vermont, and the similar "Health Care is a Human Right" campaign in Maryland, provide encouraging steps toward that goal.

But even that is a political fight few of our politicians seem to have the gumption to wage right now. Keeping the debate truthful will at least level the playing field.

BERNIE SANDERS FOR THE WIN

Bernie Sanders makes the best sense for America says Hopkins surgery professor.

THE BALTIMORE SUN   **MAY 13 2015**   BY JAMES BURDICK

Sen. Bernie Sanders is in the presidential race; this is wonderful news. The dissatisfaction people feel with what the government is doing and where we are going as a country has been the conservative's territory to exploit, but no longer. Fear is growing that the opportunities for the richest Americans to buy the 2016 election, from the president on down, have never seemed better.

But Bernie Sanders, a Vermont independent, cannot be bought. And as president he can bring helpful, healing answers to address that dissatisfaction. Recently I talked with him about health care reform. He had just gotten off the Senate floor after another attempt to instill some thought into a debate. The issue was whether large employers should be able to avoid providing health coverage to employees by changing the definition of full-time work from 30 hours to 40 hours a week. Senator Sanders—forceful, energetic, full of camaraderie and common sense as always—declared that in other countries people would not have the faintest idea what the senators were talking about.

"The argument of whether you provide health insurance for people who work 30 hours a week or whether they work 40 hours a week—whoa!" Mr. Sanders said on the floor. "In every major country on earth, health care is a right of all people."

At the Senate hearing that morning he got three witnesses, two of them Republicans, to agree with him about the advantages of a national health care program. The educator from Maine, the restaurant CEO and the pizzeria owner, the only Democrat, agreed that their efforts would be better if they did not have to provide health care for their employees as well. Said the restaurant CEO: "From your lips to God's ear."

In talking with Senator Sanders, author of the Senate single payer health care bill, I could see his clear unremitting view of what's wrong in the country and where to go. The country needs to hear his convictions—and really listen.

He understands that financiers and their business cronies exploited and evaded government intentions, broke the bank for almost everyone in 2008, and have not been punished for their actions. If the U.S. had ramped up needed spending on government projects, the anemic recovery from the Great Recession could have been far better for us—except maybe for the richest 1 percent. And Republican gerrymandering has already rendered many more districts automatically red for the 2016 elections, as it appears on the charts right now, at any rate.

We need Senator Sanders to intervene. In spite of the improvements achieved by the Obama administration, we still have the highest joblessness in recent history, minimal opportunity for our disadvantaged to get housing and education, millions of citizens still without health care coverage and nearly unchecked, expensive American violence across the globe, which only worsens our best international interests.

The straightforward Sanders approach involves appropriate government intervention where needed. No market-based democracy can be sustained without government rules to keep it in line with the interests of the country. This is contrary to the Republican mainstream in principle, although if you mention roads, food safety, Medicare—or, of course, defense—their opposition to government involvement melts away. That makes no sense.

Bernie Sanders makes sense. That is why I, as a medical doctor, support his views on health care reform and why he will be a great president. And we must not let anyone representing the 1 percent get us hung up on the label during the primaries. He is certainly not a socialist. As a Democrat I agree that he embodies the best in that party, but even if you call him an independent, he has the best interests of 100 percent of the country in mind. And he has the vision and political craftsmanship to achieve his goal.

All it will take is just over half of the voters choosing Mr. Sanders. Of course it has to be the majority that will tip the electoral college, and no interference from hanging chads and so on. The country needs everyone to get out and vote for Senator Sanders in this one to overcome those past heartbreaks. In spite of our troubles, we have made real progress in the past eight years. We cannot afford to let that promise slip away.

NOTES

CHAPTER 1

1. The Physicians for a National Healthcare Program is the most prominent advocacy group, with voluminous publications on single payer. The term single payer should be reserved for those systems in which a government reimburses providers of health care for all of its citizens:

Diamond F 2013. A Conversation With Uwe E. Reinhardt, PhD: Health Care Deserves More Respect Managed Care http://www.managedcaremag.com /linkout/2013/11/21.

Hussey, P. Anderson, G. 2003. A Comparison of Single- and Multi-payer Health Insurance Systems and Options for Reform. Health Policy 66:215.

Lewin, J. 2014. Reverberations About a Single-Payer (Communist?) Health System. The Lewin Report, May 26, 2014.

Skuka, R. 1994. Health Care Reform in the 1990s: An Analysis of the Problems and Three Proposals. Social Work 39:580.

Sparer, M. et al 2009 Exploring the Concept of Single Payer. J of Health Politics, Policy and Law, 34: 447.

But it is less complicated to use the term single payer more generally for any government program that provides universal coverage, as long as shortcomings in any variation on the basic definition are recognized. Some distinguish single payer as funding completely by the government but with private delivery of care (as in Canada) from "socialized medicine" as in the United Kingdom where the doctors and hospitals are also owned by the government (Tuohy, C. 2009. Single Payers, Multiple Systems: The Scope and Limits of Subnational Variation under a Federal Health policy Framework. J Health Politics, Policy and Law 34:453). In this book I emphasize universal access, which leads at least to consideration of a national single payer program as most cost-effective.

2. Levy, J. 2015. U.S. Uninsured Rate Continues to Fall. http://www.gallup.com /poll/167798/uninsured-rate-continues-fall.aspx. This Gallup Poll found 15.9% uninsured in early 2014, down from a high of 18%, and figures show it is dropping more.

3. Wilper, A. 2009. Health Insurance and Mortality in US Adults. Am J Public Health. 99:2289.

4. Healthday 2009. Most Insured Adults Worry about Health Care Costs [homepage on the Internet].; 2009 [updated March 09, 2009]. Available from: http:// healthday.com/Article.asp?AID=624749.

5. Kaiser Family Foundation. 2009. Kaiser Health Tracking Poll. February, 2009.

6. Fronstin P, 2006. Survey Finds Rising Costs a Prime Driver in Americans' Increasing Dissatisfaction with U.S. Health Care System. Washington, DC: Employee Benefit Research Institute; 2006 October 25, 2006. Report # 752.

7. Mahar, M. 2008. Getting Health Care Polling Right. Health Beat by Maggie Mahar http://www.healthbeatblog.com/2008/07/getting-health/.

8. See note 5 above.

9. Himmelstein, D. 2009 Medical Bankruptcy in the United States, 2007: Results of a National Study. Am J Med. 122:741.

10. Abelson R. 2009. Many with Insurance Still Bankrupted by Health Crises. The New York Times. July 1, 2009.

11. See note 4 above.

12. Pear, R. 2015. Health Insurance Companies Seek Big Rate Increases. The New York Times Jul 6, 2015.

13. Long, S. 2014. QuickTake: Number of Uninsured Adults Continues to Fall under the ACA: Down by 8.0 Million in June 2014 The Urban Institute Health Reform Monitoring, Survey July 10, 2014.

14. McCanne, D. 2015. Has Obamacare Turned Voters Against Sharing the Wealth? QOTD 20 April, 2015 in ref. to Thomas B. Edsall, The New York Times, April 15, 2015.

15. Anderson, G. 2007. Health Spending in OECD Countries in 2004: An Update. Health Aff (Millwood). 26:1481.

16. Weimer,D. 2010 Medical Governance. Values, Expertise and Interests in Organ Transplantation. Washington DC: Georgetown U. Press.

17.Weisbart, E., 2011. A Single Payer System Would Reduce US Health Care Costs. http://virtualmentor.ama-assn.org/2012/11/oped1-1211.html. Other PNHP documents include:

McCanne,D. 2015. Doctors Group Hails Reintroduction of Medicare For All Bill. Quote-of-the-Day February 4, 2015.

Drasga, R, Einhorn, L. 2014. Why Doctors Should Support Single Payer J Oncol. Practice 10:7–12.

Dvorak, D. 2013. Beyond Obamacare. How a Single-Payer System Can Save Health Care in the United States. Minnesota Medicine, April, 34.

Sullivan, K. 2009. Two-thirds of Americans support Medicare-for-All (#1 of 6) PNHP Blog Dec. 6, 2009.

McCormick, D. 2004. Single-Payer National Health Insurance. Physicians' Views. Arch.; Int. Med. 164:300.

Physicians Working Group. 2003. Proposal of the Physicians Working Group for Single-Payer National Health Insurance. JAMA 290:798.

Over the past quarter century, there have also been a variety of contributions to this thinking from non-physicians and others not writing from a PNHP soapbox, particularly just before and during the Clinton years, often stressing an urgent need for single payer reform:

DeGrazia, D. 1996. Why the United States Should Adopt a Single-Payer System of Health Care Finance. *Kennedy Institute of Ethics Journal* 6.2: 145.

Grumbach, K. 1989. National Health Insurance in America—Can We Practice With It? Can We Continue to Practice Without It? West. J. Med. 151:210.

Jost, T. 1993. Selling Cost Containment. American J of Law and Medicine, XIX: 95.

Karpatkin R, 1993. Single-payer Plan Provides Best Health Choice. (President, Consumers Union) NYT Letter to the Editor Nov.16, 1993.

Lightfoote, J. 1996. Single-Payer Health Insurance Systems: National Myths and Immovable Mountains. J Nat. Med. Assoc. 88:217.

McIlrath, S. 1994 Surgeons back single payer. ACS says national plan would protect patients' choice of doctor. (American College of Surgeons) American Medical News | February 28, 1994.

(BUT note the response then: Montague, Jim 1994. Surgeons Support for Single-Payer System Fuels Flare up Over Reform. Hospitals & Health Networks 68.6 (Mar 20): 114).

Nichols, L. 2008. On the Moral Superiority of a Single-Payer System The Hastings center Report 38: 36.

Skuka, R. 1994. Health Care Reform in the 1990s: An Analysis of the Problems and Three Proposals. Social Work 39:580.

Weil, T. 1992. A Universal Access Plan: a Step Toward National Health Insurance. Hospital and Health Services Administration 37:37.

The legal preference for tax-based health care financing was expounded upon comprehensively by: Bodenheimer,T., Sullivan, K. (1997. The Logic of Tax-Based Financing for Health Care. Int. J. of Health Services 27:409–425.) and Kip Sullivan has followed with several articles on developments over the years, including with PNHP.

With the prospect and commitment by President Obama to reform came renewed advocacy for single payer:

Barrett, B., Stiles, M. 2006. Yes to Single-Payer Reform. Health Affairs 25:293.

Tara Culp-Ressler, 2014. Beyond Obamacare Health Care as a Human Right. ThinkProgress

19 July 14.

Fein, O. 2010. Keep the Single Payer Vision. Medical Care 48:759.

DelReal J. 2014. Tom Harkin: We Should Have Done Single Payer Health Reform. The Washington Post Dec. 3 2014.

18. Institute of Medicine, 2001–4. Consequences of Being Uninsured (six volumes) IOM Committee on the Consequences of Being Uninsured. Other reviews have looked at details of implementation. An extensive review (Tuohy, C. 2009. Single Payers, Multiple Systems: The Scope and Limits of Subnational Variation under a Federal Health policy Framework. J Health Politics, Policy and Law 34:453) of the Canadian system with regard to balance between national and subnational control, showing provincial variability in drug coverage but more uniformity in paying doctors and hospitals, contains lessons for the U.S. in moving forward with a national health system. A Hastings Center report provides a proposal by DeGrazia (DeGrazia,D., 2008. Single Payer Meets Managed Competition: the Case for Public Funding and Private Delivery. The Hastings Center report 38:23.) for single payer with managed competition that strays far from the freedom from copayments that most associate with single payer (which he justifies by the morality argument that it is the feasible alternative) with commentaries:

Kaebnik, G. 2008. Reforming Health Care Reform. Hastings Center Report 38:2.

Menzel, P. 2008. A Path to Universal Access. The Hastings Center Report 38: 34.

Newhouse, J. 2004. The Institute of Medicine's Clarion Call for Universal Coverage. Health Affairs Web Exclusive W 4:179.

Several have predicted the "conservatives worst fear," that problems with the complexity of the Affordable Care Act will lead the U.S. to a government-run national health system:

Krugman P. 2014. Stealth Single Payer. New York Times July 30, 2014.

Jasper, W. 2013 ObamaCare: the Plan is to Transition to Single-Payer Socialized Medicine. The New American Friday, Nov. 8 2013. www. thenewamerican. com.

Folbre, N. 2013. The Single Payer Alternative. Today's Economist. November 25, 2013, 12:01 am.

American nurses, particularly from California, have been in favor of single payer (Keepnews, D. 2009. U.S. Health Reform: A Continuing Imperative. Policy Politics Nursing Practice 10:92.).

19. Physicians Working Group 2003. Proposal of the Physicians Working Group for Single-Payer National Health Insurance. JAMA 290:798.

20. Some advocate that the funding for a national system of universal care be through

insurance companies with a public option, giving as examples the Federal Employees Health Benefits Plan and the system in Switzerland and The Netherlands, rather than a federal fund (Menzel, P. 2008. A Path to Universal Access. The Hastings Center Report. 38: 34.). But the need for tight regulation to control costs and avoid risky patients accumulating in the public option would leave these companies unrecognizable as anything like the insurance business in the U.S. now. Batistella opposed the concept that medical professionals can be relied upon to control care decisions but he would require instead a complicated safety net strategy that would defeat much of the simplicity of a straight-forward single payer system (Battistella, R. 1993. Universal Access to Health Care: A Practical Perspective. J. Health and Human Resources Administration 16:6.). Steinmo described implacable U.S. institutional obstruction to comprehensive national health insurance to explain the failure of attempts to establish it in 1948, 1965, 1974, and 1978 as well as in 1990 (Steinmo, S. 1995. It's the Institutions, Stupid! Why Comprehensive National Health Insurance Always Fails in America. J Health Politics, Policy and Law 20:329.).

Other measured perspectives on the single payer option have appeared, generally indicating its inapplicability to America:

BruceMcF 2014. The Health Care Exchanges and Plan A Health Care Reform Economic Populist Jan 25, 2014.

Hussey, P. Anderson, G. 2003. A Comparison of Single- and Multi-payer Health Insurance Systems and Options for Reform. Health Policy 66:215.

Kemble, S. A Better Idea for United States Health Care—The Balanced Choice Proposal. Hawaii Medical Journal 69: 294.

Norato, J. 1997. National Health Care Reform and a Single-Payer System: Messiah or pariah? J. Health and Human Services Admin. 19:341.

Sparer, M. et al 2009 Exploring the Concept of Single Payer. J of Health Politics, Policy and Law, 34: 447.

Wolfe S. 1992. Universal Access in Canada. Questions of Equity Remain. Health PAC Bull. 22:29.

Newhouse, J. 2004. The Institute of Medicine's Clarion Call for Universal Coverage Health Affairs Web Exclusiive W 4:179.

Addressing these skeptics: Reinhardt, U. 2007. Why Single-Payer Health Systems Spark Endless Debate. BMJ 334:881.

21. Lu, J. 2007. Horizontal Equity in Health Care Utilization: Evidence from Three High-Income Asian Economies. Soc.Sci.Med. 64:199;

Schoen,C. 2004 Inequities in Access to Medical Care in Five Countries: Findings from the 2001 Commonwealth Fund International Health Policy Survey Health Policy 67:309;

van Doorslaer,E. 2006 Inequalities in Access to Medical Care by Income in Developed Countries. Canadian Medical Association journal 174:177;

van Doorslaer,E.; 2008. Horizontal Inequities in Australia's Mixed Public/Private Health Care System. Health Policy 86:97.

22. Zuesse, E. 2014. Hillary Clinton likes Obamacare and Opposes Single Payer

Health Insurance. The Huffington Post/ Politics. Posted 03/01/2014, updated 5/01/2014.

23. Emanuel E. 2008 The Problem with Single-Payer Plans. Hastings Center Report 38:38. The Heritage Foundation, lambasting the Canadian system (Frogue, J. et al 2001. Buyer Beware The Failure of Single Payer Health Care. Heritage Foundation), is against single payer (Book, R. 2009. Single Payer. Why Government Run Health Care Will Harm Both Patients and Doctors WebMemo #2381 on Health Care April 3, 2009.) joining with the AMA, at least historically (Palmisano D. 2004. The Danger of Single Payer Health Insurance. Arch Intern Med. 164:228.) Ackermann (Ackermann R. 2003. Support for National Health Insurance among US Physicians: a National Survey. Ann Intern Med 139: 795.) disputed the PNHP poll showing that 63.5% of doctors think that single payer would work best (McCormick, D. 2004. Single-Payer National Health Insurance. Physicians' Views. Arch. Int. Med. 164:300.), citing a poll showing physician support at 26%, a result that has since been criticized by Sullivan in the PNHP bulletin (Sullivan, K. 2009. Two-thirds of Americans support Medicare-for-All (#1 of 6) PNHP Blog Dec. 6, 2009.)

Incidentally, this battle of polls is instructive, and for those wondering why there are not more poll data cited in my book—read, in addition to Sullivan, Maggie Mahar's expose about their treachery (Mahar, M. 2008. Getting Health Care Polling Right. Health Beat by Maggie Mahar http://www.healthbeatblog.com/2008/07/getting-health/).

Articles and discussion against single payer also cite foreign problems with health care:

Hogberg, D. 2014. Statement before the Senate HELP Subcommittee on Primary Health and Aging March 11, 2014.

Frogue, J. et al 2001. Buyer Beware The Failure of Single Payer Health Care. (Heritage Foundation)

Book, R. 2009. Single Payer Why Government Run Health Care Will Harm Both Patients and Doctors WebMemo #2381 on Health Care April 3, 2009.

Other criticisms of single payer claim absence of its inclusion in discussions of "respected policy centers and stakeholder coalitions":

Lewin, J. 2013 The Elusive Path to Health Care Sustainability. (JAMA 310:1669.),

Some aver that it lacks ability to achieve savings or improve simplicity and quality:.

Jones, W. 1994. Single Payer: Do Government-Run Programs Meet America's Needs? Benefits Quarterly 10:13.

Waldman D 2014. The Health of Healthcare Part VI Be Prepared. J Med Pract Manage. 30:64.

Zycher, B. 2007. Comparing Public and Private Health Insurance: Would a Single-Payer System Save Enough to Cover the Uninsured? Medical Progress Report No. 5, Oct. 2007. Center for Medical Progress at the Manhattan Institute.

24. Porter, M. 2013. The Strategy That Will Fix Health Care. Harvard Business Review October 2013 Issue. Reprint: R1310B

25. Burdick, J. 2014 Getting Serious about a Single Payer System. The Baltimore Sun May 1, 2014. (See Appendix)

26. See note 25 above.

27. Salkever, D. 1983. Economics, Health Economics and Health Administration. J Health Adm Educ. 1:225.

28. Diamond F 2013. A Conversation With Uwe E. Reinhardt, PhD: Health Care Deserves More Respect. Managed Care http://www.managedcaremag.com /linkout/2013/11/21.

CHAPTER 2

1. Krugman, P. 2014. Secret Deficit Lovers. New York Times Oct. 9.

2. World Bank 2015: Health expenditure, total (% of GDP) | Data | Table http:// data.worldbank.org/indicator/SH.XPD.TOTL.ZS accessed 8 Feb 2015.

3. Mahar, M. 2006. Money Driven Medicine. NY,NY: Harper Collins.

4. Rosenthal, E. 2014. Paying Til it Hurts. New York Times articles from June 2, 2013 to DEC. 18, 2014.

5. Brill, S. 2013. Bitter Pill. Time Magazine. April 4, 2013.

6. Brill, S. 2015. America's Bitter Pill. NY,NY: Random House.

7. CMS, Office of the Actuary, National Health Expenditures Data. 2013. highlights accessed Feb., 2015

8. Schroeder, S. 2011. Personal Reflections on the High Cost of American Health Care. JAMA 171:722.

9. Abelson, R. 2012. For Hospitals and Insurers, New Fervor to Cut Costs. New York Times May 23, 2012.

10. New York Tomes 2014. Editorial Obamacare Deserves Some Credit for the Good News About Healthcare. 22 November 2014.

11. Bernstein, J. 2009. Impact of the Economy on Health Care Robert Wood Johnson, Changes in Health Care Financing and Organization Issue Brief, August, 2009.

12. Krugman P. 2011. The Hijacked Commission. November 11, 2010 New York Times

13. Halverson, G. 2007. Health Care Reform Now! San Francisco: John Wiley and Sons

14. Brookings Engelberg Center for Health Care Reform. 2013. Bending the Curve Person-Centered Health Care Reform: A Framework for Improving Care and Slowing Health Care Cost Growth

15. eHealthinsurance 2009. Health Insurance eeeeHealthnnin 11 minutes! [Internet].;

updated 30 September, 2009. Available from: https://www.ehealthinsurance.com.

16. Halle M. 2009. Hidden Costs of Health Care. Healthreform.gov June 22,p. 1–3.

17. Haynes V. 2009. Area Firms Tweak Benefit Plans. The Washington Post, 2009 June 23, 2009.

18. Reinhardt, U. 2011. The Economics of Privately Sponsored Social Insurance. http://economix.blogs.nytimes.com/2011/04/01/the-economics-of-privately-sponsored-social-insurance/ accessed 8 May, 2011.

19. Sessions S. 2009. The Proposed Excise Tax on Employee Health Insurance: Good idea, or Too Clever by 40%? JAMA 302:2252.

20. Casalino L. 2009. What does it cost physician practices to interact with health insurance plans? Health Aff (Millwood). 2009 Jul–Aug;28(4):w533–43.

21. Dobson, A. 2014. Health Care Spending Slowdown: The Consumer Paradox Report. Prepared for the Federation of American Hospitals, July 23.

22. Potter, W. 2009. Testimony before the U.S. Senate Committee on Commerce, Science and Transportation, U.S. Senate Committee on Commerce, Science and Transportation, U.S. Senate, (June 24, 2009, 2009).

23. Carson B. 1999. The Big Picture. 1st ed. Grand Rapids, MI: Zondervan Publishing House; 1999.

24. Pear, R. 2014. Administration to Investigate Insurers for Bias Against Costly Conditions. New York Times, 22 Dec., 2014.

25. Kaiser Foundation 2015. Premium Changes in the ACA's Health Insurance Marketplaces, 2014–2015. VISUALIZING HEALTH POLICY The Kaiser Family Foundation.

26. McCanne, D. 2015. Open Enrollment 2015. Re-Enrollment Snapshot. Quote-of-the-Day, 2 March 2015.

27. Shin, P. 2015. Community Health Centers and Medicaid at 50. Health Affairs 34:1096.

28. Song, K. 2009. Big Demand, Grim Outlook for State Basic Health Plan. Seattle Times Nov. 24, 2009. http://www.seattletimes.com/health/big-demand-grim-outlook-for-state-basic-health-plan/

29. Wolfe,R. 2010. Budget Cuts Dilute Children's Health Coverage. USA Today May 25, http://www.usatoday.com/news/washington/2010-05-24-children-coverage_N.htm

30. Rowland D. 2006. Medicaid: Facing the facts. Healthc Financ Manage. 60:66.

31. McCanne D. 2007. Extra Benefits of Medicare Advantage Plans. Qotd 23 Mar 2007.

32. Institute of Medicine (US) 2003 Committee on the Consequences of Uninsurance.

A Shared Destiny. Community Effects of Uninsurance. Washington (DC): National Academies Press: "*A Shared Destiny* is the fourth in a series of six reports on the problems of uninsurance in the United States. This report examines how the quality, quantity, and scope of community health services can be adversely affected by having a large or growing uninsured population. It explores the overlapping financial and organizational basis of health services delivery to uninsured and insured populations, the effects of community uninsurance on access to health care locally, and the potential spillover effects on a community's economy and the health of its citizens. The committee believes it is both mistaken and dangerous to assume that the persistence of a sizable uninsured population in the United States harms only those who are uninsured."

In a followup six years later (IOM 2009 America s Uninsured Crisis Consequences for Health and Health Care.Institute of Medicine (US) Committee on Health Insurance Status and Its Consequences. Washington (DC): National Academies Press) the IOM found:

"Evaluating the effects of community-level uninsurance rates on insured populations and health care delivery systems is challenging. Even when the rates of uninsurance are comparable, uninsurance may not affect all communities in the same way.

The available research suggests that when community-level rates of uninsurance are relatively high, insured adults in those communities are more likely to have difficulties obtaining needed health care and to be less satisfied with the care they receive. . . . The specific contribution of uninsurance to these problems is not well-established. Nevertheless, well-documented fault lines in local health care delivery are particularly vulnerable to the financial pressures that may be exacerbated by higher uninsurance. . . .

These problems can only worsen existing disparities between communities in the supply of provider services and other health care resources and may have potentially serious implications for the quality and timeliness of care for insured people, as well as uninsured people, in these communities."

Inadequate health care and a history of incarceration track together in states and this harms health of others in those states (Schnittker J, 2015. The Institutional Effects of Incarceration Spillovers From Criminal Justice to Health Care. Milbank Q. 93:516). Even in China, recent advances in urban health care for the poor was shown to benefit others who are better off in the community (Pan, J. 2015. Health Insurance and Health Status Exploring the Causal Effect from a Policy Intervention. J Health Econ. 2015 Sep 8. doi: 10.1002/hec.3225. [Epub ahead of]). As an extreme example, the rapid spread of Ebola in poor African countries compared with the relative ease from a public health standpoint of controlling it and preventing an epidemic here in the U.S. is testament to the value of a strong public health system for everyone.

33. McCanne, D. 2009. Private insurers, Wall Street, Tiny Tim, and my Granddaughter Quote-of-the-Day, 23 Dec. 2009.

34. Aaron, H. 2003. The Costs of Health Care Administration in the United States

and Canada—Questionable Answers to a Questionable Question. NEJM 349:801.

35. Robinson, J. 1997. Use and Abuse of the Medical Loss Ratio to Measure Health Plan Performance. Health Affairs 16:176.

36. Yoest P. 2009. Group Tallies Families' 'Hidden Health Tax'. The Wall Street Journal, 2009 May 28, 2009;Sect. Article. 46. McCanne, D. 2009 Is Health Insurers Profit 2% or 22%? quote-of-the-day@mccanne.org 26 Oct. The Affordable Care act specifies that, for any year with a lower medical loss ratio than the approximately 15–20% that is negotiated, the insurance companies will pay back the difference to their subscribers, and end of the year checks have begun to arrive. Nevertheless, economic arguments that challenge the calculations comparing U.S. private health care administration costs with, e.g. the Canadian single payer system exist. For instance, a calculation noted above by Dr. Aaron of relative earning power and salaries (Aaron, H. 2003. The Costs of Health Care Administration in the United States and Canada—Questionable Answers to a Questionable Question. NEJM 349:801), seems to allow the insurance business to wiggle out of the charge of excess administrative costs. The Brookings Institute recently reviewed how to "Bend the Curve" of rising health care costs downwards with mention of other administrative costs. Perhaps revealing bias, it did not identify the possibility of large administrative costs of running private insurance as a target for savings (Brookings Institute 2013. Bending the Curve. Person-Centered Health Care Reform: A Framework for Improving Care and Slowing Health Care Cost Growth Engelberg Center for Health Care Reform. Report April, 2013.).

37. Brownlee S. 2008. 5 Myths About Our Ailing Health-care System. Washington Post. 2008 November 23, 2008;Sect. B (B03).

38. See note 37 above.

39. PNHP; 2008. Is Administrative Savings a Myth? [Internet]. [updated 21 November, 2008.] Available from: quote-of-the-day@mccanne.org.
    The various administrative costs due to the complexity of health care in the U.S. are included in the comparison by Steffie Woolhandler and colleagues of American and Canadian administrative costs (Woolhandler S. 2003. Costs of Health Care Administration in the United States and Canada. N Engl J Med. 349:768. They document administrative costs for health care in the U.S. that are three times those in Canada. They say that we could save $209 billion annually (Woolhandler S, 2004. Health care Administration in the United States and Canada: Micromanagement, macro costs. Int J Health Serv. 34:65), although Aaron has disputed that figure (Aaron, H. 2003. The Costs of Health Care Administration in the United States and Canada—Questionable Answers to a Questionable Question. NEJM 349:801).
    Medicare saves on administrative costs, but even that has been subject to "privatization" and so may not be a best case. It has been argued by some, including the AMA, that Medicare administration has an advantage in comparison to private insurance because of federal activity outside of Medicare costs. Maybe so, but that would hardly be enough to erase the clear superiority of Medicare with

its low administrative costs. Moreover, if this truly is an advantage, it is hardly an argument against a government health care program.

Reinhardt notes that excessive administration costs in the U.S. would be about $150 billion (Reinhardt, U. 2011. The Economics of Privately Sponsored Social Insurance. http://economix.blogs.nytimes.com/2011/04/01/the-economics-of -privately-sponsored-social-insurance/ accessed 8 May, 2011.). Extrapolating from California, a bastion of lean third party payers, James Kahn estimates billing and insurance related costs at 20% of private insurance payments (Kahn, J. 2005. The Cost Of Health Insurance Administration In California: Estimates For Insurers, Physicians, And Hospitals. *Health Aff* 24:629.), which extrapolated nationally give $230 billion spent on insurance administrative expenditures that would be better spent on health care.

There are many other similar estimates:

Paul Krugman estimates we could save $200 billion (Krugman, P. 2005. One nation, Uninsured. The New York Times. June 13, 2005;Sect. OpEd).

Fein, O. 2007. professor at the Weil Medical College of Cornell, citing Wool-handler, http://www.medscape.com/viewarticle/553998, stresses the problems insurance creates for doctors, and estimates that insurance takes $350 billion from patient care and shifts it into "marketing, collections, paperwork, underwriting, and inflated CEO salaries."

In December 2009 a Lewin Group report (Sheils J, 2009. Comparing the Cost and Coverage Impacts of the House and Senate Leadership Reform Bills: Long term costs for governments, employers, families and providers. The Lewin Group; 2009 December 7, 2009. Report No.: 498093) predicted from analysis of the House and Senate Leadership reform bills that they would result in an increase of over $80 billion in administrative costs.

McCanne, reviewing all of the budget impact studies, concludes that we could "free up enough funds to cover our nation's unmet health care needs" merely by recovering the $4000 billion in wasted administrative costs predicted over the next decade (McCann, D. 2009 citing Sheils and Haught Analyze the House and Senate bills [homepage on the Internet]. Quote-of-the-Day: Physicians for a National Health Program; 2009 (updated December 15, 2009. Available from: quote-of-the-day@mccanne.org).

So the contrary arguments by private health insurance proponents notwithstanding, this business involves large, unnecessary administrative costs in the U.S.

40. Burdick, J. 2013. Medical Advertising Hurts Health Care The Baltimore Sun, April 8, 2013. (See Appendix)

CHAPTER 3

1. Lazris, A. 2014. Curing Medicare. CreateSpace Independent Publishing Platform, N. Charleston, S. Carolina.

2. Dusheiko, M. 2008. Explaining Trends in Concentration of Healthcare Commissioning in the English NHS. Health Econ. 17:907.

3. Stempniak, M. 2014. Clinical Leaders Urged to be More Transparent with Patients. 08.25.14 Hosptals and Health Networks Daily Staff Writer hhnmag.com/display/HHN-news-article.dhtml?dcrPath=%2Ftemplatedata%2FHF_Common%2FNewsArticle%2Fdata%2FHHN%2FDaily%2F2014%2FAug%2F-stempniak-IHI-transparency-patient-costs.

4. MacDonald, I. 2014. The Role of Clinical Leaders in Accountable Care Organizations. Fierce Healthcare July 10, 2014.

5. Carrier, M. 2012. Hospitals' Geographic Expansion in Quest of Well-insured Patients: Will the Outcome be Better Care, More Cost, or Both? Health Affairs 31:827.

6. Baker, L. 2014. Vertical Integration: Hospital Ownership Of Physician Practices Is Associated With Higher Prices And Spending. Health Aff. 33:756.

7. Friedberg, M. 2015. Effects of Health Care Payment Models on Physician Practice in the United States Rand/AMA http://www.rand.org/content/dam/rand/pubs/research_reports/RR800/RR869/RAND_RR869.pdf

8. McGinnis T. 2015. A Unicorn Realized? Promising Medicaid ACO Programs Really Exist. http://www.commonwealthfund.org/publications/blog/2015/mar/unicorn-realized-medicaid-acos. Wednesday, March 11, 2015.

9. Hartzband P. 2014. How Medical Care is Being Corrupted NYT Nov. 18, 2014.

10. Bodenheimer T. 2007. The Primary Care-Specialty Income Gap: Why it Matters. Ann.Intern.Med.146:301.

11. Pena-Dolhun, E., 2001. Unlocking Specialists Attitudes Toward Primary Care Gatekeepers J.Fam.Pract. 50:1032.

12. Jones,I. 2004. Is Patient Involvement Possible When Decisions Involve Scarce Resources? A Qualitative Study of Decision-Making in Primary Care. Soc.Sci.Med. 59:93.

13. See note 1 above.

14. See note 9 above.

15. See note 12 above.

16. Hall,M. 2008. Learning from the Legal History of Billing for Medical Fees J Gen Intern Med. 23:1257.

17. Jepsen, B. 2014. As Long As Doctor Is Quarterback, AMA Set To Endorse Team-Based Care. Forbes Jun 6, 2014. http://www.forbes.com/sites/brucejapsen/2014/06/06/as-long-as-doctor-is-quarterback-ama-set-to-endorse-team-based-care/

18. MacDonald, I. 2014. The Role of Clinical Leaders in Accountable Care Organizations. Heritage Medical Systems President Mark Wagar: Physicians key to ACO Success. Fierce Healthcare July 10, 2014.

19. See note 2 above.

20. Emanuel E. 2008. The Perfect Storm of Overutilization. JAMA 299:2789.

21. Gawande, A. 2009. The Cost Conundrum. The New Yorker www.newyorker.com/magazine/2009/06/01.

22. Wennberg, J. 2010. Tracking Medicine NYC: Oxford University Press.

23. Yasaitis, L. 2009. Hospital Quality and Intensity of Spending: Is there an Association? Health Aff (Millwood). 2009 Jul–Aug;28(4):w566–72.

24. Fisher, E. 2003. The Implications of Regional Variations in Medicare Spending. Part 2: Health Outcomes and Satisfaction with Care. Ann Intern Med. 138:288.

25. Dunn, A. 2013. Geographic Variation in Commercial Medical-Care Expenditures. J. Health Econ. 32:1153. Recently it was reported that there is a reciprocal relationship in spending patterns, with higher private spending in locales with lower public spending (Quealy, K. 2015. The Experts Were Wrong About the Best Places for Better and Cheaper Health Care, The New York Times Dec. 15, 2015), This could complicate the overutilization issue. But it probably represents different patterns of the same problem of unexplained variability in the different segments of the population receiving health care through private vs. public sources. Peter Orszag (former Director of the Office of Management and Budget) noted that this report does not negate the significance of overuse (Blog "Today's New York Times piece on health spending variation". New York Times Dec 15, 2015). Moreover, the Quealy article does not mention the impact on patients of this variability in spending on care.

26. Sheiner L. 2014. Why the Geographic Variation in Health Care Spending Can't Tell us Much about the Efficiency or Quality of our Health Care System. Final Conference Draft to be presented at the Fall 2014 Brookings Panel on Economic Activity Sept. 11, 2014.

27. Nye, G. 2014. Geographic Variations in Health Care Costs. Report for the Jayne Kaskinas and Ted Giovanis Foundation for Health and Policy.

28. See note 22 above.

29. Mahar, M. 2006. Money-Driven Medicine. New York: HarperCollins

30. Wulff, K. 2011. Can Coverage be Rescinded When Negative Trial Results Threaten a Popular Procedure? The Ongoing Saga of Vertebroplasty. Health Aff. 30: 2269.

31. Cooper, R. 2009. States with More Physicians Have Better-Quality Health Care," Health Affairs 28: w91–w102.

32. Baicker, K. 2009. Cooper's Analysis Is Incorrect. Health Aff. 28 w116–w118.

33. Skinner, J. 2009. The Elusive Connection Between Health Care Spending and Quality. Health Aff. 28:w119–123 4 Dec. 2008.

34. As an example of the PNHP view, a paper about incorrect care is cited (McGlynn, E. 2003. The Quality of Health Care Delivered to Adults in the United States.

NEJM 348:2635.) because although it convincingly demonstrates a problem with quality shown by underuse of indicated care, the paper also concludes that overuse was low. The problem is that, while this study used appropriate, accepted criteria for underuse, there are no statistically validated tests to score for overutilization, so that conclusion is wrong because this was not really measured. In fact how to recognize overuse patient by patient is an important area for further research. But the PNHP persists in citing that McGlynn paper and claiming that overutilization is not a problem (Sullivan, K. 2014. Why Obamacare Can't Lower Costs Truthdig, May 9, 2014 http://www.truthdig.com/report/item/why_obamacare_cant_lower_costs_20140509. Reprinted Fall, 2014 NEWSLETTER of the PNHP.).

This resistance by the PNHP to the need to curb overutilization is frustrating because, in addition to improving quality, it would save billions of dollars more. The otherwise excellent economic analysis by Gerald Friedman: (http://www.pnhp.org/sites/default/files/Funding%20HR%20676_Friedman_final_7.31.13.pdf) ignores these savings, leaving Presidential Candidate Bernie Sanders's Campaign overestimating the costs and decreasing this actual appeal of his single payer proposal. This may partly be due to inability of non-medical policy experts to envision the control that doctors can exert by a self policing national doctors board.

35. Hadler, N. 2004. The Last Well Person. Montreal: McGill-Queens University Press, and 2009 Stabbed in the Back. Chapel Hill: The University of North Carolina Press.

36. See note 1 above.

37. Hall, B. 2009. Does Surgical Quality Improve in the American College of Surgeons National Surgical Quality Improvement Program: An Evaluation of all Participating Hospitals. Ann Surg. 250:363.

38. Lomas, S. 2001. Cutting Healthcare Costs Without Rationing at the Bedside: Preserving the Doctor-Patient Fiduciary Relationship Healthc.Pap. 2:38.

39. See note 1 above.

40. Newman, D. 2008. Hippocrates' Shadow. New York: Scribner

41. Gawande, A. 2015. Overkill. The New Yorker May 11, 2015.

42. The available data are conflicting. There may not be a complete all physician-public+private database, even the state medical societies are not complete. But the MGMA reviews a large fraction of MGMA member administrators' input corrected for practice costs: Medical Group Management Association. 2009. MGMA Finds Physician Primary Care and Specialty Compensation Not Keeping Pace With Inflation. Englewood, CO; June 23, 2009. The MGMA has other similar more recent reports, in which incomes for specialists are down and for general practice more level or up. For surgeons, normalized billed charges of common surgical procedures have trended down an average of 3.5% per year over the last 100 years. Physician Reimbursement for General Surgical Procedures in the Last Century: 1906–2006. J Am Coll Surg. 206:670).

On the other hand, in Glied, S., 2015 Understanding Pay Differentials Among Health Professionals, Nonprofessionals, and their Counterparts in Other Sectors. Health Aff. 34:929, the finding is that the average nurse earns 40% more than the median comparable worker and the physician earns about 50% more than the median comparable worker now, and concludes that there is room to reduce these to save on costs. The given "comparable worker" to a doctor is a lawyer, which may be suspect if for no other reason than the generally-accepted decreased job availability for lawyers in recent years that might skew this comparison.

43. Zweig D. 2014. Kaiser Permanente's Jack Cochran on the path to value-based care. Fierce Health Payer Aug. 1, 2014.

44. Smith, Adam, 1776. An Inquiry into the Nature and Causes of the Wealth of Nations. I.10.22.

45. Meyer, H. 2012. How Much Should Doctors Really Make? Medscape. Sep 25, 2012.

46. See note 10 above.

47. Kerber 2014. Is Physician Work in Procedure and Test Codes More Highly Valued Than That in Evaluation and Management Codes? Ann Surg 262:267.

48. In data from the 2007 McKinsey report, using Organization for Economic Cooperation and Development data for an international comparison, in the U.S. specialists averaged $274,000 then—specialist incomes have been rising rapidly since then—and general practitioners, $173,000. To put that in perspective for each country's overall economy for international comparison, this was expressed as a multiple of the income of the average patient. For U.S. specialists that turns out to be 6.6 times the income of the average patient and for general practitioners, 4.2 times as much In other countries on average, specialists and general practitioners respectively were paid only 4 and 3.2 times as much as the average patient's income. By comparison, those incomes relative to the patients' incomes were also about 30 to 60% greater than in other countries. On the other hand, U.S. doctors were each treating more patients—a 60% higher volume of business on average. So in this way of looking at it, increase in productivity for U.S. doctors would just about even out the differences in incomes with other countries.

49. Berwick D. 2005. 'A Deficiency of Will and Ambition': A Conversation with Donald Berwick. interview by Robert Galvin. Health Aff. 2005 Jan–Jun;Suppl Web Exclusives:W5,1–W5–9.

50. Terry K. 2007. Rx for Health Care Reform. First ed. Nashville: Vanderbilt University Press; 2007

51. Reinhardt, U. 2008. cited by Rampell, C. Doctors' Salaries and the Cost of Health Care. Economix NYT November 14, 2008.

52. Rosenthal, E. 2014. Long Waits for Doctors' Appointments Have Become the Norm. New York Times July 4, 2014.

53. Rosenthal, E. 2014. Doctors Salaries Are Not the Big Cost New York Times May 17, 2014.

54. Rosenthal, E. 2014. Paying Til it Hurts New York Times 28 May, 2014.

55. Bai, G. 2015. Extreme Markup: The Fifty US Hospitals with the Highest Charge-to-Cost Ratios. Health Aff. 34:922.

56. Sullivan, K. 2014. AHA Exec: Hospitals Must Reduce Non-Beneficial Care. FierceHealthcare July 7, 2014.

57. Hochman, M. 2013. Payer Agnosticism. NEJM 396:502.

58. Rajcumar, R. 2014. Maryland's All-Payer Approach to Delivery-System Reform. NEJM 370:493.

CHAPTER 4

1. McDermott, W. 1982. Social Ramifications of Control of Microbial Disease. The Johns Hopkins Medical Journal. 151:302–312.

2. Sauerland, S. 2010. Laparoscopic Versus Open Surgery for Suspected Appendicitis. Cochrane Database Syst Rev. 2010 Oct 6;(10):CD001546

3. Xu, T. 2015. Hospital Cost Implications of Increased Use of Minimally Invasive Surgery. JAMA Surg. Research Letter Published online March 25, 2015.

4. Breeden J. 2013. Statement on Robotic Surgery by ACOG President James T. Breeden, MD March 14 http://www.acog.org/About-ACOG/News-Room/News-Releases/2013/Statement-on-Robotic-Surgery. Accessed Sept. 2015.

5. Barbash, G. 2010. New Technology and Health Care Costs. The Case of Robot Assisted Surgery. N Engl J Med 363:701. Makary, M. 2011. The Advent of Laparoscopic Pancreatic Surgery Using the Robot Arch Surg 146:261.

6. Brooks, D. 2013. Is Proton Beam Therapy for Prostate Cancer Worth the Cost? Expert Voices, the American Cancer Society. Feb. 20, 2013.

7. Hedberg, 2009. North Idaho Robot Connects Doctors and Patients. http://usatoday30.usatoday.com/news/nation/states/idaho/2009-04-04-1722716023_x.htm.
   Also see http://www.nbcnews.com/id/4946229/ns/health-health_care/t/robot-doctor-gets-thumbs-up-patients/ for a picture of the robot making rounds.

8. Cott, E. 2015. A Talking Teddy Bear Practicing in the Pediatric Hospital. The New York Times. June 3, 2015

9. Farrell, D. 2008. Accounting for the Cost of Health Care in the United States. McKinsey & Company; December 2008.

10. [no au] New Drugs from Old. 2006. Drug Ther. Bull. 44:73. PMID 17067118

11. Lurie P. 2009. DTC Advertising Harms Patients and Should be Tightly Regulated J. Law Med. Ethics. 37:444.

12. Moynihan R., 2006. Selling Sickness: How the World's Biggest Pharmaceutical Companies Are Turning us All Into patients. First Nation Books paperback edition July 2006 edition. New York, NY: Nation Books; 2005.

13. Gagne, J. 2014. Comparative Effectiveness of Generic and Brand-Name Statins on Patient Outcomes: A Cohort Study. *Ann Intern Med.* 161:400.

14. Kantarjian, H. 2013. Cancer drugs in the United States: Justum pretium—the just price. J Clin Oncol 31:3006. These authors document, for instance, the case of imatinib ("Gleevec"), generally curative for chronic myelogenous leukemia, a disease for which the only other promising treatment was a bone marrow transplant. The cost for Gleevec at first was $30,000 a year but soon rose to $80.000 to $90,000 a year. Several "look alikes" were developed, which arguably might help occasional patients when Gleevec failed, but are much more expensive (over $150,000 a year) and not demonstrably better for first line therapy. Similarly, other expensive drugs to treat solid tumors may improve end points like disease free survival but generally do not prolong the patients' lives very much.

15. WCBA. 2008. White Coat, Black Art. September 22, 2008. CBC Radio.

16. Giaccotto, C. 2005. Drug Prices and Research and Development Investment Behavior in the Pharmaceutical Industry. J. Law Econ. 48:195.

17. Pink, D. 2009. DRiVE. New York: Riverhead Books.

18. Light, DW. 2009. Global Drug Discovery: Europe is Ahead. Health Aff (Millwood). 2009. 28(5):w969–77.

19. Hurley, D. 2014. Why Are So Few Blockbuster Drugs Invented Today? The New York Times. Nov. 13, 2014.

20. Gøtzsche, P. 2013. Screening for breast cancer with mammography. from The Cochrane Collection Editorial Group: Cochrane Breast Cancer Group Published Online: 4 JUN 2013: "If we assume that screening reduces breast cancer mortality by 15% and that overdiagnosis and overtreatment is at 30%, it means that for every 2000 women invited for screening throughout 10 years, one will avoid dying of breast cancer and 10 healthy women, who would not have been diagnosed if there had not been screening, will be treated unnecessarily. Furthermore, more than 200 women will experience important psychological distress including anxiety and uncertainty for years because of false positive findings. To help ensure that the women are fully informed before they decide whether or not to attend screening, we [Cochrane] have written an evidence-based leaflet for lay people that is available in several languages on www.cochrane.dk. Because of substantial advances in treatment and greater breast cancer awareness since the trials were carried out, it is likely that the absolute effect of screening today is smaller than in the trials. Recent observational studies show more overdiagnosis than in the trials and very little or no reduction in the incidence of advanced cancers with screening."

Also see Carroll, A. How to Measure a Medical Treatment's Potential for Harm—Feb. 2, 2015. New York Times. Using the statistics of Number Needed to Treat and Number Needed to Harm they calculate that: ". . . for about every 1,500 women assigned to get screening for 10 years, one might be spared a death from breast cancer (though she'd most likely die of some other cause). But about five more women would undergo surgery and about four more would undergo radiation, both of which can have dangerous, even life-threatening, side effects.

21. Prince, C. 2012. CancerScope; To Screen or Not to Screen Brawley commenting on US Preventive Services Task Force's draft guidelines add to prostate cancer screening debate Cancer April 15, 2012: p.1959–1961. Also note the frustrating dissonance between different studies on detection and treatment of prostate cancer (Kim, E. 2015. Prostate-specific Antigen-Based Screening: Controversy and Guidelines.BMC Med. 24;13:61.) and the strong pronouncement by the American College of Physicians that screening for prostate cancer not be done except after discussion with the informed patient (. Qaseem, A. 2013. Screening for Prostate Cancer: A Guidance Statement From the Clinical Guidelines Committee of the American College of Physicians. Ann Intern Med. 158:761.)

22. Ladapo, J. 2014. Physician Decision Making and Trends in the Use of Cardiac Stress Testing in the United States: an Analysis of Repeated Cross-Sectional Data. Ann Intern Med. 161:482.

23. Emanuel, E. 2015. Skip Your Annual Physical. The New York Times. Jan. 8, 2015.

CHAPTER 5

1. Pronovost P. 2010. Safe Patients, Smart Hospitals. First Printing ed. New York, NY: Hudson Street Press, Penguin Group; 2010.

2. Dixon-Woods, M. 2011. Explaining Michigan: Developing an Ex Post Theory of a Quality Improvement Program. Milbank Quarterly. Volume 89:167.

3. See note 1 above.

4. Note to Dr. Anderson's statistic: the IOM estimated that between 44,000 and 98,000 deaths occurred in U.S. hospitals annually (Kohn, L. 2000 Institute of Medicine (U.S.) Committee on Quality of Health Care in America. To Err Is Human: Building a Safer Health System. Washington, DC: National Academy Press; 2000). The American College of Physicians disputed the certainty of the exact numbers although not the thrust of the finding. (Sox, H. 2000. How Many Deaths Are Due to Medical Error? Getting the Number Right. Effective Clinical Practice http://ecp.acponline.org/novdec00/sox.htm).

5. Goff, S. 2015 A Qualitative Analysis of Hospital Leaders' Oinions About Publicly Reported Measures of Health Care Quality. The Joint Commission Journal on Quality and Patient Safety 41:169.
Nicolay C. 2012 Systematic Review of the Application of Quality Improvement

Methodologies from the Manufacturing Industry to Surgical Healthcare. Br J Surg. 99:324.

In the absence of defined criteria, health insurance business groups feel justified in disputing essential benefits with patient advocates (Caramenico A. 2014. Tug-of-War Develops Over Essential Benefits. Fierce Healthcare July 23, 2014. http://www.fiercehealthpayer.com/story/tug-war -develops-over-essential-benefits/2014-07-23).

The regular ranking of hospitals, such as by the U.S. News and World Report, has been overhauled but it is still under fire as incorrect and irrelevant. ("Why healthcare quality measures don't go deep enough: Hospitals need to focus on functional outcomes instead of processes." Expert tells Wall Street Journal. Fierce-Healthcare March 23, 2015 | By Zack Budryk).

From a practicing doctor: "To Medicare and ACA reformers, quality and value are broken down into discrete measurements that must be entered into a computer exactly as Medicare dictates. Failure to do so could lead to crippling fines. I have been audited twice already in the past year, with more audits to come. No wonder patients must face doctors who stare at computer screens and do not have time to listen." (Lazris, A. 2015. Medicare Quality Indicators Diverge from Quality Care. The Baltimore Sun 29 Jan., 2015).

6. Lee, V. 2015. Redesigning Metrics to Integrate Professionalism into the Governance of Health Care. JAMA 313:1815. Although providing an accurate description of good care, the article then holds that transition to value, the ratio of the outcomes to total costs to the payee, is undermined because professionalism has not provided the basis for considering costs. Needless to say, payers are embracing the value concept (Overland, D. 2014. 40 per cent of Provider Reimbursements Are for Value Based Care. Fierce Health Player September 30, 2014; Overland, D. 2014 Aetna Drives Value Based Reform by Collaborating With One Provider in Market. Fierce Health Player, October 14, 2014; and CMS is also thinking in terms of value (payment) as part of good care (CMS 2015. Health Care Payment and Learning Action Network. http://innovation.cms.gov/initiatives/Health -Care-Payment-Learning-and-Action-Network/). Some use the term value imprecisely by presuming it means only quality (Schwartz, A. 2014. Measuring Low Value Care in Medicare. JAMA Intern. Med. 174:1067), which at least is closer to how a medical professional needs to think about patient care.

7. After the concern about cost, the second most consistent barrier found to adaptation of EMR in the U.S. included "impedes competition." (Kruse, C. 2014. Barriers over Time to Full Implementation of Health Information Exchange in the United States. JMTR Med Inform 2(2):e26.) Forty-four % of doctors' practices adopting EMR found that it improved the use of on-formulary medications, certainly not the preference of the pharmaceutical industry.

(Jamooom, E. 2012. Physician Adoption off Electronic Health Record Systems: United States, 2011. Revised Jan. 11, 2013. NCHS Data Brief No. 98). And Don McCanne in Quote-of-the-Day, April 16, 2015: "We blew this one. We turned HIT over to the private sector while failing to provide adequate government oversight. We ended up with just what I predicted a decade ago, when David Brailer was predicting a decade leading to HIT nirvana. . . . It is amazing that it has taken a decade for us to discover officially that placing control of HIT in the hands of the private sector is not serving us well."

The most mysterious and frustrating thing is that, confirming what "T.T." said in this story, HHS had publically declared Thompson's plans over a decade ago, which confirms that HHS did indeed have this well underway, based on IOM standards and SNOMED (Anderson, L. 2003. HHS Unveils Electronic Plan for Tracking Medical Records, The Wall Street Journal, July 2, 2003). Through what lurking "shadow government" could this (and perhaps other harmful impairments to modernization of health care delivery) have occurred?

8. Gawande, A. 2011. The Hot Spotters [Internet].; 2011 [updated Jan 24, 2011. Available from: http://www.newyorker.com/magazine/2011/01/24/the-hot-spotters

9. Pilon, B. 2015 Evidence-Guided Integration of Interprofessional Collaborative Practice Into Nurse Managed Health Centers. J. Prof. Nursing 31:340.

10. Burdick, J 2013. Rx for electronic records. The Baltimore Sun, June 17, 2013. (See Appendix)

   The Brookings institute has pointed out the fundamental ways health care informatics must change to achieve real interoperability (West, D. 2014, The Emerging Revolution in Health Care. Center for Technology Innovation at Brookings, August 2014).

   Regarding resistance to interoperability, one of the major EMR systems, EPIC, was spurred to try to defend itself when a Rand report deemed that billions of dollars had been spent on EPIC although it is a "closed system."

   Carl Bergman of EHRSelector, in a FierceHealth Care Interview,(Hirsch, M. May 15, 2014) criticized the federal Office of the National Coordinator for electronic medical records: "They screwed up royally," for not having interoperability as a principle goal from the first.

11. The President's Council of Advisors on Science and Technology in a May 29, 2014 report called for HHS to lead a new systems engineering effort to establish interoperable medical records.

   The AMA has called on the administration to stop penalizing physicians who do not adopt digital records.   At the 2014 National AMA meeting physicians' assessments of EMR revealed general support for EMR but considerable problems that require remedy.

12. A review by National Library of Medicine staff estimated that clinicians lose about 4 hours per week due to electronic medical records (McDonald, C. 2014. Use of Internist's Free Time by Ambulatory Care Electronic Medical Record Systems. JAMA Int. Med. 174:1860.).

13. Coffron, M. 2015. Big Promise and Big Challenges for Big Health Care Data. Bulletin of the American College of Surgeons 100:10.

14. Nan, L. 2014. BMI and Coronary Heart Disease Risk Among Low-Income and

Underinsured Diabetic Patients. Diabetes Care. DOI: 10.2337/dc14–1091.

15. Exmples of the platform process include Pathak, J. 2013. Normalization and Standardization of Electronic Health Records for High-Throughput Phenotyping: the SHARPn Consortium. J Am Med Inform Assoc 20:e341–e348, and Kohane, I. 2012. A Translational Engine at the National Scale: Informatics for Integrating Biology and the Bedside. J Am. Med. Inform. Assoc. 19:181.

  A Plan-Do-Study-Act collaborative quality improvement model is under assessment for creating physician interaction strategies: McAlearney, A. 2014. Evidence-Based Management of Ambulatory Electronic Health Record System Implementation. Int. J. Med.Inform. 83:484.

16. Sharfstein, J. 2015. Using Health Care Data to Track and Improve Public Health. JAMA 313:2012.

17. Sternberg S. 2015 Risks are High at Low-Volume Hospitals. U.S. News and World Report May 8, 2015. Multiple statistical questions are raised in this article, including the nearly universal use of comparison of percentages rather than numbers, noted by David Newman (in his book *Hippocrates' Shadow*) to be misleading. For instance, if a given death rate nationally is 1 in 2000 but 4 times higher in a small hospital that did 250 of the procedures, that increased risk sounds like a lot, but only one death in 250 would make that hospital's death rate 4 times the national average. Any death is a serious issue to be addressed by the institution, whether large or small, but the statistic is not up to the implications of the U.S. News and World Report. Moreover, mortality measurement, although particularly important (see Dr Foster "Mortality Measurement: the Case in Favour." 15 July 2014), may not be valid as the only quality measure to consider in isolation since the risk adjustment of any measure may be misleading. One has to know the total number of cases done in these low volume hospitals and the results for many types of care to justify censure of all low volume settings. Extrapolation by Birkmeyer, a supporter of the article, stated that, if corrected (by stopping low volume centers from doing the procedures) "as many as 11,000 death nationally might have been prevented" over 3 years." Of course, not all of these might have been prevented, but even given up to 4,000 deaths a year in low volume hospitals, in view of estimates of 100,000 preventable hospital deaths per year, there are bigger threats than small hospital size to patients. And it is not given whether the results in all 3 years were in the same hospitals and not merely statistically capricious results, partly for different hospitals for each year. Previously Birkmeyer and his colleagues published a scientific article showing increased mortality for some general surgical procedures in low volume hospitals (Reames et al 2014 Volume and Operative Mortality in the Modern Era. Ann. Surg. 260:244.). That analysis does not provide potent evidence that small size per se is contraindicated. It was restricted to Medicare billing data; the case mix looks favorable to large hospitals which could leak through risk adjustment; the size of the differences, although statistically significant, were not as important as it may seem; given that these are low volume hospitals treating a lot fewer patients; and there is a problem with statistics of small vs. large samples. Smaller hospitals are more likely by chance to be higher and lower than an average

of the statistically dominant mid-to-large volume institutions. Because this wider range about the mean, were there any small volume hospitals with data better than the high volume hospitals? How much variability by chance is there from year to year? The possibility that the National Surgical Quality Improvement Program, with data collected very differently, would be informative was not mentioned. So the principle is justified scientifically, but use of these findings to close down all low volume hospitals and procedures without further study is not. In fairness, this article by Reames, Birkmeyer and colleagues does temper the conclusions to correctly point out the value for continuous quality improvement, unlike the much more public and unquestioned U.S. News and World Report piece.

Years ago we addressed this problem with center size with transplant programs in connection with the public release of patient and graft survival in every U.S. organ transplant program, using the complete data available on every donor and recipient in the country. This calculation to determine poorly performing programs used the size and significance of the difference in results for each center compared with the national average. Because a larger difference in the case of a smaller center did not reach the statistical significance that it would have with the bigger numbers from a large center, we developed a formula describing a continuous range of smaller size with less significance (higher p value). Smaller programs that fell below the line defined by this formula were defined as needing further evaluation, whereas regardless of size, programs with only arbitrarily small differences from the national average were not selected, regardless of how highly significant the difference (17). The trend over time was then followed, which strengthens the data and carries CQI information.

So to use as data for CQI, the poorer results in small volume institutions and practices needs to be considered carefully. But only with a national EMR using ongoing analysis by my proposed Health Security Board will we be able to be more certain about the implications.

18. Burdick, J. 1997 Identification of poorly performing transplant centers using the UNOS ceter-specific data. Transplant Proc. 1997 Feb–Mar;29:1495.

CHAPTER 6

1. Fielding, J. (editor), 2013. Public Health Practice. New York: Oxford University Press, New York, 2013.

2. Cookson, P. 2004. Expect Miracles. Boulder CO: Westview/Perseus

3. Atkinson, H. 2015. Treat Traditional Schools like Charters. The Baltimore Sun 9 July 2015.

4. See note 3 above.

5. Chetty, R. 2015. The Impacts of Neighborhoods on Intergenerational Mobility: Childhood Exposure Effects and CountyLevel Estimates. Harvard University Working Paper 2015: "Approximately 4,600 families living in high poverty public

housing projects were randomly assigned to one of three groups: an experimental voucher group that was offered a subsidized housing voucher that came with a requirement to move to a census tract with a poverty rate below 10%, a Section 8 voucher group that was offered a standard housing voucher with no additional contingencies, and a control group that was not offered a voucher (but retained access to public housing)."

6. American Hospital Association. 2009. Uncompensated Care Continues a Steady Rise for U.S. Hospitals www.ahanews.com December 7, 2009.

7. Stiglitz, J. 2012. *The Price of Inequality* New York: W. W. Norton & Col. See especially Chapters Four and Five.

8. Chomsky, N. 1988. *Manufacturing Consent* New York: Pantheon Books: discusses the Propaganda Model and failure of media to provide information that a successful society needs.

9. As discussed also in Chapter 1., muliple studies, books and papers by members of the PNHP have defended the concept of single payer but it has been a favorite target for opposition by mainstream health policy establishment. Jones in 1994 observed it does not meet America's needs (Jones, W. 1994 Single Payer: Do Government-Run Programs Meet America's Needs? Benefits Quarterly 10:13), echoed recently by Emanuel: "I just don't see health care for all," he said, adding that it was "just not an American value." (Windemuth, A. 2014. Emanuel says traditional health care companies obsolete by 2025. The Daily Princetonian Feb. 24, 2014). In the stir in the late 20th Century leading up to the failure of the Clinton plan, Norato noted that "the single-payer proposals were treated like pariahs like most of the Congress (Norato, J. 1997. National Health Care Reform and a Single-Payer System: Messiah or Pariah? J. Health and Human Serv. Admin. 19:341.) and during debates before the ACA was passed the national health plan initiative was also summarily dismissed (Blesch G. 2009. Left out of the discussion single-payer advocates still striving to be heard. Modern Healthcare June 8, 2009.) even in the face of a modest but vivid bit of social disobedience on the part of Dr. Flowers and her PHNP colleagues at a Senate hearing. The Heritage Foundation has predictably marshaled big arguments against single payer (Frogue, J. 2001. Buyer Beware: The Failure of Single-Payer Health Care. May 4, 2001 http://www.heritage .org/research/lecture/buyer-beware-the-failure-of-single-payer-health-care), but, more harmful, very respected investigators have also been dismissive (Newhouse, J. 2004. The Institute of Medicine Committee's Clarion Call for Universal Coverage. Health Aff. W-4 179). Recently, there are finally more public voices in favor of single payer (Burdick, J. 2014 Getting serious about a single payer system. Now that Obamacare has shown the country can accept health care reform, it's time for real reform. [Commentary The Baltimore Sun May 1, 2014] See Appendix)

10. Krugman, P. 2015. Slavery's Long Shadow. New York Times June 22, 2015.

11. Cullen, E. 2016. A Countervailing Voice in the South: Future Doctors on Medicaid Expansion. Research Letter, JAMA Internal Medicine 175:254.

12. Rodericks, D. 2016. High Court Ruling Hits Close to Home. Affirmation of Fair Housing Too Late for Arundel Plan but Warns Against Future Discrimination. The Baltimore Sun 29 June, 2015. The setting tells a lot; there are large racial differences in where people live: higher income African Americans are more likely to live in lower income areas (Reardon, S. 2015. Neighborhood Income Composition by Household Race and Income, 1990–2009 *Annals of the American Academy of Political and Social Science* July 660:78).

13. The community in Charleston showed remarkable grace and dignity in the face of a fierce ongoing fight over the Confederate flag (Goldberg J. 2015. Southern grace, dignity. The South Showed its Heart After Charleston Shootings. The Baltimore Sun. 28 June, 2015).

14. Glied, S. 2009. Single Payer as a Financing Mechanism. J. Health Politics, Policy and Law 34:593. Among the issues to be considered, she points out: Subnational competition can limit the monopsony power of a single national payer particularly if there is competition among the units for pricing; there is moral hazard because of danger of excessive use of services with a single budget, but subnational payment may lead to underfunding; and if subnational governments—such as states—continue to compare their results, it may lead to improved performance.

15. Ziff, L. 1988. *The Responsible Reader*. New York: St. Martins Press/Macmillan. I am indebted to her book for reproducing these marvelous pieces: Krutch, J.W. "The Individual and the Species," and King, M.L.K., Jr., "Letter from Birmingham Jail."

16. See note 15 above.

17. Freud, S. 1917. *Civilization, Society and Religion* (Penguin Freud Library 12 p. 131 and p. 305). Cited in http://psychology.wikia.com/wiki/Narcissism_of_small_differences.

18. Yancy, G. 2015. American Racism in the White Frame New York Times. The Stone. July 27, 2015. George Yancy interviewed Joe Feagin about the unrealized racism that pervades all of American society: "Prejudice is much less than half the story. Because prejudice is only one part of the larger white racial frame that is central to rationalizing and maintaining systemic racism, one can be less racially prejudiced and still operate out of many other aspects of that dominant frame. That white racial frame includes not only racist prejudices and stereotypes of conventional analyses, but also racist ideologies, narratives, images and emotions, as well as individual and group inclinations to discriminate shaped by the other features. Additionally, all whites, no matter what their racial prejudices and other racial framings entail, benefit from many racial privileges routinely granted by this country's major institutions to whites."

    Feagin argues that the history of the U.S. has cemented this social aberration in place. "Most whites, and many others, do not understand that about 80 percent of this country's four centuries have involved extreme racialized slavery and extreme Jim Crow legal segregation. As a result, major racial inequalities have been deeply institutionalized over about 20 generations."

19. Quadagno, J. 2005. *One Nation, Uninsured*. New York: Oxford University Press. In

this powerful exception to the usual absence of much about it, she documents the powerful impact of racism against health care reform from the 1930s to the 1960s, but additionally, the "coded messages implying that minorities are undeserving beneficiaries of social programs." that have continued to infect progressive attempts since the dawn of the civil rights movement, including the Clinton Health Plan. Also: see Derickson, A. 2005 *Health Security for All* Baltimore, MD: the Johns Hopkins University Press. He documents the endemic resistance to including African Americans in health care and other social supports during the first half of the 20th century; and Williams, A. 2007 *Eliminating Healthcare Disparities in America: Beyond the IOM Report* Totowa, N.J.:Humana Press, Inc. (reviewed by Gasjun. D. 2007 JAMA 298:2917), which has chapters on race and disparities.

20. Puggliucci, M. 2014. On the Biology of Race. Scientia Salon, 19 May 2014. Based on a review of a book by Nicholas Wade that claims a biological explanation for racial ideas, this article by Massimo Puggliucci has many references to thinking about this from different viewpoints. In summary, the conclusion debunks the idea (and Wade's book) as representing speculation and pseudoscience, akin to claiming a genetic basis for the convention of the diatonic scale in Western music. From Puggliucci and his colleague Jonathon Kaplan: "While in nonhuman biology the term 'race' has been and is being used in a variety of ways, the best way of making sense of systematic variation within the human species is likely to rely on the ecotypic conception of biological races. In this sense, there are likely human races (ecotypes) of biological interest. But again, biology provides no support for the very strong, essentialist-style conception of 'race' that has, both historically and at present, underwritten racism (of both the individual and institutional varieties), and indeed, biology reveals that the assumptions underlying such a conception of race are false."

21. The Dec.16 2005, cover of AAAS Science magazine showed two strains of a fish species, one dark and the other fish nearly transparent as a result of a mutation of a particular gene for color in the dark fish. With the elucidation of the human genome it was shown that the same gene, carried over the vast phylogenetic separation as are many genes, is present and active in African Americans from our distant ancestors, but present as a later mutation to the unexpressed form in humans as they migrated north, explaining the relative absence of skin pigment in European Americans.

CHAPTER 7

1. Wulff, K. 2011. Can Coverage be Rescinded When Negative Trial Results Threaten a Popular Procedure? The Ongoing Saga of Vertebroplasty. Health Aff. 30: 2269.

2. The Conyers Bill includes the requirement that: ". . . at least one member shall be a representative of health care providers, including nurses and other nonphysician advisors." The Wyden-Bennett bill includes a brief mention of "Finding what works in health care." It assigns the responsibility without much detail to

researchers at medical schools. (Well, at least one might presume this could include input from practicing physicians on the faculty.) An interesting variation is the Dingell bill (MI-15) from 2005, which specifies a National Health Insurance Board, requiring at least one member to be a licensed physician. Included in this bill is a National Medical Advisory Council to advise the Board on effective health care, which would include six providers among its members. There is not much insight in any of these bills about the degree to which doctors could help. And the advisory committee provided for in the ACA will not be much of an improvement. The ACA, however, does leave room for flexibility that could allow more effective professional input.

3. These include: *Putting our House in Order,* by George Schultz and John Shoven; *Crisis of Abundance*, by Arnold Kling; *Lives at Risk*, by John Goodman, Gerald Musgrave and Devon Herrick; and *The Cure*, by David Gratzer. More aligned with the views in this book about the problems with insurance for coverage of the poor and the value of a national single-payer approach, are: Ezekial Emanuel's *Healthcare, Guaranteed*; *The Politics of Health Policy*, by Vincente Navarro; *Dead on Arrival*, by Colin Gordon; and *Health Security for All*, by Alan Derickson. Advocacy for the single national payer viewpoint of the Physicians for a National Health Program is documented in Bob LeBow and C. Rocky White's *Health Care Meltdown*; *Bleeding the Patient*, by David Himmelstein, Steffie Woolhandler and Ida Hellander, and *How "Obamacare is Unsustainable; Why We Need a Single-Payer Solution For All Americans* by John Geyman. These and many other books represent a variety of carefully argued and substantial views of the reasons, and possible solutions, for the problems of health care in the U.S. But I have not seen any writings place reliance on doctors as a fundamental source of help with a reform effort.

4. The excellent call for a major overhaul of the system, *Critical*, by Tom Daschle, Scott Greenberger and Jeanne Lambrew, envisions a realistic role for clinicians in the Board of National Health Care. But this would operate more as advisory to Congress for legislation than by providing physician expertise for making and enforcing rules. Another book is *A Second Opinion*, by Arnold Relman, former editor of the New England Journal of Medicine. This describes the system that he has devised to provide a reasonable way to cover everyone. Many of the provisions, as he notes, are like those of The Physicians for a National Health Program (PNHP). Dr. Relman's proposal differs from the PNHP in how doctors are paid. It has stronger controls against the amount of private care to be allowed. In his book, control of costs is stressed and included as an important ingredient in the system. The Board described in my book is a lot like the National Medical Care Agency that Relman envisions for overseeing the system. Nevertheless, although experts are specified, the particular importance of clinician input is not stressed there. *Health Care Reform Now!* is by George Halvorson, the Chairman and CEO of Kaiser Foundation Health Plan. His book has index entries under "Physicians." These have excellent background on some of the issues regarding doctors including systems that include medical autonomy. He has a realistic view of public and

private systems in parallel which is a feature of the Open System. The difficulty in keeping up with new information is described. As a famous leader in working with doctors and making health care happen cost-effectively, his views must be reckoned with. But there is no mention of covering everyone or why private markets will not provide the answer. And he does not have the vision that doctors can be much more effective than insurance for controlling health care.

5. *One Nation, Underinsured* is by Jill Quadagno, who is a government policy expert. She has an extensive set of index entries to descriptions of the difficulties physicians have caused and the problems they have suffered as the managed care process evolved.

   In *Critical Condition* by Donald Barlett and James Steele, the index has a long section with multiple entries under "physicians." From their investigative reporting background these tough experts discuss the problems doctors have had (and the misbehaviors of some). Their Chapter, "Curing the Ills," envisions a role for physicians in cost-containment—one of the only strong calls for this as an explicit part of a national system that has appeared. On the other hand the book appeared in 2004 but has as yet had apparently little effect regarding a doctors' role on what has appeared in the newspapers or in legislative proposals.

   The third book advocating fundamental physician involvement is *Money-Driven Medicine*, by Maggie Mahar—or watch her excellent, compelling video of the same name. This is a rousing, massively documented picture of the problems with U.S. medicine and health care coverage. She dedicates the last few pages of the book to the reasons that we must re-engage the medical profession at a national organizational level for reform. Unfortunately, like the two other calls for doctors to take a fundamental role, this seems to have fallen on deaf professional and political ears.

6. Stiglitz, J. 2012. *The Price of Inequality* New York: W. W. Norton & Col. See particularly Chapter One.

7. Pinker, S. 2011. *The Better Angels of our Nature. Why Violence Has Declined.* New York: Viking.

8. Burdick, J. 2015. Sanders for the Win. The Baltimore Sun 13 May 2015 (see Appendix).

9. Sanders, B. 2015. Why Not? Reader Supported News, 01 July 15.

ABOUT THE
INTERVIEWS

Starting in the summer of 2014 I contacted possible interviewees and explained that, as part of my project writing a book on health care reform, I was asking knowledgeable people to allow me to interview them for a half hour on health care reform in light of the ACA, including their thoughts on single payer. Most of the interviews were done by phone, but some were in person. I explained that it would be relatively unstructured because the goal was to see what each individual considered most important to discuss. I asked and was granted permission to record each interview. I promised that anything that would be specifically attributable to the person I would show to them first. In general, the interviews started with an invitation to say what the person thought about single payer, then extended widely into health care policy, politics and professional issues. After each interview I transcribed all of the responses verbatim, plus enough of my questions and comments to clarify the interchange, yielding 30 documents of between 1,000 and 3,000 words. Statements from interviewees in quotes are copied from those transcriptions.

Not everyone whom I felt it would be desirable to talk with granted an interview. Some refused personally, in some cases discussion within the person's institution ended with a more anonymous refusal, and in a couple of cases I was frustratingly unable to make contact. Since in all of those cases I did not have permission, I do not include anything about those attempts in the book. I did not approach one likely possibility because apparently when asked about single payer during a book signing this elicited such an agitated degree of refusal to discuss it by the author that I figured nothing informative would come of an interview, even if it were to be granted.

The list below alphabetically summarizes those interviewed. I have given more details about the person and the interview in each case at appropriate points in the book.

THE INTERVIEWEES

Adams, Owen, PhD.   Chief Policy Advisor in the Canadian Medical Association.

Anderson, Gerard, PhD.   Professor, Johns Hopkins Bloomberg School of Public Health.

Boling, Philip.   Property/casualty claim manager and a former insurance salesman in Baltimore, MD.

Bond, Charles, J.D.   an attorney who has litigated and discussed health care and its reform widely.

Boufford, Jo Ivey, MD.   Professor of Public Service, Health Policy and Management at the Wagner Graduate School of Public Service, NYU, President of the New York Academy of Medicine and member of the Institute of Medicine who served in the Office of the Assistant Secretary for Health in the Clinton Administration.

Cohen, Joshua, PhD.   Research Associate Professor, Tufts Center for Drug Development.

Cooper, Richard A. "Buz," MD.   Oncologist, Senior Fellow in the Leonard Davis Institute of Health Economics at the University of Pennsylvania and Clinical Professor in the Medical College's Institute for Health and Society. Sadly, Dr. Cooper died in January, 2016.

Daschle, Thomas.   U.S. Senator from South Dakota, former Senate Majority Leader and now Chair of the Center for American Progress Board of Directors.

Drasga, Ray, MD.   Practicing oncologist and PNHP member, also started a long-standing free clinic in Crown Point, IN.

Duderstadt, James, PhD.   President Emeritus and University Professor of Science and Engineering, The University of Michigan; Member of National Academy of Engineering and Chair of the Policy and Global Affairs Division of the National Academies of Science, Engineering, and Medicine; Former Chair of the Board of the University of Michigan Health Center.

Fielding, Jonathan E., MD, MPH, MBA.   Distinguished Professor of Health Policy and Management, UCLA Fielding School of Public Health, Distinguished Professor of Pediatrics, UCLA Geffen School of Medicine, Former Massachusetts Commissioner of Public Health and Los Angeles County Director of Public Health.

Hadler, Nortin M., MD, MACP, MACR, FACOEM.   Emeritus Professor of Medicine and MicrobiologyImmunology at the University of North Carolina at Chapel Hill and author of several books on flaws in U.S. health care: *The Last Well Person*, *Worried Sick*, *Stabbed in the Back*, *Rethinking Aging*, and *Citizen Patient*.

Hellander, Ida, MD.   Director of Policy and Programs, Physicians for a National Health Program.

Katz, Matthew.   Executive vice president and CEO of the Connecticut State Medical Society.

Laupacis, Andreas, MD.   Canadian internist and health services researcher; First Chair of the Canadian Expert Drug Advisory Committee and Editor of "Healthy Matters," a public discussion site on Canadian Health Care.

Lewin, Jack, MD.   President and CEO of the Cardiovascular Research Institute, Chairman of the National Coalition on Health Care (of Washington DC), formerly CEO of the American College of Cardiology.

Opelka, Frank, MD.   Colon and Rectal Surgeon, Medical Director for Quality and Health Policy, American College of Surgeons, Washington DC; Professor of Surgery and Executive Vice President for Health Care Quality and Medical Education Redesign, Louisiana State University; Chair, Surgical Quality Alliance, American College of Surgeons; and Chair, AMA Physician Consortium for Performance Improvement Foundation

Orsolini, Liana, PhD, RN, ANEF, FAAN.   Care Delivery and Advanced Practice System Consultant, Bon Secours Health System, former Robert Wood Johnson Health Policy Fellow.

Ostrich, Jack, MD.   General medicine physician with Kaiser Permanente, Sacramento, CA.

Pronovost, Peter, MD.   Professor and Johns Hopkins Medicine Senior Vice President For Patient Safety and Quality and President of the Armstrong Institute at Johns Hopkins Medicine.

Ransom, Gene, Esq.   CEO of MedChi, the Maryland State Medical Society.

Rowe, John "Jack," MD.   Gerontologist, Professor at Columbia University School of Public Health, member of the IOM and former Chairman and CEO of AETNA, inc.

Sanders, Bernie.   U.S. Senator from Vermont, a staunch single payer advocate, running for the Democratic Nomination for President of the United States.

Schroeder, Steve, MD.   Professor of Health and Health Care at U.C. San Francisco, former Chair of the Robert Wood Johnson Foundation and IOM member. Prominent in U..S. smoking cessation effort.

Sherman, Arloc.   Senior Fellow at the Center for Budget and Policy Priorities, formerly at the Children's Defense Fund, author of "Wasting America's Future," and an expert in studies on poverty and welfare.

Thompson, Tommy.   Former Governor of Wisconsin and U.S. Secretary of Health and Human Services under President George W. Bush.

Warshaw, Andrew, MD, FACS.   Gastrointestinal surgeon, Past President of the American College of Surgeons, formerly Chairman of the Department of Surgery at the Massachusetts General Hospital.

Wells, Samuel A. Jr., MD.   Surgical Oncologist, formerly the Chair of the Department of Surgery at the Washington University School of Medicine.

Young, Quentin, M.D.   Chicago internist, a leading single payer advocate, an early member and officer in the PNHP, prominent in many civil rights and social improvement causes. Sadly, he died in March, 2016.

Zorza, Richard, JD.   After a childhood in England, now a U.S. lawyer working for the right to legal process and effective self representation for the disadvantaged.

INDEX

ABOUT THE AUTHOR

Dr. Burdick obtained an MD in 1968 at Harvard Medical School, followed by a Surgical Residency at the Massachusetts General Hospital. After Fellowships in the Public Health Service and in Transplantation at the Massachusetts General Hospital, he had a career doing vascular surgery and abdominal organ transplants for 25 years at the Johns Hopkins Hospital. His academic work has included laboratory and clinical research in controlling the allograft immune response. He was on the Board of the Mid-Atlantic Renal Coalition (ESRD Network 5), the Council of the American Society of Transplant Surgeons and is a Past President of the SouthEastern Organ Procurement Foundation and Past President of UNOS, the Organ Procurement and Transplant Network contractor. Starting in 2003, he served for five years as Director of the Division of Transplantation in the Healthcare Systems Bureau of the Health Resources Services Administration, an agency in the US Department of Health and Human Services. Presently he is on the Board of the Baltimore City Medical Society of the Maryland MedChi and is a Professor of Surgery at the Johns Hopkins School of Medicine.